D0078079

FEMINISM AND THE CONTRADICTIONS OF OPPRESSION

FEMINISM AND THE CONTRADICTIONS OF OPPRESSION

CAROLINE RAMAZANOGLU

London and New York

First published 1989
by Routledge
11 New Fetter Lane, London EC4P 4EE
29 West 35th Street, New York, NY 10001

Reprinted 1990, 1993

© Caroline Ramazanoglu 1989

Phototypeset in 10pt Baskerville by
Mews Photosetting, Beckenham, Kent
Printed and bound in Great Britain by Biddles Ltd,
Guildford and King's Lynn

All rights reserved. No part of this book may be reprinted
or reproduced or utilized in any form or by any electronic,
mechanical, or other means, now known or hereafter
invented, including photocopying and recording, or in any
information storage or retrieval system, without permission
in writing from the publishers.

British Library Cataloguing in Publication Data

Ramazanoglu, Caroline, *1939–*
Feminism and the contradictions of oppression.
1. Feminism
I. Title
305.4′2

ISBN 0–415–02835–3
ISBN 0–415–02836–1 Pbk

Library of Congress Cataloging-in-Publication Data

Ramazanoglu, Caroline, *1939–*
Feminism and the contradictions of oppression / Caroline
Ramazanoglu.
p.   cm.
Bibliography: p.
Includes index.
ISBN 0–415–02835–3   ISBN 0–415–02836–1 (pbk.)
1. Feminism. 2. Patriarchy. 3. Women's rights. I. Title.
HQ1154.R34   1989
305.4′2–dc19   88–18509
CIP

CONTENTS

CONTENTS

PREFACE AND ACKNOWLEDGEMENTS

This book is addressed to serious problems in the connections between feminist social theory and feminist political strategy. The enormous popularity of feminism in recent years has made improvements in the relations between men and women a real possibility, but has also provoked considerable opposition. Some are now arguing that feminism was an idealistic political movement born of the 1960s which has failed to measure up to the harsh realities of the 1980s. Yet the potential of feminism for the transformation of society has hardly been realized. Feminism is far from dead or dying, but feminists are often divided, confused and weary. The last twenty years or so have generated a diversity of feminist activity all over the world, but this activity, which started by asserting women's common interests as women, has drawn increasing attention to the differences *between* women. It is only if these differences can be identified, clarified and dealt with that effective strategies for the liberation of divided women can be clearly worked out. This book is intended as a positive contribution to the process of clarification.

During the 1960s and 1970s, radical feminism made the person behind the book at least partly visible. The author was no longer an impartial conveyor of general truths, but a subjective woman or man with a particular social position in a particular society. In writing on feminism I cannot take a universal standpoint, I can only look out from my own position and try to see beyond the boundaries that this imposes. I have written as a white, western, middle-class sociologist, now into middle age, married late to a foreigner and with two young sons. I write, therefore, as a woman exhausted by combining paid work and motherhood in a patriarchal society, but also as one of the most privileged of women attracted to feminism, and from a class and race that has received a great deal of criticism from less privileged women in recent years. Given this lack of objectivity, the problems of how diverse women can arrive at general feminist political strategies appropriate to the liberation of all women are considered throughout the book.

In the 1960s, feminists began to write in the first person and to speak of women as 'we', on the grounds that we all shared common interests as women oppressed by men. This use of 'we' has since been criticized by women who felt that their own lives were not included in many feminist generalizations. Since the basis of these criticisms, and the problems for feminism which they raise, form the theme of this book, I have not used an unqualified 'we'. I have used 'we' on some occasions when the points made seemed appropriate; when 'we' could be clearly qualified, or could be used of all women. I have used 'they' when writing of the feminists who have (regrettably but unavoidably) become constructed as the objects of this book. In practice it has been difficult to decide when it is appropriate to identify women as 'us'. The often uncertain line between 'them' and 'us' has come out of women's struggles against each other. 'I' has been used to indicate personal positions and opinions which have shaped the particular approach to feminism taken here. I have, however, tried to evaluate feminism from the perspective of feminist politics, rather than from my personal stance.

Feminist politics makes the choice of initial capitals or lower-case letters of some significance. I have opted in general for lower-case letters where there is debate on this issue. I have used lower case for both black women and white women. Although Black has been used in recent years to emphasize the importance of black experience and iden-tity which had been made invisible in racist societies, the problem with using Black and white is that it renders white politically unproblematic. I think the category of white is extremely problematic and needs critical attention. However, using Black and White seems politically no improvement on black and white, so I have simply used the latter and consider that neither term should be taken for granted. On the same grounds, I have used lower case for the west, the east and the third world. While I have generally retained the convention of capitals for some categories of women such as Muslims and Asians, I have used lower case for all categories of feminism. Otherwise the convention of referring to Marxist feminism and radical feminism seems to unbalance the relative importance of these versions of feminism.

PREFACE AND ACKNOWLEDGEMENTS

I am grateful to those who have offered support and encouragement so that I could write this book. Colleagues in the department of sociology at Goldsmiths' College covered my teaching during a year's leave of absence. Various comments on draft sections of the manuscript, on personal conversations, telephone calls and cries for help were made by Priscilla Alderson, Janet Bujra, Betsy Ettorre, Janet Holland, Huseyin Ramazanoglu, Sue Scott, Vic Seidler, and Angela Stock. To all of these I am grateful for their responses, and none of them bears any responsibility for what I have written. Thanks too to personal tutees, and students on the sociology of sex and gender course at Goldsmiths' College, for making me think, and to Emre and Jem for (mostly) letting me get on with it.

Part One

FEMINISM AS A THEORY OF OPPRESSION

INTRODUCTION
TO PART ONE

The outburst of feminist theory and practice, which has affected so many women's lives since the 1960s, differed from previous forms of feminism. It started from assertions of women's common sisterhood in oppression. Sisterhood expressed the idea that in general women have interests opposed to those of men, that men generally dominate women, and generally benefit from this domination. During the 1970s, however, feminists produced new knowledge of women's lives. Instead of establishing women's shared oppression as women, they began to emphasize the differences between women. Once attention was given to the diversity of women's experience, to the power of some women over other women, and to the political and economic interests shared by some men and some women, problems were created for feminism. Differences of interest between women challenged feminist theory of women's shared oppression. They also undermined the basis of feminist political practice. If women do not have interests in common, then it is not clear how feminist politics can change all women's lives for the better. The problems for feminist politics raised by these areas of difference constitute the main theme of the book. Part One serves to clarify preliminary problems in approaching recent feminist analyses of women's differences.

Opinions differ on how feminism may be dated, according to how it is defined. In order to avoid constant qualification, I have termed the period of feminist thought which developed from the 1960s to the time of writing, new-wave feminism, but elsewhere it may be referred to as second-wave, be divided into second-wave and third-wave or be labelled feminism and post-feminism. In Part One, new-wave feminism is presented as inherently contradictory. As it developed, theoretical accounts have been given of male dominance and female oppression which focus on the relationships between women and men. But in order to understand women's situations fully, it is also necessary to account for women's relationships with other women.

New-wave feminism has brought to light the many divisions between women which cut across our common experiences as women, and so has a contradiction at its heart. Women are very generally dominated by men, and live in societies in which such domination is taken to be natural and desirable, but women also oppress each other, and new-wave feminism has no clear means of resolving these divisions between us.

Chapter 1 reviews the problems of defining feminism and indicates the contradictions both in the experiences of ordinary women around the world and also in the ways in which feminists have come to understand these experiences. In chapter 2, the question of what is wrong with feminism is dealt with by examining critical problems in feminist explanation of women's oppression. These problems have led to the diverse rather than unanimous understandings of women's oppression. Given these weaknesses, the problems of why anyone should take feminist knowledge seriously are considered in chapter 3: the difficulties faced by feminists attempting to reinterpret the whole of human history, and to challenge the bases of existing knowledge. In chapter 4, I give a necessarily brief overview of the knowledge produced by new-wave feminism. This is not dealt with in depth as it is available elsewhere. It is reviewed here to show how developing knowledge of men's oppression of women has led both to knowledge of women's oppression and to the elaboration of differences and divisions between women.

The idea that new-wave feminism's problems spring from its development as a generalized theory is developed in Part Two. I argue that recent feminist thought has led towards the discovery of the diverse ways in which women experience oppression and the extent to which many forms of oppression are shared with men, rather than with other women. Feminist social theory has developed as a theory of women's oppression which divides women against women and feminists against each other.

In Part Three, the possible connections between feminist theory and feminist political practice are reassessed. Divisions between women indicate a rather different feminist politics from that envisaged at the start of the new wave. Liberation need not be a uniform or noncontradictory process. But feminism cannot hope to be taken seriously if the implications of liberation are not clearly related to the actual contradictions of women's lives.

Chapter One

FEMINISM
AS CONTRADICTION

There have been many versions of feminist thought throughout human history, and these are being shared and rediscovered after years of isolation and neglect. This book is an evaluation of some of the problems raised by the new wave of feminism which arose primarily in North America and Europe at around the time of the Vietnam War. This approach to feminism is inevitably ethnocentric, and does not give a full appreciation of the diversity of women's thought and women's struggles over the last twenty years or so, let alone throughout history. Naomi Schor (1987: 99) has commented that a focus which started geographically close to Britain, but from the standpoint of French feminism, would be no less ethnocentric, but would be different. Feminism does not have an agreed meaning or content around the world, and is in many ways so diverse that it cannot be easily characterized. The point of focusing on new-wave feminism is to try to explain both the diversity and the potentiality of feminism as an international phenomenon.

New-wave feminist ideas were launched over a very few years, often in ignorance of earlier struggles over the same issues. They were spread very rapidly, largely by educated young women moving between different countries (see e.g. Dahlerup 1986). These ideas provoked an enormous public response, both positive and negative, in societies already shaken by race riots, civil rights movements, anti-war protests, student demonstrations, pressure for sexual liberation, gay rights movements and the rise of drug and hippie cultures. Feminist ideas quickly spread to societies with rather different internal struggles and to the third world. Nowhere was women's political activity as women new, but new-wave feminism made the very general subordination of women to men all over the world political in many new ways.

The term third world is inadequate for encompassing the complex connections within and between the different countries of the world, but it is used here to indicate approximate areas of difference in women's situations and histories. New-wave feminism logically and politically requires that the ideas and practices developed in the west become part of the experience of women everywhere. The problems inherent in this position are recognized in feminism now and constitute one theme of this book.

The early euphoria produced by politicizing the shared oppression of women by men provoked hostile media reactions to the castrating, bra-burning, unfeminine women's libbers. Much more seriously, the new wave of feminism soon stimulated feminist critiques of feminist ideas and very diverse responses to such criticism. New-wave feminism split almost immediately into different schools of feminist thought, which offered different explanations of women's oppression and different strategies for liberation. Each school has attracted its own criticisms and generated its own practical problems.

WHAT IS FEMINISM?

Although many definitions of feminism have been attempted and a variety can be found in textbooks and dictionaries, and in general use, attempts to provide a general definition of feminism are inevitably confusing. Women's emancipation, or liberation, has developed numerous meanings over the years, not least because the ideas and political aims of those who have struggled for women have varied. Nineteenth-century European and American movements were split between socialist and liberal movements favouring either working-class or middle-class women. Some struggles were confined to white women, while others fought for rights for blacks or for the working class as well as for women. Organized women's movements had developed by the early twentieth century in most parts of the world. In addition, there have been many spontaneous women's struggles which are now forgotten, or are unknown outside local areas.

In the light of this diversity there are various possible approaches to the definition of feminism. These tend to vary according to the period and to the way in which they define 'woman'. Leaving aside popular and mass media definitions, which are generally limited or hostile, feminists themselves have recognized problems in defining feminism. For example, feminism can be defined in terms of American 1970s radical feminism, or nineteenth-century bourgeois movements. Writers early on in the new wave tended to take this narrow approach. A similarly narrow approach is also taken, however, by liberal feminists, and by those male commentators who identify feminism as an organized political movement. Alternatively, a broad definition can be offered which attempts to encompass all versions of feminism. This approach is more typical of feminists writing after new-wave feminism had clearly diversified into schools.

Neither of these solutions is particularly satisfactory. The narrow version excludes a variety of political practices and schools of thought which are widely regarded as feminist, and which have fought for women. At its worst it can lead to increasing concern with the exclusion of those who are not 'proper' feminists, rather than with political strategies to achieve unity. Narrow liberal definitions, which define feminism as a quest for equality with men, exclude most of new-wave feminism. Narrow definitions of an organized political movement exclude the wealth of feminist knowledge and practice which lies outside any organized movement, and is opposed to organization.

The broad version, however, fails to convey the variety and contradictions of feminist thought. A unified version of feminism cannot reconcile the conflicting struggles within feminism. Rather than attempting to impose uniformity on diversity, some feminists have simply accepted feminism as a loose term for a variety of conceptions of the relations between men and women in society, their origins and how they might be changed for the better (Mitchell and Oakley 1986). Further explanation of these differences is then needed to demonstrate the extent to which the different versions of feminism have any common characteristics.

Defining feminism is then clearly a question of taking a political stance. The way in which feminism is defined is contingent upon the way the definer understands past, existing, and future relationships between women and men. This book is an attempt to achieve a positive but critical evaluation of new-wave feminism which will make the nature and causes of these problems of definition somewhat clearer. Ultimately a conception of feminism rests upon a vision of the future and, as with all such visions, the relations between what we can understand of human history, of present societies, and of what might be, become critical strengths or weaknesses. Feminism has many weaknesses, and many critics to point these out. But it is the only social theory at present which retains some optimism for the future. In the

1980s this optimism, which owed much to western culture in the 1960s, has been faltering (Segal 1987), but it is by no means extinguished. The first generation of new-wave feminists are older and more tired than when they began, but not down and not out. Defining feminism remains difficult because feminism entails rethinking the past and the future, and seeing women as active agents in achieving change. Feminists share at least some understanding of what women's oppression might mean, but they differ enormously over what could constitute women's liberation.

I think it is possible to generalize about feminism, but only within limits and with very careful qualification. It is possible to generalize about women, but again only to a limited extent. When I use the terms 'woman' or 'women' without qualification, I refer to all people who are, were, or will be physically female, but it is frequently necessary in discussing the oppression and liberation of women to qualify the term and to specify which categories of women are being discussed.

At this stage it is sufficient to state that feminism comprises various social theories which explain the relations between the sexes in society, and the differences between women's and men's experience. Without giving a precise definition, it can be said that the various versions of feminism share certain common characteristics:

1 all versions of feminism assert that the existing relations between the sexes, in which women are subordinated to men, are unsatisfactory and ought to be changed;
2 feminism challenges much that is taken for granted as natural, normal and desirable in our various societies;
3 feminism consists of ideas which raise fundamental problems of explanation. The whole history and future course of human society is brought into question;
4 feminism is not simply ideas. Its point is to change the world, to transform the relations between women and men so that all people can have more chance to fulfil their whole human potential; feminism is logically then a set of ideas which are also a political practice;
5 feminism comprises very varied political practices but these are all aimed at changing the relations between the sexes by giving women control over their own lives; they may vary from consciousness-raising groups and struggles over the washing up, to struggles for separation from men, to organized demands for civil liberties and

economic and political power; feminism is then by definition provocative;

6 feminist proposals for change always encounter resistance, although the nature and strength of this resistance is variable;

7 feminism does not start from a detached and objective standpoint on knowledge of the relations between women and men. Even the most moderate advocates of women's rights must take the view that men have rights which are unjustly denied to women. This commitment does not mean that feminist knowledge is not valid knowledge, but it does entail asking what we mean by knowledge, and why some forms of knowledge are seen as more valid than others. Feminism implies a radical critique of reason, science and social theory which raises serious questions about how we know what we think we know.

Once feminism is seen both as social theory and also as practical politics, as an engagement in struggle to change the world, the goals of change have to be defined. But the political strategies of different groups of feminists vary very widely, which makes any common definition of feminist aims problematic. There are considerable differences in social theory and political strategy between campaigns to get more women into prominent positions in public life, 'reclaim the night' marches aimed at making public spaces safer for women, campaigns for more liberal abortion laws, campaigns against sterilization and infanticide, and attempts to draw low-paid women into trade unions. The problem of finding a common definition for feminism is not then simply one of finding the correct form of words which will cover everything satisfactorily, it is a problem *with* feminism. The problem can best be seen clearly in two main areas of contradiction: in feminist social theories that explain the relations between the sexes; and in the nature of women's lives and experiences in society.

CONTRADICTIONS IN FEMINISTS' CONCEPTIONS OF WOMEN'S LIVES

The main contradiction in new-wave feminism is between the different schools of feminist thought and different strategies of feminist political practice. Not every feminist can be assigned to a particular school of thought. In practice it is getting increasingly difficult to label individuals or to identify boundaries between schools as feminists struggle to learn from each other and to bridge our differences. Yet the development of different versions of feminism with distinctive theoretical positions has given new-wave feminism acute political problems which are still with us. It is still useful to distinguish between these schools of thought in order to clarify the contradictions inherent in feminism.

There is a convention of grouping different theorists loosely together on the basis of the assumptions they make about human nature, the relative importance of biology, ideology and material conditions in determining social practices, and on the basis of their strategies for change. These groupings vary somewhat between different countries. The radical feminism of the 1970s, with its emphasis on unstructured organization, lack of hierarchy and lack of leadership, was a particularly American product which has had a limited impact in, for example, Scandinavia (Dahlerup 1986) compared to Italy (Hellmann 1987) or in many spontaneous political conflicts in which women are involved (Ridd and Callaway 1986). Marxist feminism has been stronger in Europe than in America, but with numerous variations. There are some unique schools, such as the French 'Psycho et Po' (Duchen 1986).

A brief review of three main categories, however, brings out key differences within feminist thought and practice. These categories should properly be further subdivided distinguishing, for example, between different strands of radical and revolutionary feminism or between varieties of marxist and socialist feminism, but these three groupings suffice here to show the main contradictions inherent in feminist theory and practice.

Liberal feminism

Liberal feminists have followed a long tradition of campaigning for improved rights and opportunities for women without seriously questioning the existing organization of society. This strand of feminist thinking and political practice is widespread around the world, and is the version of feminism most clearly understood by non-feminists. Liberal feminism can be very threatening when it arises in conservative societies (UNESCO 1984), but in the west it is much more generally approved than new-wave feminism. Liberal feminism poses particular problems for general definitions of feminism as there are important differences between liberal versions of the relations between the sexes and the more radical and marxist feminist views, which are discussed below. Liberal feminism overlaps with non-feminist analyses of social relations which are concerned primarily with concepts of justice and equality (for example, Midgley and Hughes 1983). Liberal feminism assumes that women suffer injustices because of their sex (Richards 1982: 14) and is organized around campaigns for equality and redistribution: equal pay, equal civil rights, equal access to education, health and welfare, equal access to the democratic political process. Liberal feminist movements can be found wherever women fight for health, work, education, legal rights, decent housing, and an improved standard of living for women in general. These struggles do not, however, seriously challenge non-feminist understandings of the causes of the inequalities between women and men.

Liberal feminism acknowledges that women are widely discriminated against because of their gender, but does not identify the relations between the sexes as specific power relations. In this respect it differs both theoretically and politically from radical and marxist forms of feminism which are both directly concerned with power relations within sexual politics. One reason for the difficulty of defining feminism satisfactorily, then, is the problem of whether or not to include liberals as feminists. If they are excluded then many women who have given up their lives to fighting for women's rights are summarily dismissed as non-feminist by women who claim a theory of universal sisterhood. If they are included, the definition of feminism has to be stretched to cover theories and political practices of quite different sorts, which are addressed to radically different visions of liberation. This stretching renders the definition of feminism of limited political use.

Radical feminism

Radical and revolutionary feminists have been the real innovators in establishing new-wave feminism as an understanding of social relations to be reckoned with. Radical feminism is the most difficult version of feminism to define because it has always been diverse, and has become more so over the years. Yet radical feminists can be identified as sharing some common assumptions which differentiate their approach to women's oppression by men from other groups of feminists (Jaggar 1983). While liberals campaigned for specific rights for women, radical feminists launched an assault on the whole of male-dominated

11

society. Women's common political interests were identified in our general condition of subordination to men. The conventional wisdom in western culture that women's place is in the home and at the service of men was torn apart by the revelation of women as unnaturally confined and restricted by the institutions of patriarchal society.

Many radical feminists have adopted an explicitly anti-intellectual stance. They have objected to the intellectual evaluation of feminism (Hellman 1987: 200). But, as many radical feminists have recognized, if you want to change the world, you need to get your theory right. Male categories of thought, and male knowledge of social life, have had to be tackled explicitly, and evaluated as knowledge. The feminist evaluation of radical feminist knowledge and practice is one of the many contradictions thrown up by the diversity of feminism.

Radical feminists in the 1960s and 1970s, especially a few small and extremist groups, attracted the most distorted, outraged and virulent media coverage. But it was the radical feminists who inspired an international movement which differed substantially from nineteenth- and twentieth-century liberal and socialist women's movements. Radical feminism has had such an impact on thinking about gender and about women's lives that it is sometimes hard to realize just how radical it was at the time. Susan Griffin (1982: 39) notes of her earlier work on rape,

> I wrote 'The Politics of Rape' in 1970. During this time rape was not generally perceived as a political issue, and to call it one seemed a daring and extreme act. And it was not then common to use the pronoun 'I' in a political essay, nor to begin such an essay by describing one's emotions.

Radical feminism focused directly on women's relation to men as politically problematic. It brought sexuality and reproduction into the political arena and transformed women's political consciousness.

The radical feminist strategy of small, non-hierarchical, consciousness-raising groups allowed women to share their personal experiences of oppression. The radical feminist slogan, 'the personal is political', allowed women to make sense of their own lives as part of common experiences in male-dominated societies. This turned rape and other forms of male violence into public political issues. Radical feminism focused political attention on patriarchal oppression in every area of women's lives, from the most private to the most public. For those of us brought up in the 1950s, women's struggles were not unknown and feminism was not entirely new (Spender 1983), but radical feminism blew our minds.

American radical feminists drew on a long tradition of women's challenges to conventional accounts of society and human behaviour, from the eighteenth century up to the 1960s. But works such as those of Morgan (1971), Millett (1977) and Firestone (1979) broke new ground in feminist theory, and stimulated new forms of political activity among women. Some radical feminists began to move in a different direction by celebrating women's essential difference from men, and by revaluing creative and nurturing aspects of femininity which had become devalued or distorted in patriarchal society (Daly 1978: Griffin 1978; Rich 1980). This development has made it particularly difficult to generalize about radical feminism. The separatist politics to which this theory gave rise also led to problems in connecting feminist theory and political practice. I take up these problems in later chapters.

Radical feminists produced knowledge of women's oppression by challenging conventional assumptions. By redefining the most intimate of human relations as political, rather than as private, radical feminists politicized sexuality and exposed men's normal, everyday behaviour as a widespread social problem. By questioning what was taken for granted in existing understandings of nature and society, they revealed such knowledge as male knowledge which gave a spurious legitimacy to women's inferiority. Radical feminists rejected liberal strategies of gaining more justice for women within the existing social order. They questioned the legitimacy of any social order which created and maintained the oppression of women by men.

Although radical feminism sprang from issues affecting mainly young, middle-class, American and European women in the 1960s and 1970s, it was conceived as a theory, and thus as a set of political practices which could be applied to the struggles of women everywhere. The radical feminist theory of what was wrong in the relations between women and men was intended to be applicable all over the world and through most of human history. Radical feminism defined women as universally oppressed, as sisters in oppression, in a world owned, controlled and physically dominated by men.

Marxist feminism

Marxist feminism is in a way more inherently contradictory than radical feminism. Socialism is a struggle for the interests of a particular class at a particular historical stage of human development. Marxist feminists are, therefore, in the contradictory situation of having a commitment to struggle for the interests of women as women, regardless of our class, power or economic interests, while at the same time having a commitment to struggle for the interests of the exploited working class, which entails struggling with some men and against some women. New-wave marxist feminism grew out of reactions to marxism, inspired by radical feminism. Radical feminist assertions of women's common oppression were incompatible with classical marxist analysis. The new radical feminist insights which exposed women's common oppression as women, and celebrated sisterhood in oppression, had a powerful influence on marxist women's thinking. The rise of radical feminism, for example, raised women's consciousness of the subordinate roles they were expected to play in left-wing political organizations and protest movements. Reactions to the sexism of left-wing and black men brought awareness of conflicts of interest between women and men, and of class and racial divisions in capitalist societies. While marxist analysis could not explain women's oppression by men, radical feminist analyses did not address the problems of divisions between women.

Previously, socialist women had taken up the cause of oppressed working-class women, but had seen the struggle for women's issues as subordinate to the more general class struggle within capitalism. Feminism was dismissed as a bourgeois expression of women's interests, which did not act in the real interests of working-class women. The explosion of radical feminism allowed socialist women to become feminists in pursuit of women's goals which, to some extent at least, transcended class. This made marxist feminism inherently problematic from its inception.

Different marxist feminists have taken up different versions of marxism. These differences are crucially important in determining the exact relationship between marxism and feminism. Since they require a major review of marxist scholarship and practice around the world, they cannot be adequately dealt with here. I have only been able to draw on a highly simplified version of a relatively sympathetic interpretation of Marx's theory and method as a means to a fuller understanding of what is entailed in the liberation of women. This simplified interpretation does not elucidate the exact positions of marxist feminists who draw explicitly on the work of later marxists, nor does it clarify differences between marxist feminists which are rooted in their different interpretations of socialism.

Marxist feminists questioned the adequacy of marxist theory and politics, since socialism, although it could produce improved material conditions for women, clearly did not produce women's liberation from men. But at the same time, they also reacted against what they saw as the unjustified universality of radical feminist analysis. Because they were very conscious of the class divisions between women, and of the legacy of colonialism and imperialism, the assumption of one form of oppression affecting all women equally was treated as problematic. Marxism and feminism have not been integrated (Rowbotham *et al.* 1979; Sargent 1981), but radical feminism's influence on marxism led marxists to ask new questions. Marxist feminism came into conflict with radical feminism, particularly in Britain, and has remained in a state of some tension ever since.

Like radical and unlike liberal feminism, marxist feminism focused on power differences between women and men. Marxist scholarship offers little analysis here, so marxist feminists drew on radical feminist notions of patriarchy (the generalized power of men over women) and on the notion of sexual politics (the general struggle of women against men's power over them). Both radical and marxist feminists drew on Engels's essay on the family although not uncritically.[1] The concept of patriarchy then became one of the most central, but also one of the most confused terms in feminist use. It is discussed further in chapter 2.

My own inclination favours marxist feminism. My bias in this direction has come largely from working in South Wales, Uganda and Turkey, where I experienced both the limits of other social theories in explaining labour migration and, at a personal level, the enormous differences of interest between women. But this is a statement of my bias, rather than an assertion that marxist feminism provides everything we need to know in order to change society. There is, however, no way of being all things to all women within feminism, and if my biases had been more towards radical feminism, the balance of this book would, no doubt, have been different.

I prefer the term marxist feminism to the politically more ambivalent socialist feminism, because it was Marx's method of social analysis that enabled feminists to produce knowledge of the wider context of women's varying oppression through history. I do not think that a commitment to marxist feminism need entail commitment to a masculine vision of socialism, nor approval of the quality of women's lives in male-dominated, totalitarian states. Nor does it mean that marxist feminism is independent of radical feminism. All versions of feminism have strengths and weaknesses, and marxist feminism could not exist in the forms that it does now if there had been no liberal or radical feminism. Radical feminism was in part a reaction against marxist explanation. But radical feminist ideas have also been taken into marxist feminism, creating new contradictions, but also positive and creative understandings of society. It is through debates between schools that we have to find effective political strategies for feminism.

Each of the three general approaches outlined above will offer different political strategies. Liberals struggle for reforms to the present system, radical feminists struggle for the overthrow of patriarchy (which will entail capitalism) and marxist feminists struggle for the overthrow of capitalism (which will entail patriarchy). The immediate objects of struggle are different. The philosophical problems implicit in each of these positions then become of great practical importance.

Radical and marxist feminism are both clearly feminist in that they question every aspect of the power relations between women and men, although in different ways. Liberal feminism is very different to the extent that so much more of what now exists is taken for granted. The main argument against liberal feminists is that because they neglect the realities of male power over women, their political strategies are largely ineffective. Legal changes to promote equality do not tackle the underlying economic causes of inequality. In practice, however, most people who read this book will owe their education, civil rights, health, and personal liberty to liberal women's struggles. Radical feminism emerged in countries where women have considerable intellectual freedom within the constraints of patriarchal ideologies. It is the masculine convention of contrasting reformism with radical or revolutionary change which leads to liberal activity being seen as ineffective. If we treat the reform/revolution dichotomy as yet one more male dualism which should be questioned (Harding 1986), liberalism can be seen to edge into a broadly based view of feminist politics. A more telling argument against the efficacy of liberal feminism is Jaggar's point (1983: 48) that liberal feminism is incapable of conceiving of women's liberation. Liberal feminism has appealed to bourgeois or middle-class women within national movements, rather than to the millions of working-class, rural, and destitute women who make up the majority of the world's female population.

16

CONTRADICTIONS IN WOMEN'S LIVES

The difficulty of defining feminism has illustrated some of the contradictions of feminist theory. The circumstances of women's lives illustrate further problems for feminist theory and political practice. While all schools of feminism are agreed that men very generally dominate women, the question of the divisions between women is more controversial. Marxist feminists have criticized liberal and radical feminism on the grounds that their political strategies ignore the different class interests of working-class and bourgeois women. Working-class women are economically exploited in ways that the women of the bourgeoisie are not. Black, ethnic-minority, and third-world women have criticized radical and marxist feminists for their ignorance and insensitivity to racial and ethnic differences between women. Radical feminists have criticized liberals for trying to share male power rather than to transform it. Liberal feminists have seen radical feminists as unnecessarily hostile to men, unwilling to let men share in struggles for women's liberation, and marxist feminists as too left-wing. Disagreements within and between these schools over the extent to which women differ from men vary from some liberal calls for freedom to be as like men as possible, to some radical feminist struggles for freedom as total separation from men in action, thought, and culture.

These contradictions within feminism are clearly related to contradictions in women's lives. Women have been active in resistance and struggle all over the world but, as Omvedt (1980: 163) comments, it is one thing to spread the consciousness of women's oppression, it is another to create a women's movement among women who have no common political perspective. Even a cursory look at the variety of women's experiences, around the world and through history, shows the limited extent to which women's experiences are shared. The Icelandic notion of women's strikes (Styrkarsdottir 1986) (in which even the prime minister of Iceland joined for a day in 1987) would be improbable in India, but then Icelandic women do not experience the kinds of oppression that many Indian women suffer (Kishwar and Vanita 1984). Indian women's struggles against male violence may have some parallels in Iceland, but dowry deaths, female infanticide, debt bondage, child labour, the particular conditions of domestic servants, the consequences of land reform, and the personal wealth of the very rich have no obvious counterparts in Iceland. Indian women are divided by class and caste, by religion, and by region. There are differences of interest between mothers-in-law and daughters-in-law, mothers of sons and the childless, employers and servants, landowners and the landless, those who have some hope for the future and those who have none. It is perfectly possible to argue that Icelandic women are subordinated to Icelandic men in ways which make their sisterhood with Indian women, as women, a reasonable concept — they can all be raped, they can generally be subordinated as housewives — but this ignores other significant differences between women's lives in Iceland and in India. The sources of oppression which affect women's lives in India are more varied and contradictory than those found in Iceland.

The gulfs between privileged women who can exercise considerable choice over the course of their lives and women who have to struggle alongside men for their subsistence, let alone for any further rights, are enormous. Take, for example, the need for adequate day care for children of parents who work outside the home. Large American companies are finding that with women now reaching high levels of management, and with a new generation of management fathers beginning to suffer from paternal guilt, adequate day care for management's children is essential. It can be cheaper to send a paid nurse to care for a sick child at home than to allow a highly paid mother time off to care for her own child (Chapman 1987). This situation is hardly comparable with that of Guatemalan Indian families for whom day care for their children would mean the right for small children *not* to work for their own subsistence on coffee and cotton plantations (Menchu 1984). While executive mothers agonize over whether their children will be adequately emotionally adjusted, Guatemalan mothers agonize over whether their children will survive hard labour, inadequate food, pesticide spraying, and the violence of plantation owners and the state. It is hard to see that Guatemalan Indian women and high-flying American executives have common interests in any present struggle. While this example is one of extreme contrasts, its existence does raise problems for any universalistic theory of women's common oppression.

It is true that both executive and Guatemalan Indian women can be subjected to male dominance, male violence and rape. The dangers should not be underestimated, but executive women can buy themselves considerable protection from male violence. They still face enormous practical and emotional problems in combining stressful executive jobs with marriage and motherhood in a culture where

18

most men have yet to discover what equal domestic labour means, but they have considerable resources with which to identify and tackle these problems. While Guatemalan women may well be subject to male domination, their overwhelming struggle is for physical survival against the terrorism of the state, the landowners and the military, a struggle in which their hopes for survival lie with their menfolk rather than with American women.

> Women work picking coffee and cotton, and on top of that, many women have taken up arms and even elderly women are fighting day and night; so it isn't possible to say now that we're setting up an organisation so that women can rebel, work or study women's problems.
>
> (Menchu 1984: 221)

Women's lives are contradictory in the sense that we are not an oppressed minority who can clearly see our oppression as women. We are biologically distinguished from men by our sex. The cultural meanings and social practices which have become attached to the two sexes are not, however, uniform or fixed. Being a woman or being a man is not the same experience in all places and at all times. The knowledge and skills needed to survive, the value attached to what is defined as masculine and what as feminine, the choices exercised over personal action, and the power exercised over others are all variable. While it may be very generally established that men exercise power over women it is not universally so, and such power is variable and can be resisted. Sometimes men have little power over anyone, sometimes women have power over men, as for example in slave societies, in racially divided societies, or as employers.

New-wave feminism produced overwhelming evidence of widespread social discrimination against women, and restrictions on women's freedom, in favour of men's liberty and control. Feminists were able to find this evidence because their social theories encouraged them to ask questions and to look for answers in ways which were not part of conventional wisdom, but they differed in the ways in which they interpreted the answers that they found. In addition to divisions between feminists in the ways in which they accounted for evidence of women's oppression, there was increasing evidence that treating women as a non-problematic category was an improper approach. If it is not immediately obvious what the term 'woman' means in empirical terms, then the term needs qualification. Are black and

19

white women in racist societies, destitute women in affluent societies, women dying of famine and women political leaders, affluent western housewives, and teenagers forced into prostitution all 'women' in anything more than the biological sense of the term? That is, do they all stand in the same relationship to men? Are they all oppressed by men in the same way? Once such questions began to be asked, the enormous diversity of women's lives, the variability of our relationships to men and to each other make the problems of defining oppression in general terms apparent. Sisterhood in oppression can then be seen as a much more limited concept than had originally been intended.

The main categories of division between women are examined in Part Two. Marxists and marxist feminists have always argued that women are divided by our relationships to the ways in which production systems are organized. In capitalist societies, working-class women do not have the same interest in maintaining capitalism as do women of the bourgeoisie. Women are clearly divided by class. Some women benefit both directly and indirectly from the exploitation of other women. Where women are exploited, their interests in resisting oppression may lie more clearly with similarly exploited men than with other women who have no knowledge or experience of exploitation.

Sources of division between women can be found in many other circumstances in which women share interests with men. In addition to class, women have different interests as members of different races and ethnic groups, or as adherents of different religions. Even the ways in which kinship groups are organized can divide women against each other (Whitehead 1984: 8). Women in some instances are divided by the powers allocated to different age groups, which can give dominant older women considerable power over young subordinates. They may, for example, favour their sons' interests at the expense of those of their daughters-in-law. Feminists have argued that sexuality is the basis of women's unity in relation to men, but sexual differences between women have proved to be the source of bitter divisions. Women are also divided by conflicts between nations which are maintained through differential access to power.

Women's emotional attachments to men have also proved divisive. Where women's ambitions are limited to marriage and motherhood, and where these are the only respectable achievements that are socially permitted, feminism can seem a frightening prospect. New-wave feminism tried to show women that we all have interests in common in spite of the obvious differences between us. The foundations of

20

sisterhood lie in the politics of gender, in women's common struggle against men's power. Feminism was intended to develop as a universal theory to show women the nature of our oppression and as an international political practice to achieve our liberation. From this optimistic start feminists had to come to terms with the diversity of women's experience, and women with diverse interests had to come to terms with feminism. It has been a very considerable problem for new-wave feminism that it emerged among the most privileged women in a divided society, and in the most powerful nation of a divided world.

UNIVERSAL FEMINISM AND WESTERN CULTURE

New-wave feminism was the product of privilege and power produced within a particular western culture with its own values and its own battles to define oppression, freedom, truth, science, and individual rights and liberties. Feminism is itself a cultural product of a particular historical period. This does not of itself make the theory unconvincing, but it does raise very considerable problems in generalizing across cultures about what women's liberation could consist of. The difficulty of defining women's liberation (which has perhaps been explored most directly in feminist science fiction) is an inherent weakness of western feminism. Feminist theories of oppression can only be evaluated in relation to some cross-cultural conception of liberation, but the problems in attempting such an evaluation have scarcely begun to be faced. If we turn from attempting to establish that women are very generally oppressed to trying to establish what women's liberation ought to, and in practice could, consist of, the many serious divisions of interest between women are revealed.

The divisions which have developed within feminism ensure that even the term 'oppression' is disputed, so that the terms used to conceptualize the relations between women and men vary from the liberal conception of inequalities to more radical conceptions of the universal exploitation of women. I take oppression to mean the various ways in which men have been seen to dominate women, and in which social structural arrangements have been seen to favour men over women. Oppression is not wholly satisfactory as a term, but it is useful as a single concept which conveys the political impact of recent feminist thought. Lerner (1986: 233–5), for example, objects to the use of a single term as confusing the interpretation of women's history. She argues that the term oppression implies forceful subordination, with women as passive victims. She prefers the term subordination as not entailing evil intent by men, allowing for collusion by women and being neutral as to cause, but demands different terms for different historical situations. A single term is limited, but oppression is a relatively loose concept which can be qualified in different situations. It does not need to entail evil intent on the part of men nor passivity on the part of women. It indicates the very general case that feminists have made in establishing the general dominance of men over women, and does not preclude the use of qualifying terms such as subordination, discrimination, and exploitation. The point of conceptualizing recent feminist thought as a challenge to conventional knowledge is to argue that this approach to feminism is politically problematic. I am not disputing that women are very generally oppressed by men, but I am arguing that the focus of new-wave feminist work on women's shared oppression as women has had the contradictory effect of emphasizing the divisions between women.

Rather than try to impose an assumption of shared oppression on the diversity of women's situations, it would seem realistic to accept that feminism is contradictory. It is a *universal theory* in that it is a general theory of the oppression of women by men. While feminists disagree on exactly how uniform such oppression can be, without some element of universality there can be no feminism. It is as women *vis-à-vis* men that, feminists argue, women have shared interests in transforming society. But, as has been very dramatically shown by its critics, feminism is also a *historically and culturally specific set of practices* in social situations where women have conflicting interests and diverse experiences. It is when women begin to struggle against oppression that they discover the contradictory obstacles they are 'really' up against — which can include one another.

LIBERATION AND CONTRADICTION

If the oppression of women is contradictory, the prospects for women's liberation must also be contradictory. Once women begin to define visions of liberation, it is quite clear that one woman's view of the perfect society can seem appalling to another. Different experiences of oppression not only lead to different conceptions of liberation but they are complicated by male ideological dominance over women's access to visions of liberation. Women in male-dominated societies have had limited ideas and language with

22

which to conceive of social transformation.

With all its limitations and contradictions, however, we need feminism, first, in order to produce knowledge of what we could not see before, and second, to encourage us to act on situations which were previously confused, frustrating, depressing, isolating, or threatening. There are many situations where women need to struggle with men against external threats or oppression, as well as many situations in which women need to struggle against men. The production of feminist knowledge should provide specific and accurate accounts of these situations which can be used as effective guides to liberation. This leaves the problem of how far feminism can provide an adequate social theory for total social transformation, a point to which I shall return in chapter 8.

My purpose in exploring the relation between oppression and liberation is not to attack feminist theory, nor to devalue any version of feminism. It is only by facing divisions between women honestly, and by accepting that some women are oppressed not only by men but also by other women, that the implications and desirability of liberation can be approached. We should not then be afraid of, or ashamed of, our contradictions. If they exist we need to understand them before we can tackle them. Ignoring or denying the salience of the divisions between women has stimulated hostile criticism of new-wave feminism by women. The connection between oppression and liberation is a central problem for feminist theory and practice, and is the focus of the rest of the book.

Chapter Two

WHAT IS WRONG
WITH FEMINISM?

One problem with feminism has been that many prominent feminists who have generated tremendous political excitement have not been particularly rigorous as social theorists. Criticism of feminism can often mean picking on two or three more extreme radical feminists, for whom the philosophy of social science was not a primary concern (e.g. Daly 1978; Firestone 1979; Spender 1980), and then generalizing these criticisms to feminism as a whole. Many books like these have had a tremendous impact on women's lives because they have caught women's imaginations, enabled them to ask new questions, and connected previously disconnected strands of experience, but they have proved vulnerable to the analyses of those who are not convinced by their arguments. The explosion of American radical feminism in the 1970s was not usually presented as carefully articulated social theory, but more as what Midgley and Hughes (1983: 222) have termed stink bombs: outbursts which ensure an audience, but put little emphasis on patient, reasoned argument. Stink bombs can attract attention where patient arguments are ineffective, but they do not necessarily continue to be effective once the logic of the arguments is worked through in relation to practice. Nevertheless these radical texts, in spite of their logical and philosophical flaws, generated political excitement, anger and enthusiasm on a scale never matched by the more carefully qualified texts which followed. It is only in the recent texts of black and third-world women (see chapter 6) that a comparable level of passion can be found.

It is only to be expected that feminist work which is directly critical of the power of men, in societies where access to the mass media is dominated by men, will be blocked, discredited, distorted, and mocked. Feminist work survives its critics because women want it, and so have created feminist knowledge as a marketable product. It is yet another contradictory aspect of the development of new-wave feminism that its subversive knowledge, in certain conventional forms, sells.

New-wave feminists cannot afford to ignore their critics, even though criticisms of feminism are very uneven and their targets somewhat varied. The question of what is wrong with feminism is not always as obvious as might be thought. Some criticisms are couched in terms of more or less conventional academic disputes. Some are wholesale but relatively uninformed dismissals of everything feminist. Sometimes the behaviour and lifestyle of particular feminists is criticized, or particular movements, such as abortion rights campaigns, are taken to represent the whole of feminist thinking. The diversity of these criticisms reflects the problems of defining feminism, which have been discussed in chapter 1. This has left us with difficulties in evaluating the strengths and weaknesses of recent feminist thought. Criticisms can be useful though, as they have identified real problems in the ways in which feminists explain the oppression of women by men.

The gulf between feminism and male-dominated thought is so wide that there has been little close engagement between feminist thought and many of its critics, as compared with the critique of men's thought by feminists. In focusing on problems in feminism, I have drawn as far as possible on feminist critics who are familiar with what they are criticizing, and for whom the liberation of women remains both a necessity and a possibility. The criticisms of feminism which are dealt with in this and subsequent chapters do, therefore, constitute problems for feminism, but they do not invalidate the knowledge produced by feminist social theory. The feminist challenge to existing forms of knowledge and existing power relations remains.

The problems of making feminist knowledge convincing are taken up in chapter 3, but it should be clear that I cannot give an objective evaluation of feminism which is independent of my personal passions. I cannot give an impartial account of the 'facts' about feminism, but I can criticise feminism as part of an argument for taking feminist politics seriously. Because of the enormous numbers of women who have contributed to the theory and practice of new-wave feminism it has not been possible to give this knowledge back to its subjects for checking, as part of the process of validation. It is, therefore, only through publication that a critical contribution to debate can be made and differences made explicit.

While there are a number of points which might have been reviewed here, I have picked only four. Clarification of these issues can illustrate the main problems in connecting feminist social theory with coherent political practice. In the rest of this chapter, I deal in turn with the problem of the relationship between feminism and marxism; the problem of how to take account of biological differences between the sexes; the problems inherent in the concept of patriarchy, and the contradictions of universal generalizations. Although I have treated them as separate issues for discussion, in practice these problems are closely interrelated.

THE PROBLEM OF THE RELATIONSHIP BETWEEN FEMINISM AND MARXISM

The theoretical and political impetus for new-wave feminism was radical feminism. From radical feminism came the idea that women, regardless of class, race, or other differences, shared oppression as women. Marxist feminism took its socialism from Marx, and its feminism from radical feminism, but it questioned both. When Marx's analysis was applied to an understanding of women's place in capitalist society it led to the conclusion that women's liberation was subordinate to the goals of class struggle. Marxism could not explain what had happened to the relations between women and men during the rise of capitalism in Europe. It could not explain whether what happened to gender relations elsewhere in the world, as capitalism expanded, was similar or different. Marxist feminists of the 1970s challenged this absence of gender in Marx's analysis by looking again at women's situations, using ideas from the new radical feminism. The attempt to incorporate marxism into feminism, however, has proved extremely problematic. It has given rise to very serious practical and theoretical problems for feminism. The development of marxist feminist concepts led clearly to the conclusion that, far from being sisters in oppression, women were very much divided. Their opposing class interests cut right across their common problems as women in a world dominated by men.

This idea of oppression shared with some men rather than with all women exposed contradictions in trying to unite marxism and feminism. It has led to political divergence in feminist strategies for change (Segal 1987). The impact of marxist feminism (together with black and third-world criticisms which are discussed in chapter 6) was to counter the radical feminist view of women as universally

oppressed with a view of women as oppressed in multiple and contradictory ways.

The early phase of 1970s marxist feminism was labelled a 'marriage'
and, not surprisingly, this was seen to be an unhappy marriage (Hartmann 1981; Sargent 1981). Marxist feminism was far from being a
union of two compatible theories. Some early attempts to draw on
marxist insights to address feminist problems were philosophically quite
removed from classical marxism. More recently Cockburn (1986: 85)
has suggested that cohabitation rather than marriage might be
achieved, while Hamilton (1978: 104) had already proposed 'a decent
period of shacking up perhaps under the same roof but with separate
bedrooms'.

Radical feminists have been critical of the use of marxist analysis.
Marxism was clearly located within patriarchal institutions and
confined by patriarchal modes of thought. Marxist feminists need to
make careful distinctions between the conceptual inadequacies of
marxist theory, the sexism of male marxists, the political poverty of
western socialism, and the positive potential contribution of marxist
analysis to feminism. Marxist feminism is not simply marxism with
women put in, but a theoretical and political critique of marxism. A
theory which cannot account for women's history and experiences is
an inadequate theory and leads to ineffective attempts to change the
subordination of women. Marxism simply cannot distinguish women's
experiences from men's experiences, because it does not have the
necessary concepts. But while marxism is inadequate to explain the
oppression of women, versions of feminism which have ignored the
integration of gender relations into systems of production are also
inadequate. This is the dilemma for feminism posed by marxist
feminism.

The ways in which marxist feminists dealt with the problems of connecting feminism with marxism did not necessarily make for greater
clarity. For example, the issue of how men's domination of women
was interrelated with capitalists' domination of workers was initially
taken up as a general abstract issue, which would have one general
answer. This version of Marx's method led to deep but quite
unnecessary divisions, not only between marxist and radical feminists
but also among marxist feminists themselves. Some claimed patriarchal ideology as the underlying cause of women's oppression, some
biological differences between the sexes, and others the operation of
the mode of production. More recent work in marxist feminism has

tended to focus on much more historically specific analysis, with more limited grounds for generalization. I discuss some of the ways in which these arguments developed below, in relation to biology, patriarchy, and universal generalizations. The tension between marxism and feminism runs right through these problem areas.

Marxist feminists have criticized radical feminists explicitly for biological reductionism and overgeneralization, and have questioned the usefulness of patriarchy as a feminist concept, but marxism cannot account for men's power over women, We are still left with the problem that neither marxist nor radical feminism can stand alone as a solution to what is wrong with feminism. Radical feminism provides the main political thrust of feminist politics for all women. Speaking as a socialist feminist, Barrett (1984: 128) has commented, 'in a wider context it must be recognized that feminism in its non-socialist forms is immensely more powerful and influential than we are.' Marxist feminists are not politically united, but they have some degree of commitment to socialism. Radical and liberal feminists are generally critical of socialism, but these schools of feminism do not provide any political resolution of women's opposing class interests. Radical feminism does not have a theory of capitalism, and it cannot simply absorb a marxist theory of capitalism into feminism. The tensions between marxist theory and practice and feminist theory and practice still remain, leaving feminism with no clear political focus.

THE PROBLEM OF BIOLOGY

Why is it that women are so very generally dominated, oppressed and exploited by men? Why do men beat and rape women, rather than the other way around? Why do men go to war rather than women (although women's active role in warfare throughout history is now much better known than previously)? Why was women's labour less valuable than men's prior to large-scale industrialization? Behind these questions lies the problem of the importance of human biology in men's ability and willingness to dominate women. It is not clear that the relations between the sexes can be wholly independent of our biology. Men's physical dominance at the level of sexual relations, their ability to rape by force, is not a choice open to women, just as childbearing is not an option for men. At the same time, though, biological processes — sexual relations, puberty, childbirth — are given form and meaning only through social beliefs and practices.

28

While feminism is built on the premise that gender, or what societies recognize as normal male and female behaviour, is socially constructed, feminists have also tried to consider how far the physical differences between the sexes are socially significant. Feminists have been extensively criticized from within as well as from outside feminism because of the various ways in which they have tried to take the biological difference between women and men into account. Criticisms are sometimes aimed at biological reductionism, sometimes at biological determinism and sometimes at biological essentialism. For the purpose of this chapter, these differences of emphasis are not particularly important.[1]

Biological explanation became a way of thinking for some feminists in the process of rejecting previous knowledge of women's nature. It has been criticized as an inadequate way of understanding gender relations because it ignores historical variations in the ways societies have organized relations between women and men. The issue of biological reductionism (in the sense of reducing explanation of social relations to biological factors) has become a major problem in the ways in which feminists have tried to rethink the relations between people.

When feminists are accused of biological reductionism, they are being accused of being unable to explain what their theories purport to explain. As Bhaskar has put it (1978: 115), 'as a means of discovery reductionism must fail.' This is because if we try to reduce women's oppression to biological explanation, our biological knowledge will be of no practical use in enabling us to predict or control human affairs. Reducing explanation to the level of biology is only useful if we already know a good deal about how human society works. Elsewhere Bhaskar (1979: 126) comments:

> What the reductionists forget is that every historically
> successful example of a reduction (such as that of chemistry to
> physics) has depended on the prior existence of a well
> developed body of knowledge in the domain of the to-be-
> reduced science which, in a reduction, is then 'explained'. But
> of course the very problem in the human sciences is that there
> is no such body of knowledge: so that there is nothing (or at
> least as yet very little) for a reduction to explain. (Bhaskar
> 1979: 126)

Biological explanations were particularly characteristic of 1970s radical feminist explanations. There have been two main approaches.

1 arguments that men, determined by their masculine nature, are
   doomed to be women's oppressors (Brownmiller 1975; Dworkin
   1981), and conversely, that women are doomed to be men's victims;
2 arguments that once women can discover their own biological
   natures, concealed up until now by the dominance of male
   knowledge, they can positively celebrate their essentially creative,
   nurturing female nature and capacity for motherhood (Daly 1973;
   Griffin 1978; Rich 1980).

Both the negative and the positive approaches assume that women
share an innate, essential, female nature that distinguishes them from
men, and gives them interests in common with each other (even though
such apparent barriers as racial and class differences may obscure their
view of these common interests).

It is clear that many radical feminists have made statements which
imply that the behaviour of men towards women can be explained by
biological factors. It is less clear that these authors explicitly defended
biological reductionism in the face of criticism, as an essential ingre-
dient of feminist social theory. Shulamith Firestone, who has been one
of the most widely criticized of popular feminist authors, did not
attempt to sustain her original thesis (Firestone 1979) in the face of
criticism of her biological determinism. Her book was extremely
influential, when it was first published in America in 1970, in setting
off debates and further exploration of the nature of women's oppression, and in stimulating debates within feminism on the relation
between biology and oppression.[2] The more positive aspects of her
argument tend to have been forgotten, since as Spender (1985: 4) has
commented, 'classic texts are quickly lost — what endures are the
criticisms.'

Since early and more extreme versions of biological determinism
were quickly criticized, later writers were able to modify this position
to take account of some of the complexities of assigning causal
power either to biology or to social forces (rhodes and McNeill
1985: 7). Adrienne Rich (1980: 282) warned against naivety and self-
indulgence in developing political strategies from a radical feminist
theory of motherhood. She says (283), 'it can be dangerously simplistic
to fix upon ''nurturance'' as a special strength of women, which need
only be released into the larger society to create a new human order.'
She argues that women remain potentially both creative and
destructive.

Marxist feminists have been particularly critical of the biological reductionism of certain radical feminists, and of the difficulty of escaping biological reductionism in any radical feminism. Fox-Genovese (1982: 15) has argued that women have had to be actively excluded from the corridors of power, so they have not been naturally barred by their biology. Jaggar takes the view that much radical feminism, even if it is not explicitly determinist, has a constant tendency to slip into biological determinism because it treats human biology as a constant, without reference to historical contexts (Jaggar 1983: 113). But once radical feminists had raised the problem of how to take biology into account, marxist feminists were faced with the same problem. Marxist feminists had to recognize that it is the variable relations between the organization of production, the sexual division of labour, and the social construction of biological difference which makes the explanation of women's oppression so difficult.

Brenner and Ramas (1984), in criticizing Barrett (1980), looked at the problems of explaining how the working class had developed during the rise of capitalism. Within this class there was a structured gender hierarchy in which men were more valuable than women both at work and in the home. Women were subordinated to men. They worked outside the home but still retained responsibility for domestic labour and childcare.[3] Brenner and Ramas trace women's inability to compete effectively with men in the first industrial labour market to women's biological capacity to bear and nurse children. They reject the power of patriarchal ideology as an explanatory factor. They conclude (1984: 71) that the combination of the capitalist class system and biological reproduction combined at a particular point in time to create a family-household system which assured both women's subordination to men and their exploitation as workers. Barrett replied (1984) that the biological facts of reproduction were themselves mitigated by class factors. The superiority which men gained over women at this period cannot be understood as a simple consequence of the material capitalist base; the intervention of ideology must also be taken into account. It is the relationship between ideology and women's place as wage labourers which needs to be explained (Barrett 1984: 127).

In commenting on this debate, Lewis (1985) points out the historical difficulty of separating the causes of patriarchy (and patriarchal ideology) from the rise of capitalism, since they are now so thoroughly intertwined. Where there is evidence from socialist feminist historical research on Britain, the evidence does not support Brenner and

Ramas's generalizations. By arguing for the importance of biological reproduction they underestimated the complexity of the changing social relations in which women were involved.

The attempt by Brenner and Ramas to raise the problem of women's role in reproduction for marxist theory did, however, reveal the problems of explanation raised by marxist feminist rejection of biological explanations. Lewis (1985: 108) comments, 'If as Barrett says, feminists have been "squeamish" in the face of biology (Barrett 1984: 123) it is largely because of the difficulty they experience in skirting the minefield of biological determinism.' Lewis concludes, following Lown (1983), that class and gender are constructed simultaneously and must be investigated historically.

In practice, this conclusion is harder work than constructing causal generalizations without investigating variations. The level of generalization that results is very much more limited. We simply do not know in general how far women's capacity to bear and breastfeed babies has limited their economic roles. We do not know if men and women have essentially different natures which make women more caring and nurturing and men more aggressive and competitive. The extent of variation in how our biological capacities have been socially valued, invested with meaning and mediated by the social organization of production, makes generalization premature. We should be able to arrive at qualified general statements as the historical complexity of the interrelations of production systems, ideology, and biology become clearer. There are no obvious grounds for attributing general significance to biological or ideological or material factors without some explanation of *why* they should have had an overriding effect in a particular place at a particular time.

Soper argues (1979: 63) that in its zeal to escape biological reductionism, marxism has argued for the dominance of social over natural factors. This position has weakened marxist explanation, because biology still has to be taken into account even though it is always socially mediated. Although natural factors which constrain or affect human society cannot be explained wholly as natural (78) they are rendered as cultural products, such as motherhood, which do need to be explained.

There is a difference between slipping into philosophical traps (and feminists have often slipped) and defending entrenched philosophical positions. While those who have used constant biological forces as explanations for variable social behaviour have not adequately

defended their explanations, they have identified a major problem
which lies at the heart of feminist political practice. If women are not
to be identified as having common political interests through our
membership of the biological category 'woman', then on what grounds
can common political interests be identified (Delmar 1986)? It was
the 'discovery' of women as a biological category with common political
interests which gave radical feminism its political force in the 1960s
and 1970s. The subsequent acceptance by many feminists that
biological explanation is an inadequate basis for explaining the
historical variability of male domination, and no basis at all for
explaining the domination of some women over others, divides
feminists into different theoretical camps. This poses serious problems
for the coherence of feminist political practice. Both radical and
marxist feminists have made attempts to deal with the social meanings
of biological factors through the concept of patriarchy, which in itself
raises further problems.

THE PROBLEM OF PATRIARCHY

Patriarchy is a key concept used by feminists in recent years. It
encapsulates the mechanisms, ideology and social structures which have
enabled men throughout much of human history to gain and to maintain their domination over women, Any term with such a wide-ranging
task is likely to present problems. Patriarchy is not only a central concept
in feminist thought, it is also the term most disputed between feminists,
and it is used by different feminists in very different ways. Different
versions of the concept of patriarchy are used to present different
accounts of the nature and causes of men's domination of women.

Patriarchy, in the sense of the power of the father over his kinship
group, had been developed in social theory prior to feminists' use of
the term and had been used by anthropologists. But in the early 1970s
the use of the term was transformed as it took on political significance
in new-wave feminist discourse. Since the concept of patriarchy was
developed as a means of both identifying and challenging men's power
over women, theories of patriarchy are, implicitly or explicitly, theories
which explain the creation and maintenance of men's social,
ideological, sexual, political, and economic dominance.

The term patriarchy was taken up by radical feminists because
existing social theories had no general concepts to account for men's
domination. Social theories which had developed in the west from views

33

elaborated in the eighteenth and nineteenth centuries took men's superiority for granted. The absence of concepts for understanding male domination followed from the lack of questioning of male dominance. Men's dominant position in society was publicly taken for granted as the normal and desirable state of affairs. The unequal relations between men and women were not seen as needing explanation. (Though it should not be forgotten that throughout this period such complacency was repeatedly challenged by women at all levels of society, albeit with varying results.) Once feminists asked questions about why the relations between men and women were as they were, and how they could be changed, they had to create new concepts for answering their questions.

However patriarchy is defined, it is a concept used to attempt to grasp the mechanisms by which men in general manage to dominate women in general. It refers to ideas and practices ranging from the most intimate of sexual encounters to the most general economic and ideological factors. It came to mean not only the power of men in general over women in general, but also the hierarchical character of male power, and the ideological legitimation of this power as natural, normal, right, and just. It enabled feminists to 'see' the common oppression of all women in relation to all men. Radical feminists initially treated patriarchy as a universal characteristic of human society. Marxist feminists tried to take account of both mode of production and patriarchy in their understanding of men's dominance. This gave them the problem of approaching the universal concept of patriarchy historically.

Patriarchy as universal

The assumption that male dominance could be explained in general terms initially led feminists to search for a single overriding source of male power over women (e.g. Millett 1977; Daly 1978). This ahistorical view of patriarchy is most characteristic of 1970s American radical feminism, but has variants and qualified versions in America and elsewhere. It is this view of patriarchy which has probably attracted the most criticism, because it raises very directly issues of biological reductionism and conceptions of the innate essences of being male and being female. Because this approach is particularly vulnerable to criticism, attacks on this version of patriarchy have often been seen as disposing of the power of radical feminist argument in general.

The overgeneral use of patriarchy, however, was politically very effective in drawing women's attention to the extent of male dominance. It drew attention to the existence of power relations between men and women, not only in the public but also in the private domain of family, household, and sexual relations. The idea of patriarchy enabled women to see their personal experiences as part of a general sexual politics in which they shared interests with other women. It made the subordination and oppression of women by men visible and illegitimate, and stimulated political action.

The problem of treating patriarchy as socially constructed but still as universal is that it is difficult to avoid falling into the trap of biological determinism. If, for example, feminists are dealing with immediate practical issues, such as that of male violence towards women, they may assert that patriarchy is a cause but without being able to explain variation in male violence. Patriarchy does not just label men's power over women, it also creates a need for explanations of why men have this power and of how they maintain it. Where patriarchy is taken to be a universal characteristic of the relations between men and women, then, since all that women have in common is their biological sex, it is hard to avoid the assumption that patriarchy must be rooted in an essential masculine nature.

The conception of patriarchy as universal is logically based on the conception of woman as a universal category. Whether or not women are explicitly conceived of as a class whose interests are opposed to those of men as a class (a position taken, for example, by Firestone (1979) and Millett (1977)), men are seen as having and defending power over women. Criticism of biological determinism has been countered to some extent by those who have defined patriarchy as the institutionalization of male power, rather than as an innate property of being male (e.g. Spender 1985: 36). Spender argues that all men derive benefit from patriarchy so that all men are politically in opposition to women, but she qualifies this universalizing position by claiming that politics is only one dimension of existence so that individual men need not be treated as personal enemies (Spender 1985 and Spender 1986: 217).

Delphy (1984: 17–18) also modifies the initial radical feminist position. She rejects the universal notion of patriarchy in favour of patriarchy defined as the system of subordination of women by men in contemporary industrial society. This system has an economic base rooted in what Delphy terms the domestic mode of production. Where women have been subordinated elsewhere, or in the past, separate explanations are needed. Although Delphy's conception of the domestic mode of production has attracted criticism (e.g. Barrett and McIntosh 1979) Delphy maintains (1984: 22), against the radical feminist position, that it is useless to seek a single cause of women's oppression. But she also argues (180), against marxist feminists, that women do constitute a class with interests antagonistic to those of men.

Radical feminists also successfully used the conception of patriarchy to challenge conventional knowledge of society as patriarchal, that is, as constructed by men in men's interests. This conception of patriarchal ideology as a characteristic of western thought, however, has been more enduring than initial attempts to use an abstract concept of patriarchy to explain the whole history of relationships between women and men.

Patriarchy slipped into feminist discourse as a loose general category of explanation, particularly as 'patriarchal society'. Radical feminist approaches to patriarchy as an explanation of male dominance were mainly countered by feminists who drew more directly on marxist thinking. The influence of Marx's analysis of human history led marxist feminists to see patriarchy as a historical product, created by people in the course of their daily lives. This approach meant that patriarchy could not be taken for granted as a characteristic of the relations between men and women, but needed to be identified and explained in a variety of different historical situations.

Patriarchy as historical

In the 1970s, there were varied feminist attempts to treat both patriarchy and capitalism as generalized abstractions with the consequent problem of having to explain in very general terms the relationships between them. This was done either by locating patriarchy as an intervening variable between the mode of production and the oppression of women or by conflating patriarchy and capitalism into a system of capitalist patriarchy, or patriarchal capitalism (Patriarchy Conference 1978; Kuhn and Wolpe 1978; Eisenstein 1979; Sargent 1981). The way in which this was done varied between different authors, but is always problematic (Brittan and Maynard 1984: 58-9). All these attempts faced common problems of specifying the relations between capitalism and patriarchy *in general*. In these approaches, capitalism is seen as historically intertwined with patriarchy in characteristic ways, giving rise to a patriarchal family/household system, a patriarchal state, the domination of education by patriarchal ideology, and so on.

Hartmann (1981: 18–19) argued that capitalism and patriarchy were two different forms of oppression each with its own material base: 'the material base of patriarchy is men's control over women's labour power.' The way in which men gained and exercised this control through marriage, childcare, domestic labour, economic dependence on men, and social institutions constituted capitalism as patriarchal capitalism. McDonough and Harrison (1978: 11) took a somewhat different view, arguing that patriarchy should be seen as a historical concept, but that in general, 'patriarchal relations take their form from the dominant mode of production'. The problem with this view is that there is no clear way in which we can know how, or even whether, these variables are interconnected. How can we determine whether patriarchy is independent of capitalism, or any other mode of production? Is patriarchy produced by capitalism, and feudalism, but not by every mode of production? Or, is patriarchy semi-autonomous, that is, partially dependent on the way production is organized? How can such questions be answered in general? There is no reason to assume that such connections must take the same form in different situations.

These views attracted criticism within feminism. Criticisms focused on the very generalized conceptions of both capitalism and patriarchy, which resulted in the assertion of very general relations between them. Walby (1983) picked on a crucial weakness of this marxist feminist approach when she pointed out (102) that these analyses lacked any notion of contradiction: 'many existing analyses of the relation between patriarchy and capitalism, or between gender inequality and capitalism, assume that there is a harmonious articulation between the two.'

Adlam (1979) argues that conflating capitalism and patriarchy renders any explanation of male dominance insoluble. It reduces explanation to generalized abstractions, and ignores the specificity of sexual divisions which do not need to be reduced to other factors such as class, biology, or property. Adlam sees no need to treat women as a unitary category with the same essential interests (1979: 101). Rowbotham (1981: 365) goes further in rejecting the concept of patriarchy on the ground that it cannot escape being an ahistorical term. She argues that it is a word that fails to convey movement, the complexities of the relations between men and women, or the extent of women's resistance to and transformation of male power. Dorothy Smith (1983: 99) comments that any generalized conception of patriarchy, or assertion of a generalized relationship between patriarchy and mode of production, works against our ability to explain history. No matter how similar they may appear, household relationships and the articulation of households with the rest of society have changed through time. Smith goes on to claim (101) that the near universality of patriarchy has simply been produced by feminists' conceptions of social hierarchies, and by disregarding the variability of history.

Cockburn (1983) suggested replacing the ahistorical notion of patriarchy indicating generalized male supremacy with a conception of sex/gender system. A sex/gender system could produce patriarchal ideology but would require further explanation of how this ideology was produced and maintained through its historical development. Any such explanation would entail some knowledge of the organization of production. Cockburn's study of the male dominance of the British craft printing industry indicates the complexity of the historical relations between class, gender, and technological change in the struggle to establish male supremacy in printing. The situation in other industries and in other countries led to rather different struggles with different outcomes.

Other marxist feminists have been more cautious in rejecting the concept of patriarchy completely. There is always the danger of throwing the baby out with the bath water. It was the crude universality of the radical feminist conception of patriarchy which forced marxist feminists to rethink their marxism. If the relations between sexuality, production and ideology are historically variable, it is probable that the extent to which women share common interests across class lines is variable. But we still need some general concept of patriarchy to enable us to see the extent to which women are oppressed as women, although the male domination of women has to be identified and explained in each situation in which it is found.

Considerable problems remain of explaining exactly how men gain power in different situations, and in different modes of production, and whether such power has any basis in biological difference. Sylvia Walby (1986: 50) argues that the complexity of social existence is such that too many factors need to be explained in an unstructured way. This criticism, however, would be equally applicable to the whole of social theory. It can be countered by the argument that the relevant factors for explanation are identified through theoretical analysis and women's critical consciousness of their experiences.

Walby (1986: 69) conceives of patriarchy as a mode of production comprising domestic work, paid work, the state, male violence, and sexuality. Gender inequality then has to be explained through the intersection of patriarchy, capitalism and racist structures, in specific areas such as in the use of women's labour. This is useful in focusing problems of explanation on the historical connections between areas of women's lives normally seen as separate, but it is not clear how conceiving patriarchy as a mode of production successfully bridges historical and general explanation.

Radical and marxist feminist attempts to specify general connections between patriarchy and capitalism have been unsuccessful because they cannot take adequate account of history or struggle. It cannot be assumed that patriarchy routinely benefits capitalism, and Walby argues that in practice it does not, for example, where men can prevent women from undercutting their labour. Neither can it be assumed that capitalism always serves the needs of dominant men. Cockburn (1983) argues that men are robbed of warmth, creativity, full sexuality, and caring, and that they encounter tensions in their domestic lives.

Feminism at present has no agreement on a possible resolution of the problem of patriarchy. Universal theories of the general male dominance of women founder on the rocks of biological reductionism and historical variability. Abstracted marxist feminist explanations of capitalist patriarchy or patriarchal capitalism do not solve the problem of dealing with the contradictions of historical developments rather than with abstracted generalities. They do not explain why or how men have managed to oppress women in so many different situations. But if we abandon patriarchy altogether and adopt 'an historical approach to sex-gender relations' (Rowbotham 1981: 368), we are left with no general understanding of why variable historical struggles between men and women have so many similar outcomes. As Kuhn and Wolpe (1978: 9) pointed out, 'a materialist approach to the question of women's situation constantly comes up against the problem of the transhistorical character of women's oppression, which immediately problematises the relationship between such oppression and the mode of production.' Treating patriarchy historically does not resolve the problem of how biology can be taken into account in understanding men's dominance over women. The term patriarchy then leaves open historical questions of how it is that men generally dominate women, rather than female dominance or some balance of power.

Rather than patriarchy constituting a general explanation of the relations between men and women, these relations remain a problem to be explained. Patriarchy has enabled feminists to see mechanisms in sexual relations, work, and public and private life through which men dominate women, but problems of explanation remain. It is not at all clear that if it was men who bore and suckled babies they would be able to maintain their extensive dominance over women. We do not need to reduce patriarchy to biology, but equally, we do not need to ignore biology without good reasons. Yet if we abandon patriarchy we are in danger of losing our political conception of what needs to be changed. The problem of using a single term with disputed meanings to cover the enormous complexity of the relations between men and women, between sex and gender and between gender relations and mode of production, throughout history, is still with us.

THE PROBLEM OF UNIVERSALITY

A general problem with feminism is the tendency towards universal generalization which has characterized not only radical feminism but also, in somewhat different ways, marxist feminism. The use of universal generalizations derived from theory and divorced from experience are characteristic of much western social theory. I have criticized elsewhere (Ramazanoglu 1985) the ways in which universal generalizations can make women's experience invisible. The adequacy of feminist argument, however, has been weakened by the uncritical application of feminist generalizations to situations which are insufficiently known or understood.

Universal generalizations about male domination prevent us from seeing the contradictions in women's lives. The concept of contradiction is one that feminists have taken from marxism. The power of Marx lies not so much in the conclusions he drew in the 1860s or 1870s, but in the questions which his approach to human history enable us to ask today. The relevant marxist question for feminists, then, is not 'are women oppressed?' but 'what are the sources of the contradictions which determine and limit the opportunities for women (or workers or ethnic minorities) to live as whole, free, human beings in control of their own lives?' If the question is put in this way, then quite clearly there cannot be one standard answer that will apply to all women or in all circumstances.

Marxist feminism has frequently been treated as about capitalist societies, and capitalism is taken to be an abstraction which takes the same form in different places and times.[4] Marx's own sense of historical variability, his outrage at the appalling conditions in which nineteenth-century workers lived and died, and his ability to weave their individual experiences into his general analysis of the capitalist mode of production, had no place in the generalities of 1970s marxist feminism. Marx was quite clear that while the abstract concept of capitalism was a general tool for identifying the character of capitalist societies, each historical capitalist society was unique (Marx 1976: 876). More recently, Heyzer (1986) has pointed out that while women in South-East Asia are oppressed as women, the form that their oppression takes depends on the extent and manner of the integration of local production and kinship systems into the capitalist mode of production, and also on the presence or absence of grass-roots resistance by women.

Having said this, it does not follow that unique situations have nothing in common with each other. While each situation needs its own investigation and explanation, the very general occurrence of the oppression of women by men indicates that there will be shared circumstances even over time and across cultures, economies and classes. We need a general feminist theory in order to look for combinations of underlying determinants which over and over again create and recreate the circumstances of oppression. But we also need a theory which can take account of the differences and divisions that develop between women. Male domination is contradictory for women, in that patriarchal societies allow some women power over others.

The value of marxist analysis for feminism, therefore, is to end the search for a single cause of women's oppression or for a generalized relationship between patriarchy and capitalism. Rather the lessons of marxism should alert feminists to the incredibly complex and variable situations in which women come to be oppressed. Rather than taking the prevalence of oppression for granted, we should see every instance of oppression as a problem in which combinations of shared and unique factors need to be identified and explained.

We still need to establish much more clearly how women have come to be in the social situations that they are in; how the balance of power between men and women is maintained, and what forms resistance has taken and might take in future. These investigations must be clearly located in feminist theory which can take account of history and of contradiction. Historical research has already shown significant variation in women's experiences during industrialization and the variety of working experience even among working-class women (Lewenhak 1980; Sarsby 1985). What is wrong with much of feminist theory is the tendency towards abstract generalization, even though this is often grounded in personal experience and so does not necessarily seem abstract. If abstract generalizations are imposed in a variety of unresearched and unexamined situations, the understanding of why some women are more oppressed than others is actively discouraged.

THE PROBLEM OF TREATING FEMINISM AS A THEORY OF OPPRESSION

Feminists broadly agree that women are very generally dominated, subordinated, or oppressed by men and agree on what such oppression consists of. They disagree on how they explain the oppression of women. The problems revealed by feminists' struggles with explanations of oppression have divided feminism. But any effective politics of women's liberation will have to deal with the tensions and contradictions which have been revealed. While I do not believe that radical and marxist feminism can be synthesized or amalgamated in any simple way, since many of their assumptions are incompatible, I do think that the differences between them need to be approached much more constructively. Radical and marxist feminists are addressing very similar problems of explanation. Their disagreements stem from very different attempts to resolve these problems. While it is probable that many feminists will not agree with the way in which I approach possible resolutions of this division, at least further debate could be a positive step towards achieving a more effective and sisterly politics of women's liberation. Failure to resolve our problems of explanation has led to feminism developing in diverse directions in response to women's contradictory interests.

Before considering feminist knowledge in more detail, I look at the problem of taking feminism seriously as social theory.

Chapter Three

MAKING FEMINISM BELIEVABLE[1]

The problems within feminist thought raise the further problem of why feminist thought should be believed. Consideration of this question means treating feminism as social theory. Social theory may seem far removed from the daily lives of ordinary women and from the practical politics of women's liberation. Many new-wave feminists have dismissed social theory as irrelevant to feminism, as it has been equated with male modes of thought. Male domination of knowledge has been seen as part of the framework of women's oppression. While many social scientists would now identify themselves as feminists, few feminists identify themselves as social scientists. Nevertheless, feminist ideas do constitute a body of social theory and any effective connection between feminism and women's liberation needs a convincing social theory.

The following arguments summarize and simplify the essential issues of epistemology, or theory of the foundations of knowledge. Feminism has to be understood not only in terms of what feminists think and what feminists do, but also in terms of how feminist knowledge is produced, what status such knowledge has when it is produced and what is to be investigated. While it may not seem an immediate issue in the struggles of ordinary women around the world, the clarification of feminist social theory is none the less essential for an effective understanding of feminism as a practical, international political movement. (Identifying feminism as a movement does not need to imply an organized or hierarchical movement with any kind of formal membership or structure. There is no existing word for identifying a movement based on shared interests but without formal organization.)

I have taken philosophy to be necessary to any understanding of the societies we live in, but I understand philosophy to be the development of a critical awareness in the sense defined by Gramsci (1971: 325):

> For a mass of people to be led to think coherently and in the same coherent fashion about the real present world, is a 'philosophical' event far more important and 'original' than the discovery by some philosophical 'genius' of a truth which will remain the property of small groups of intellectuals.

Women are not simply a mass of people, comparable to the Italian working class of Gramsci's day, but millions upon millions of people living in very diverse circumstances and cultures, with no common language or concepts. Materially, women's situations vary from extreme affluence to destitution and starvation. Some women have considerable power over the lives of others, some have no power even over their own lives. The vast majority of women today live in hierarchically ordered social and economic structures in which some women are very much more valuable and can exercise much more choice in controlling their lives than others. For this mass of people to be able to think about the 'real present world' in the same terms would be momentous; to be able to share a vision of a better world would be almost incredible. Feminism as a social theory addresses this almost incredible task, and it is hardly surprising that considerable problems have been encountered as women's diverse voices struggle to make themselves heard.

FEMINISM AS AN ADVANCE ON PREVIOUS SOCIAL THEORIES

The assumption that feminist ideas and explanations give a better account than others of what goes on in society is common (at least implicitly) to all schools of feminist thought. Feminism is concerned with changing society for the better in at least some respects, so feminists must assume that they have an adequate understanding of what is wrong with existing societies, and of the consequences of pressing for specified changes. All variants of feminism define some version of women's oppression by men although, as was shown in chapter 2, they disagree on how far such oppression is intermeshed with other factors. Since feminism has to be taken as entailing at least a partial theory of society, it falls within the realm of the construction of social

44

theory. Although practical feminist activity takes a number of political and cultural forms, all feminism (however prosaic or poetic) implies a critique of existing social arrangements and the development of political strategies for achieving better arrangements.

The point of feminism is not to produce an abstracted theory of society only intelligible to intellectuals but, like marxism, to change societies for the better. Feminists, therefore, are necessarily engaged in understanding, more or less scientifically, the societies in which women and men now live, and in which they have lived in times past. They are also engaged in the practical transformation of societies so that in future women can live without oppression. Feminism is then partly a lived experience, a political struggle for liberation, but it is also an intellectual activity. There is no point in engaging in political struggle if we do not have an accurate understanding of what to struggle against. This intellectual activity is the development of a critical understanding of the nature of society, and thus of the sources and mechanisms of the oppression of women. It is the development of ideas which are rooted in women's daily experiences, but it is also the impact of ideas on these experiences. Feminist thought gives women new knowledge of social life, the power to think about our circumstances, and the power to act upon them. Feminism then has a claim to exist as scientific knowledge. In common-sense terms it is a form of the pursuit of truth. Existing knowledge of the social world has failed to identify and account for the power of men over women and so needs to be improved upon.

Feminists, like other social theorists who want the knowledge they produce to be regarded as convincing, need to provide statements which generally hold 'true' within prescribed limits. Since any conception of truth begs many questions I have indicated problematic concepts with quotation marks. There are reasonable objections to the notion of truth (because of problems of ever arriving at absolute proof). Yet it can still be argued that feminists, as members of their societies, have some moral obligation to show that some statements are 'better' accounts of social life than others. Both those who wish to change society and those who wish to maintain the status quo have to chose between competing accounts of what society is 'really' like.

We can all discriminate between 'better' and 'worse' theories on moral and political grounds (such as, for example, more egalitarian, more democratic, more humanitarian, more in harmony with nature, as against more oppressive, more hierarchical, more patriarchal, more exploitative of nature). We also need to be able to judge theories on their scientific adequacy, without having to invoke absolute, objective criteria for discriminating between theories. The claims to scientific status for the knowledge produced by feminists persist, because this is the only basis we have for claiming that those who do not share our starting premises should be convinced by our conclusions.

Without taking this step, feminist social theory, for example, can simply be dismissed as expressive of women's politics and of no interest to those who do not share these political convictions. I am arguing that feminism has to be understood as producing 'better' knowledge of society, whether critics of feminism like it or not.

FEMINISM AS SCIENTIFIC SOCIAL THEORY

Feminists and others have drawn attention to the conception of science which came to dominate western thought from the seventeenth century Enlightenment onwards. The term Enlightenment, like the term industrial revolution, is a convenient label for a long and complex period of change in European history. This was the period in which the ultimate authority of God finally gave way most decisively to the ultimate authority of reason, allowing nature, and later society, to be explored scientifically.

While it is impossible to summarize the development and variations in Enlightenment thinking here, there are some general characteristics of the Enlightenment which have become part of popular thought. These are the focus of feminist challenge. The dominance of reason in science gave scientists, and social theorists, a source of control over the objects of their studies. Scientists had many practical problems in carrying out their research but they were reasonably assured that their aims were sound because their methods of producing new knowledge were scientific. That is, they tried to avoid metaphysical speculation and to control human passions and prejudices as rigorously as possible, in order to collect facts accurately and to present them objectively. They used their facts to test hypotheses and so gradually to establish knowledge of the general regularities which could be used to explain, and thus to control, both nature and social life.

The logic of this approach justified the separation of reason from emotion. It allowed emotional individuals to study nature and society objectively. Mind became separated from body, culture from nature, objectivity from subjectivity, and public life from private life. This separation was not one of equality, but one of superiority and inferiority. Reason was superior to emotion, mind superior to body, culture superior to nature, objectivity superior to subjectivity. It is scarcely surprising that, given the accompanying social and economic developments of this period, men became associated with the superior qualities, and women with the inferior (Bleier 1984; Harding 1986; Seidler 1986). Reason became a masculine attribute, and scientific knowledge a masculine preserve. Feminity was natural, passive, intuitive, and subjective. Women were ruled by their hearts and their bodies rather than by their heads. These dualisms and their gendered meanings have passed into western popular thought where they remain as taken-for-granted truths, defining men's and women's natures. At the heart of reasonable, scientific detachment lie unwarranted assumptions about the natural inferiority and unreasonableness of women. The objective, scientific exploration of both nature and the social world is based on unrealistic premises of the separability of reason from other human attributes.

The extensive criticisms of this approach, which I do not have space to review here, show clear problems with this conception of science. Critics have pointed out that far from being a neutral and detached process, the production of scientific knowledge is a selective and creative social process.[2] Scientists live in societies, occupy social positions, pursue specific interests, and work in male-dominated, hierarchical institutions.

Given these criticisms, science changes from being a matter of discovering what *is*, to one of science as a *set of social practices* guided by *ideas* of what is *real* and *ideas* of what *ought* to be. What then exists can only be studied within these limitations.[3] A social theory which assumes that scientists are accountable for the knowledge which they produce, and for the way in which this knowledge is produced, is 'better' than one that treats the scientist as disengaged and morally neutral. The latter theory is not 'really' the way scientists are. This question of the nature of science is a very practical political issue for the survival of feminist social theory since feminist knowledge is generally thought of as political and irrational, rather than as accurate and scientific.

It is easy to find fault with the logic, consistency, and coherence of many feminist arguments, where women (often relatively inexperienced) have suddenly felt free to take on the most fundamental problems of explaining human nature, history, and society. It is, though, impossible to ignore the devastating impact of these arguments on the logic, consistency, and coherence of previous arguments which legitimated and actively encouraged the continuing oppression of women. Whatever its faults, feminist social theory cannot be ignored because it has made previously held beliefs untenable. It has exposed western knowledge of the relations between the sexes and of women's proper place in society as being far from reasonable or true. This knowledge is the product of particular ways of constructing knowledge at particular periods, in the context of particular power relations in which men very generally dominate women. Feminism challenges male-dominated knowledge of nature and society by putting sexual politics in its proper place at the centre of social relationships. Rational argument about the relations between women and men can no longer be thought of as separable from the rest of our lives.

FEMINIST CRITICISMS OF REASON IN SCIENCE

The feminist critique of science is more radical than the standard criticisms which have argued that science should be seen as socially constructed knowledge. Feminist scientists have questioned the validity of scientific knowledge which has been produced by men, for men, within a very constricting notion of reason. Such knowledge actively works against, or at best ignores, the interests of women (Keller 1983; Bleier 1984; Rose 1984; Birke 1986; Harding 1986). Feminists have argued that men have appropriated scientific thought and have done so without regard to the dimension of power in the social construction of knowledge. Feminists, however, have not attempted to appropriate science in a comparable way. They have attempted to change the ways in which we think about the production and evaluation of scientific knowledge, and so to change the ways in which we know nature and society.

Feminism has effectively challenged the various ways in which knowledge of society has been made believable, by questioning notions of reason as the basis of scientific knowledge. The objectivity of scientific method cannot be separated in practice from the subjectivity of the scientist. The emotions of the scientist cannot be separated from the rigour and rationality of scientific method. Since western science was developed on the basis that reason could be independent of emotion, scientists had to control their personal feelings in order to produce objective knowledge. Feminists have argued that in practice, reason cannot be separated from emotion. This has been a dramatic development which has forced reconsideration of everything reasonable that we know about social life. The importance to natural and social scientists of maintaining men's dominance over women has influenced the kind of knowledge of society that they have produced.

People are generally unwilling to believe what feminists say, not because feminism is 'bad' social theory, but because feminists' notions of what is 'really' going on in society challenge dominant versions of reality. They are politically and personally uncomfortable. Several authors have now stressed the need for a new notion of reason which recognizes reason as inseparable from emotion (Daniels 1976; Hochschild 1976; Smith 1979).

The production of feminist knowledge is an openly subversive activity. It is attempting, in its critique of existing knowledge, to undermine the foundations of male-dominated knowledge. By engaging in subversive activity it is also openly charged with emotion and provokes emotional reactions (Scott 1984; Ramazanoglu 1987a). *Feminist knowledge makes those who believe in the dominance of reason over emotion, and the superiority of rational man over emotional woman, angry and upset.* Any evaluation of feminist knowledge must, therefore, take emotions into account. Yet all conventional modes of rational evaluation leave emotions out. Feminist knowledge has to be compared with knowledge produced by other methodologies which are in the paradoxical situation of adopting a commitment to masculine rationality which clearly obstructs 'reasonable' accounts of social life and of how social scientists 'actually' work. Critics of feminist theory and methodology who do not take their own intentions, social context and emotions into account are not properly equipped to evaluate feminism. Only when reason is seen as united with emotion, subjectivity with objectivity, theory with practice, can we begin to develop adequately scientific procedures for evaluating knowledge of the contradictions of our social existence.

Since feminist conclusions and generalizations are widely socially unacceptable, feminists are faced very openly with disbelief. They are accused of being biased, political, or unreasonable. Mainstream social theories (categorized by feminists as malestream or androcentric[4]) have developed various (often esoteric) solutions to the problems of how we recognize what is scientific knowledge of society. Feminist social theory, however, has made it clear that the problem of how we make scientific knowledge convincing to others is still unresolved. At a common-sense level people want to know what is 'true'. If we accept that no one can ever know for sure what is true, then all scientists have the problem of showing why their conclusions should be believed.

PROBLEMS OF VALIDATING FEMINIST KNOWLEDGE

By validation I mean the problem of how knowledge can be made generally convincing. Since feminists cannot produce objective facts which can be proved to be true, we need clear rules on how we can produce knowledge, and on the limits within which such knowledge should be believed. Scientists have developed such rules by relying on the rigour of reason. New-wave feminism, however, challenges the assumption that we have access to rules of validation that can be arrived at solely by reason. If we lose the rigour of scientific rules based on reason, which can be divorced from the scientists' emotions, then we lose the rigour of validation procedures which safeguard scientific methods. This rigour depended on belief in the existence of logical rules which could effectively control the subjectivity of the scientist. Feminists have challenged the validation of malestream knowledge, both of nature and society. They have pointed to the impossibility of separating objectivity and reason from subjectivity and emotion.[5]

The new-wave feminist critique of science is devastating to scientists' dependence on reason divorced from emotion (which could be why so many established academics have dealt with the problem by ignoring feminist thought or by making fun of feminists). Feminist knowledge opens up again the whole question of the procedures for evaluating scientific knowledge, not as a special problem for political marxists or emotional feminists, but as a central concern for all scientists and social scientists, however 'hard' their discipline. We are left with the problem of what 'society' is really like, and why any accounts of social relations should be believed.

This gives feminism the problem of validating the knowledge produced by feminist research. Feminism has been publicly labelled as non-valid knowledge, and yet feminist means of validating knowledge are little known or understood outside academic debates. One reason for this is the difficulty of explaining them to those for whom feminist knowledge is personally painful. As Hearn (1987) warns, it is very hard for men to take feminism seriously, because to do so can seriously change their lives. The problems of validating feminist knowledge are not intrinsically different from the problems facing any social theory and they only differ in degree from the problems facing natural science. Feminism simply reveals these as still unresolved problems.

RULES FOR THE PRODUCTION OF FEMINIST KNOWLEDGE

We may have lost the rigour of a scientific method controlled solely by reason, but we do not need to abandon rigour in validation entirely. Indeed it is politically important that feminist knowledge can be rigorously established if it is to be convincing to those people who do not accept feminist political premises. Some progress in this respect is being made, for example, in the growing recognition of male violence towards women as a general social problem. Male violence cannot be presented as a social problem simply through empirical evidence of rape or of domestic violence. The statistics documenting men's violence to women only make sense as feminist knowledge because of the abstract concepts which allow us to see them as expressions of men's oppression of women. Validation is as much a conceptual as an empirical process, and inevitably proceeds with dispute, debate, and political struggle.

The rules for the production of feminist knowledge as scientific knowledge, therefore, have had to be rethought. Feminism's claims to better knowledge of society are based on the assumption that feminism is informed by theory that is more general, more coherent, and able to take account of more factors than previous social theories. The validity of feminist knowledge must be limited by feminists' starting premises, language, and conceptions of the world; nevertheless feminist knowledge can be more accurate and more useful than knowledge produced within other social theories. It follows from this that feminist methodology should be superior to other research methodologies in that it is conceived within a broader and more 'realistic' conception both of scientific activity and of social life.

This claim is still problematic because there is no general agreement on how feminists can overcome the problems of producing valid knowledge as members of the societies they study. The contradictions within feminist theory and within women's lives entail contradictions within feminist methods of producing knowledge (Harding and Hintikka 1983). Feminist theories of knowledge are, for example, divided between those sympathetic to and those unsympathetic to marxism, but marxists and non-marxists produce knowledge of society in different ways and theorize knowledge differently. Black and white women, working-class and middle-class women, western and third-world women all look out upon society from different standpoints.

Feminist social theory is addressed to the transformation of male-dominated societies and feminist methodology is addressed to the knowledge needed to liberate women from oppression. Since there is not a single feminist theory of oppression, so there cannot be a single feminist methodology. In addition to the problems of clarifying the epistemological status of feminist methodology, and the knowledge it produces, there are numerous practical problems in collecting, theorizing, interpreting, and using information. Feminist social theorists have, however, begun to specify the problem areas that remain. Feminist claims to produce 'better' explanations of social life than malestream accounts must rest on success in tackling these problems. If feminism is to produce knowledge on which major social transformations can be built, then there must be some means of showing that feminist knowledge is superior to existing knowledge. That is, not absolutely superior, but superior with reference to specified criteria of validation. Feminism has not developed any clear code of procedures but, through practice and debate, some grounds for improvement are emerging.

Expressing women's experience

The most obvious principle of improvement has been to take women's own accounts of their experience as part of their situation. The researcher as an impersonal, objective 'knower' disappears (Smith 1979), to be revealed as a person with a gender and a particular place and passions of their own in society. Allowing women (or other subjects) to express their own experience has allowed previously silent voices to be heard but it has also raised problems of how the knowledge produced can be validated. Allowing the researched to express their own experience gives a view of society otherwise inaccessible to outsiders, but still leaves the problem that the sum of personal accounts does not necessarily constitute a feminist understanding of social life. Interviews with women who have been raped or assaulted will not necessarily express a theory of patriarchy. Researchers, however sympathetic they are to their subjects, cannot avoid some selection and interpretation of people's accounts. If feminists wish to understand those to whom they are unsympathetic, right-wing women, or men in authority, for example, this problem is more acute (Cain 1986).

The need to select and interpret

The necessity of selection and interpretation remains the Achilles' heel of all science and social science. Although all schools of social science have tried ways of making selection and interpretation of evidence scientific, feminism has shown that these solutions have still only produced male knowledge of the social world. It is more realistic to see the problems of selection and interpretation as central and serious weaknesses in feminism (as in all social theory) which are still unresolved. This does not make feminist knowledge invalid, but it does mean we need to look much more critically at how feminist knowledge is produced, why, for whom, and with what consequences.

Even if the inseparability of subjective and objective knowledge is agreed, problems of validation remain. Any selection and interpretation of women's accounts of their experiences will be guided by the researcher's commitment to a prior theoretical position. Interpretations of women's expression of their experience must, therefore, remain open to criticism and modification.

Any new look at the gendering of the social world should take into account not only the way in which women can express their personal experience, which will itself depend a good deal on their relationships with researchers, but also at factors which may not be apparent to them as *general* issues. Feminists cannot logically be subjectivist (simply presenting everyday accounts of women's lives as women see them) because feminist politics depend on concepts such as patriarchy and oppression which are not in most women's vocabularies. Dorothy Smith (1986: 6), writing on feminist sociology, has argued for a method of discovery which will show women more of their own lives than they would see otherwise:

A sociology for women must be able to disclose *for* women how their own social situation, their everyday world is organized and determined by social processes which are *not knowable through the ordinary means* through which we find out our everyday world. (my emphasis)

Feminism provides concepts which enable people to interpret personal experience in terms of sexual politics — to see what could not be seen before. Allowing women to express their own experience could allow women to express racist beliefs and practices without indentifying these as racist. That is, the concept of racism has to be provided by the researcher. A feminist researcher for whom racism is a salient concept could, therefore, give a very different account of the same women's experiences from one who has no consciousness of racism. An essential part of the validation of feminist knowledge must, therefore, lie in the quality of feminist theory. Where people's very physical survival is threatened by racism, awareness of racism ought to be visible in the research process. Because of the very human problems of generating adequate self-criticism, feminist theories must be exposed to criticism from outside as well as from inside.

Taking account of power

Feminist methodologies differ from others, in the recognition of more factors as impinging on the research process, such as gender and emotion, and in particular in seeing power as central to the research process. 'Better' knowledge, by being more general and coherent, would have to take account of such issues as race, ethnicity, sex, age, and class which all structure the power of the researcher in relation to the researched (and vice versa). Other critiques of method do this, but feminism has to go further in extending the boundaries of relevant evidence. For example, *any* research on doctor-patient relations needs to take the sources of power which impinge on these relationships into account.

There is also the problem that if knowledge is power, then the researcher inevitably gains power through knowledge of the subjects of research. Where white women gain knowledge of black women, or middle-class women of working-class women, or affluent western women of third-world peasants, then power is an issue in the validation and use of the knowledge gained. The argument that feminist research is about women, by women, and for women assumes common interests between women and overlooks the power differences between them.

Validating subjective knowledge

Once feminists make their engagement with their subjects overt, the problem of how to produce scientific knowledge is evidently acute. It

54

is in this respect that the natural scientist retains some advantage, as the degrees of engagement between the scientist and her subject can vary considerably from, say, astrophysics through medical research to qualitative social investigation. These differences of degree can be quite substantial at the extremes. Feminism is located at the extreme of engagement with subjects of research, and does, therefore, have very great problems of explanation and interpretation.

Discussions of researchers' relationships with their subjects in feminist research can make the process of engagement plain but have left the problems of exactly how to validate subjective knowledge unclear (Acker *et al.* 1983; Rose 1986). Feminists have still not resolved the problem of constructing adequate knowledge of social life. The possibility of women's liberation depends on the quality of our understanding of women's lives.

Avoiding objectification of the subjects of research

While feminists have argued against the need to objectify the sub-jects of research (that is, to treat the people being studied as the researcher's objects), it does seem impossible to escape objectification entirely. Since, by and large, people do not choose to be investigated, they are logically the objects of research chosen by the feminist for purposes defined by feminists. Such research can be justified in various ways. The subjects/objects of research can be treated with honesty and the engagement of the researcher made plain; research results can be discussed with them and amended in the light of these discussions. Some degree of objectification and control of the knowledge produced seems unavoidable, however. We can attempt to mitigate the processes of objectification by making clear to our subjects what these are and why they occur. The history of socialism is a generally depressing example of the problems of giving knowledge back to its subjects.

FEMINISM AS POLITICAL PRACTICE

Although feminism clearly has problems in producing convincing knowledge of women's oppression, it has advanced on existing knowledge by making these problems clear. All other social theories have the same problems of making their knowledge convincing, but they have settled for solutions which largely exclude women's lives.

Regardless of the version of feminism which is favoured, the point of developing feminist social theory is to use it to improve women's lot. In this view, social theories are not developed simply as intellectual exercises. The kinds of theories that people draw on to explain the world they experience will affect their behaviour. Women who see the troubles of their lives as due to their own inadequacies as wives and mothers will not behave in the same ways as those who attribute their troubles to men, or to economic exploitation or to religious destiny. Any evaluation of feminism, then, will need to pay attention to the links between theory and practice. The radical feminist slogan 'the personal is political' has also been taken up by marxist feminists, but does not sit easily with liberal assumptions. The liberal analysis of the relations between the sexes is less one of oppression than one of inequality, injustice, and discrimination which works to women's disadvantage. Strategies to tackle inequality are in practice very different from strategies aimed at transforming power relations between men and women. When social analysis is translated into action, the contradictions inherent in the production of feminist knowledge become clear.

Feminism is not, then, simply a political corrective for remedying the inadequacies of other theories. If feminism is to be more generally politically effective, we need much more precision in feminist knowledge than the political conviction that it is superior to sexist knowledge, or the hope that it can ultimately be validated politically, through practice and struggle. As Midgley and Hughes have argued (1983: 219), 'Feminism was never only an eccentric fad, and it is not so today. It is rooted in serious troubles affecting the lives of large numbers of ordinary people.' A great deal of personal suffering is involved if we get our applied social theory wrong.

It is both a strength and a weakness of feminism that its analyses of women's oppression create practical strategies for changing this oppression. Feminism's weakness lies in the philosophical difficulties of producing valid feminist knowledge which have diversified our knowledge of women's oppression. Diverse conceptions of oppression lead to diverse strategies for liberation. Feminism's strength lies in new ways of thinking about the desirability of change which are opened up by questioning much that has previously been taken for granted in the relations between the sexes. It is this strength which is reviewed in chapter 4.

Chapter Four

WOMEN AGAINST MEN — FEMINIST KNOWLEDGE OF WOMEN'S OPPRESSION

It is impossible in a single book, let alone in a single chapter, to begin to do justice to the enormous production of feminist knowledge over the last twenty years or so. A trickle in the 1960s became a stream in the 1970s and a flood in the 1980s. While many works are known internationally, every part of the world and every area of social life has its own specialist and local literature as well. It is impossible to become familiar with everything that is being done before the tide sweeps on. There is no uniform perspective which encompasses this knowledge since the location of the observer affects the view that is taken. Radical and marxist, black and white, working-class and middle-class feminists do not necessarily recognize the same milestones in the development of feminist knowledge. Western feminists have built largely on western experience, but knowledge of women's lives, and of the relations between men and women around the world, is more comprehensive and more detailed than it has ever been.

All that I have attempted here is to give a brief overview of the main challenges that new-wave feminists have made to male-dominated knowledge of women's nature and of the relations between the sexes. Feminist theory, in spite of its considerable problems, has revealed much that could not be seen before, by questioning what was previously taken for granted. The knowledge produced is very varied in quality and level of analysis. Some feminist work has been explicitly anti-intellectual, and many activists have not written for publication. But I have been less concerned with doing justice to individual authors and activists than with attempting to outline a body of knowledge which has made the many facets of men's oppression of women plain.

Although this chapter is confined to the main themes of new-wave feminism, feminists soon realized that many of our struggles had been experienced by women previously. Feminism had taken new cultural forms, but was not a new phenomenon (Rowbotham 1973). With hindsight, feminists could see that theirs was not a new movement, but they could also see that women's contributions to knowledge, production, culture, and historical events had been very generally neglected. Women set out to recover their own history. The origins of women's oppression remain beyond our reach, and work on original matriarchies and matriarchal religions remains largely speculative. But historical knowledge could at least to some extent be recovered (Lerner 1973; Carroll 1976; Spender 1983; Lewis 1984).

The new feminist publishing houses produced a stream of reprints of forgotten or neglected writers, helping to establish feminist work as a marketable commodity. Earlier women writers were given new attention, and old debates were rediscovered. The impact of this recovery of women's knowledge showed that women's awareness of their oppression had long roots, but it also showed that women were far from equally oppressed. Modern history showed conflicts between bourgeois women and proletarian women, between black women and white women, between women in the capitalist countries and those in the colonies, between patriots and internationalists. The new emphasis in new-wave feminism on the common oppression of women as women was soon confronted by existing evidence of the deep divisions of interest between women.

The topics reviewed here are those where feminist knowledge, feminist questions and feminist reasoning have transformed conceptions of social relations (which is not to discount continuing vigorous opposition to many of these ideas). This is not a definitive statement which transcends the divisions within feminism discussed in previous chapters. It is a necessarily restricted attempt to review the ways in which feminists have claimed that women are oppressed by men, and that women do have political interests opposed to those of men. Inevitably several areas of feminist knowledge have had to be omitted. There has been a considerable body of feminist work on the ways in which the relations between the sexes become structured by the ideologies and practices of the state, law, and public institutions. Feminists have shown the extent of women's oppression in education, in art and literature, in our depiction in and access to the mass media, and in mental and physical illness. These areas are very generally informed by developments in feminist theory and I do not treat them here as separate issues, although they have developed as specialist fields of knowledge and activity. Many of these areas have provided essential evidence for, and much-needed qualifications to, the broader generalizations of women's shared oppression.

I have concentrated, first, on the critique of western thought which was needed in order to make new sense of women's experience. Second, I review the grounds for the main feminist argument that women are oppressed by men. Third, I consider aspects of this argument which have increasingly emerged as problematic.

THE FEMINIST CHALLENGE TO MALE BIAS IN WESTERN THOUGHT

The social construction of gender

All versions of feminism make a direct challenge to the assumption that women as a sex are naturally inferior to men. Feminists assert instead that while the sexes are biologically differentiated, the observable biological differences between the sexes are socially constructed. Men and women in societies are cultural products. If the biological process of reproduction makes women socially inferior to or economically dependent on men, then this is a problem to be explained, not a scientific account of natural difference (Sayers 1982b).

As the question of how far biology must still be taken into account is still not resolved, this remains a contested issue in every area of feminist thought. Nevertheless, the distinction between sex as largely biologically given, and gender as largely the social construction of what is male and female, is fundamental to feminist thought. The exact nature of the relationship between sex and gender remains disputed. This is because of the difficulty of specifying in general terms exactly how far biological sexual difference enters into the social constructions of gender, and how far our ideas about sex construct our biology. Mies (1986: 23) has argued that distinguishing between sex and gender leads to the treatment of sex as biological — but human sexuality is not simply biological. Some authors have attempted to avoid this dualism by using the term sex/gender, but the problem remains of determining in what respects 'women' and 'men' are biological, and in what respects social categories.

While this use of gender worries grammatical pedants, the feminist production of knowledge would not have been possible without it.

The assumption that gender is culturally constructed has enabled feminists to challenge scientific knowledge of the relations between women and men, the meanings of female and male in different societies, the social construction of femininity and masculinity, and thus dominant conceptions of nature. This most basic premise of feminism, however, is also the seat of contradiction. Women are only recognizable women in any general sense because of our biological sex and potential reproductive function. As a gender, our experiences, power or lack of power, relationships to men, economic activities, beliefs, and values are all historically and culturally variable. Our sex is what all women have in common, but it is as a gender that women are oppressed by men.

Nature versus culture

The argument that women are a culturally constructed gender category rather than simply a biological sex led to a much broader feminist challenge to existing knowledge of the relations between men and women. The idea of women's oppression was a means of conceptualizing the supposedly natural inferiority of the feminine as unnatural. Feminists challenged the conceptual separation of nature and culture which had allowed men to dominate women and had allowed women's oppression to develop in the guise of women's feminine nature. Ortner (1982: 490), in an ambitious attempt to avoid biological determinism while still explaining women's subordination as a universal phenomenon, asked what it was that would lead every culture to place a lower value on women than on men. She concluded that every society made a distinction between nature and culture. Women were seen as closer to nature while men were identified with culture. Drawing on the work of de Beauvoir and Chodorow, she argued that women's social ties to children through pregnancy and breastfeeding ensured that women appeared to be closer to nature than men. Local variations could be explained through empirical study (502), but not the universality of this subordination itself.

Later writers have challenged Ortner's assumption of subordination as universal. Karen Sacks (1979), for example, argued that motherhood can be combined with personal autonomy and with relationships of political and economic power. Women can share power with men, and are generally significant economic producers. They do not always have their activities valued as less than men's. Sacks argues that the impact of industrial capitalism has done much to diminish the social, economic, and political roles of mothers, but that the very general impact of capitalism today should not be confused with biological universals. Brown and Jordanovna (1982) also argue that the nature/culture dichotomy is not a universal one in human society. Women cannot universally be seen in their own societies as closer to nature. They locate this dichotomy as coming to dominance in western thought from the middle of the eighteenth century, when it became increasingly important in secular scientific thought for men to have progressive mastery over nature, and so over women.

Carolyn Merchant (1982) re-examined the western, scientific world view created largely by men during the sixteenth and seventeenth centuries. She shows that the emergence of modern science entailed a shift from a view of nature as organic and part of a cosmic whole to a view of nature as separate from humanity, as like a machine, and thus exploitable. Scientific progress has meant the separation of nature into parts and contributed to the oppression of women. Merchant comments (294), 'today the conjunction of the woman's movement with the ecology movement again brings the issue of liberation into focus.' Effective struggle against the 'death of nature' can only come about through 'a reversal of mainstream values and economic priorities' (295), a reversal for which feminists are also fighting.

This view needs to be distinguished from what has been termed ecofeminism (Karpf 1987). Ecofeminism is based on an acceptance of the nature/culture dichotomy, however problematic this may be, and views women as essentially closer to nature than men. In this way some radical feminists have gone on to reclaim nature for women. This is a primarily American school which has emphasized women's special and creative relationship to nature, a relationship which patriarchy has limited and distorted in men's interests (Griffin 1978; Rich 1980). Not all exponents of this view have a simplistic conception of dualism, however. Susan Griffin (1982: 16–17) discusses her difficulties in writing her book on the dualism of nature and culture (Griffin 1978). She conceived this book in the context of her experiences of American culture, and when its completion was followed by a period of depression, she found the voices both of women and nature and of patriarchal authority were inside herself.

Knowledge, science, and language

Feminist exposure of the opposition of nature and culture as a concept which developed at a particular period of western thought, rather than as a universal truth, brought the whole of modern western thought into question. The feminist critique of science, which has been referred to in chapter 3, challenged the status of supposedly scientific knowledge of the nature of male and female and of the relations between women and men. Feminists also questioned the ways in which scientific knowledge is produced, the purposes for which it is produced, and the relation of the production of scientific knowledge to the transformation and destruction of our natural environment. As Barrett (1987: 35) has put it, the white western man is now revealed behind the appearance of universality. Feminists have shown up male bias in the production and valuation of knowledge of societies, and made detailed challenges to the supposedly natural dominance of cultured man over natural woman (Sydie 1987).

In an associated critique feminists have also questioned the methods by which knowledge of the social world is produced, and so the language and concepts with which men and women can express their experience (Spender 1980; Cameron 1985). This work is a general indictment of the limitations of what we know, the restrictions of male-dominated language, and the limitations of methods of producing new knowledge which are unable to take women's experiences into account.

Public versus private

Feminist criticism not only demonstrated that the dualism of nature versus culture could be questioned, but went much further in examining the notion of public and private domains in social life. Considerable evidence has been produced to show that whereas different societies define male tasks and female tasks rather differently, it is very often the case that whatever women do is defined as being in the private or domestic domain, whereas what men do is in the public domain. Numerous social mechanisms are employed to limit and discourage women's intrusion into the public sphere (Imray and Middleton 1983). There are obviously considerable variations around the world in the nature and social value of women's work. General arguments on the boundaries of the public and the private need to be qualified. The work of some women is relatively much more valuable than the work of others. The plight of dependent, isolated western housewives, who are wholly economically dependent on their husbands and who have little defence against physical violence in the home, should not be taken as a universal model. There are both similarities and differences with women elsewhere which need to be explained. Public and private domains are not fixed over time or across cultures. Women are able, in different ways and in variable circumstances, to break into the public sphere, even if they do encounter various forms of male resistance (Stacey and Price 1981).

Modern western culture has generally ignored women's active involvement in public life. It has taken the dualism of male dominance in the public sphere and women's relegation to the private sphere for granted. Until the 1960s, western knowledge of society was primarily knowledge of the public sphere, with women confined to studies of the family, deviance, or the local community. Feminists exposed and questioned this division by looking at women's activities and showing the public significance of women's work, and men's (often violent) place in the private sphere. Feminists' conceptions of gender relations showed that the inequalities of power between men and women formed a continuum, from the most intimate sexual encounters to the most public economic and political activities. Redefining what is public and what is private raised the problem of where power lies and on what power rests. The reconnection of the public and the private also meant broadening the concept of power to show that the private domain is as political as the public. The boundaries between the public and the private, rather than being defined by male and female natures, were drawn in struggle and had to be actively maintained against women's resistance (Siltanen and Stanworth 1984). Exposing the restriction of women to the private sphere served to document and publicize the extent and nature of women's work. The extent to which men benefit from women's work, and the many mechanisms for ensuring women's economic dependence on men, could then be revealed.

Defining women as properly belonging to the domestic domain helped to legitimate their devaluation as workers. Although there was little agreement within feminism on how to theorize the oppression of women in their restriction to the private sphere, and no agreement on how general such restriction has been throughout history, a considerable challenge had been presented to conventional wisdom. Hundreds of studies around the world have established the social and economic value of women's work in the supposedly private domain, and have shown the many mechanisms which exist for keeping women out of public life. While women very generally accept their 'natural' place in the domestic sphere, there is also widespread resistance and struggle over the imposition and maintenance of the boundaries of private life.[1]

THE CASE FOR WOMEN'S SHARED OPPRESSION

Within the framework of these challenges to conventions of western thought, new-wave feminists were able to make a strong case to support the argument that women in general were oppressed by men in general.

The social construction of sexuality

A new focus on the most private area of people's lives, that of sexuality, revealed the oppression of women as central to human relationships. There is an extensive feminist literature demystifying cultural assumptions about what is normal and natural in sexuality, and showing (in the west at least) that normal sexuality is taken to be masculine sexuality. It is focused on heterosexual, genital sex, in which men are dominant. The expression of women's sexuality has been silenced or rendered abnormal except where it complements male needs (Millett 1977; Jackson 1984). There is an unresolved debate in the literature on whether sexuality is some kind of unchanging natural essence with which people are born, but on the whole the feminist challenge to existing knowledge of sexuality has come from arguing that women's sexuality, like men's, is socially and historically constructed. In this respect feminist thought has some common ground with homosexual men's challenges to the idea of sex as biologically given (Gay Left Collective 1980; Weeks 1985, 1986). It has also been influenced by the work of the French philosopher Michel Foucault (1979). While the work of Foucault has had a very considerable influence on thinking about the social construction of sexuality, it is less clear that Foucault has clarified the politics of female sexuality (Butler 1987; Schor 1987). Feminists have not just argued that sexuality is socially constructed, they have also argued that female sexuality has throughout history become systematically constructed in relation to male dominance.

Feminist analysis reveals sexuality as an area of political struggle. The politics of sexuality reveal that women's sexuality and women's sexual pleasure, like women's needs in general, have little social significance, and that women have little power in heterosexual sexual encounters (Lees 1986). This most basic area of feminist understanding of women's relationships with each other, and with men, remains, however, one of some debate (Stimpson and Person 1980; Snitow *et al.* 1984; Vance 1984). There is considerable agreement that sexuality is a critical issue in the oppression of women by men, but less than perfect agreement as to the mechanisms by which this oppression is maintained and reproduced. There is also some division over whether the way in which sexuality has developed in western cultures is a specific historical case of the oppression of women, or whether sexual relations are more generally oppressive of women (Morgan 1984: 13–14; Caplan 1987).

Rejection of the view of sexuality as an unchanging biological essence means that explanations of female and male sexuality cannot be reduced to nature, or to individual psychology. Feminists have had to look for the social processes which produce particular forms of sexuality at particular historical times. They have also looked beneath recent appearances of sexual freedom to show how these have concealed a construction of female sexuality in the interests of meeting socially constructed male sexual needs (Coveney *et al.* 1984). Feminist work on sexuality has shown the limited ways in which human sexuality has been thought about, at least in western cultures, and what new questions need to be asked (Coward 1983). These new questions also resulted in a specifically lesbian critique of heterosexual sexuality and of women's varying ability to determine their own sexuality, which is discussed below.

Male violence to women

Once attention was focused on the sexual and gender politics of the struggle to confine women to the private domain, it became clear that men were able to control women through the use of physical and sexual violence in the home, and to use violence, or the threat of violence, to control women in public places.

The study of male violence towards women has been a major and well-documented contribution from radical feminism. This is the main area in which arguments for the generality of women's oppression by men can be supported. It has been possible to show the prevalence of violence not only in western societies, but in many other parts of the world where women are dependent on men and are physically

65

abused by men. The possibility of rape, wife-beating or sexual harassment at work cuts across the boundaries of nationality, class, race, and religion. The forms that violence can take can be both general, as in the case of murder and rape, or culturally specific, as in the case of dowry deaths in India (where young wives are murdered because of their inadequate dowries) (Omvedt 1980: 167). Some forms of physical violence are widely used, such as wife-beating, others depend on broadening the concept of violence and also on the spread of industrialization, such as obscene telephone calls, sexual harassment at work, pornography, and prostitution. While it is not established that all known societies institutionalize and legitimate male violence against women, the threat and practice of violence is certainly very widespread. (It should be expected that male violence towards women would be absent or limited only where women have effective economic and political power of their own, are not dependent on men, and have means of redress in the public sphere.) It is through the use or threat of violence that men in general most clearly oppress women in general. Violence has been and still is an important mechanism for maintaining the subordination of women to men.

Anne Edwards (1987) traces a shift in new-wave feminist thought from separate accounts of specific types of male violence, notably rape, to an appreciation of male violence as a general mechanism for the subordination of women — the shift, for example, from the work of Brownmiller (1975) arguing that rape is a mechanism for the social control of women, to the more empirical work of Stanko (1985), linking several types of male violence with women's survival strategies in Britain and the United States. This was one of the main areas in which women could clearly see that the personal was indeed political. The widespread fear of being out alone at night, the need to conform to feminine patterns of behaviour at work, the need to take women's jobs rather than intrude into male public space, the shame of being beaten or sexually abused by one's nearest and dearest, were all revealed as shared problems for women rather than as personal secrets. Although there has been some dispute over how far male violence should be attributed to men's biology, that is, to some form of naturally induced aggression, feminists studying violence have generally argued against biological determinism, looking instead at the social construction and ideological legitimation of male violence. Edwards sees the work of the American radical feminist Mary Daly as a bridge between the more specific studies of the early 1970s, which concentrated in particular on rape, and the more general later analyses.

66

Daly (1978) took a broad sweep across the variety of historical and cultural ways in which women were oppressed in patriarchal society, picking on such diverse examples as *suttee* in India, footbinding in China, genital mutilation in Africa, witchburnings in Europe, and the practice of gynaecology in the United States. While Daly herself labelled her book extremist (1978: 17) she saw women's common situation as one of extremity, in which women were silenced, sacrificed, fearful and controlled within the male violence of patriarchal society. Her aim was to show (20–1) 'the interconnectedness of things' so that women could make sense of the great variety of their individual experiences and see them as common experiences of the violence of patriarchal society.

While the problem of the implicit biological reductionism of this universal conception of patriarchal violence remains, Edwards argues (1987: 20) that during the 1970s feminists uncovered the key social institutions and core social values that have historically legitimated and maintained male power over women. By the 1980s, the varied forms which male violence can take were being linked to the underlying struggle by men to retain their dominance over women. In this struggle, violence had become interwoven with sexuality, so that the institutionalization of heterosexuality in the family had become a key area for the control of women by men (Rich 1983).

The claim that male violence is very generally, if not universally, institutionalized and legitimated emerges clearly from this literature. In the west, where much of the literature has been situated, feminists have made a strong case for arguing that women's lives are normally constrained by the threat of male violence (Wilson 1983; Stanko 1985). The legitimation of male violence takes forms which treat the victims of violence as responsible for their own rapes, or assaults or harassment or murders: they asked for it, flaunted their sexuality, enjoyed it although they pretended not to, started something they could not stop, were out alone at night, hitched a lift, dressed provocatively, nagged their husbands.

The growing involvement of feminist activists in working with women who have been raped, or who have been assaulted by the men they live with, politicized male violence. The rapid, though uneven, growth of rape crisis centres and refuges for assaulted women created a new body of knowledge which challenged existing explanations of rape. They revealed the widespread extent of male violence, particularly domestic assault and the sexual abuse of children (Hanmer and Saunders 1984; rhodes and McNeill 1985).

In the west, not only rape but also assaults on women by the men they live with, sexual harassment at work, the rape and abuse of children, and child prostitution are now much more widely accepted as common occurrences which have been grossly underreported to the authorities. As a result of feminist activity, public attitudes and official procedures are beginning to change, although slowly, unevenly, and with limited effect. Elsewhere women are struggling against comparable and even worse forms of harassment, violence, and death. In the volume of articles from the Indian feminist journal *Manushi* (Kishwar and Vanita 1984), types of violence include female infanticide, dowry deaths, and rapes by the police. The *Manushi* articles differ from most western feminist analyses of violence in that they implicate women in violence. They also show links between sexual violence and land disputes, the conception of women as property, and other economic factors. The role of women in violence is dealt with by some feminist authors (e.g. Wilson 1983) but is not an issue for those who define women and men as having essentially different biological natures.

Feminist knowledge of male violence requires a redefinition of public and private boundaries. The violence that occurs in the private sphere cannot be separated from the legitimation of male dominance, the greater value of men, and the dominance of patriarchal political and economic institutions in the public sphere. Feminist studies of male violence have, therefore, gone some way towards operationalizing the concept of patriarchy through making key mechanisms of male dominance and gender hierarchy visible. While some of these mechanisms, such as hitting, are very common, others are harder to understand. The ways in which they are embedded in social and economic processes can be very complex.

The causes of male violence and its interconnection with sexuality and mode of production remain unclear in that different causes have been suggested. The explanation of male violence is not straightforward since women are still harassed in situations where they could offer physical resistance. A knee in the groin would deter most drunken husbands or workplace Romeos, but women tend not to take this option because they lack consciousness of the generality of harassment, and so do not see a knee kick as morally justified, or they fear the consequences: physical retaliation, unemployment, a charge of assault. Physical assaults on women may be accompanied by weapons, or the use of institutional power (e.g. as workplace superior, senior relative) or by economic sanctions (cutting the housekeeping) rather than depending on natural physical strength. Violence can exploit fear, guilt, loyalty, shame, and loving, caring emotions. Susan Edwards (1987: 164) cites British and American evidence to show that when women do attack or kill violent men, their attacks may be treated as premeditated because they often compensate for their physical disadvantage as women by catching the man at a disadvantage, when he is drunk, asleep, or otherwise incapacitated.

The issue remains complicated because male violence is not simply a universal phenomenon. If it was universal, then a biological factor might be looked for. In the more recent works on male violence, the possibility of biological explanation, at least in terms of essential male aggression which must be vented on women, is generally rejected. There is still a physical element in male violence, however, which should not be overlooked, and which does not entail biological reductionism. Assuming adequate nourishment and health, men are on average larger, heavier, and stronger than women. So once the ideas which legitimate violence are dominant, men *can* act violently because women often cannot physically prevent them. This point needs to be qualified to the extent that adequate health and nutrition and the relative muscle development and body weight of men and women can be varied to some extent by different socio-economic conditions, and different social evaluations of male and female worth and attractiveness. Where male violence to women is ignored or socially legitimated, male violence towards 'weaker' men is also likely to be prevalent. It does not follow that men must use, or have always used, physical superiority to subordinate women. But historically, physical superiority accompanied by social and ideological conditions which legitimate male superiority generally have *allowed* men to use violence as an effective mechanism for controlling women. Belief in the superiority of the male physique and the valuing of male muscular development over female fragility is also characteristic of societies which legitimate male dominance. In spite of these necessary qualifications, it is hard to conceive that women would be so systematically controlled through violence and fear if they were in general physically equal to or stronger than men.

Motherhood

Feminism revealed women as literally oppressed by men through the construction of female sexuality and male violence. It also showed that motherhood and childcare should be understood as cultural constructions, rather than as innate female capacities. As Coulson (1980: 35) has put it, 'It is through culture defining biology that having babies becomes a social disadvantage, that rearing children is women's work . . . .' The identification of women with the physical ability to nurture children within their bodies, and to bring them into the social world through a mysterious but messily physical process of birth, does seem to put women really closer to nature than men. Women are plainly capable of motherhood by nature rather than by the will of men. But the meanings embedded in motherhood in different societies, and the extent to which social definitions of womanhood restrict women to their reproductive role, have been challenged by feminism. All healthy women are biologically potential mothers, but not all women are mothers in practice; infertility, childlessness, conception, paternity, pregnancy, childbirth, motherhood, breastfeeding and care of dependent children are all variable social concepts of behaviour which occur in historically variable social relationships.

In the first stage of new-wave feminism, motherhood was taken to be a major form of women's oppression and was seen as of little interest to feminists. A number of women have commented in personal accounts on their unease as mothers in the early phases of the movement. Susan Griffin, when asked for a feminist theory of motherhood in 1974, could produce only some preliminary notes (Griffin 1982). The demand for twenty-four-hour state childcare took little account of the social processes of parenthood or the emotional needs of parents and children. Motherhood as experience, however, intruded very directly into women's lives. Feminists had mothers, many feminists were mothers, or became mothers during the 1970s and 1980s, while others debated whether or not they should become mothers or had to cope with the knowledge that they could not become mothers.

Adrienne Rich (1980) broke new ground in arguing that motherhood was a social institution with a history and an ideology.[2] The exhaustion and domestic isolation of American mothers were essential to the maintenance of the patriarchal system. The experience of maternity had been channelled to serve male interests, under male control of reproduction. The privatization of mothers in the home rendered them politically powerless in patriarchal society. Rich's analysis is apparently rooted in American experience, in spite of its very general frame of reference, but since it linked women's personal, private experiences to motherhood as an oppressive institution, it served to politicize the whole area of human reproduction.

Following Rich, though with a rather different argument, Mary O'Brien (1981) argued that the biological process of reproduction engenders reproductive consciousness which is cultural. Men and women experience reproduction differently so that men have had to overcome their alienation from childbirth by establishing paternity and by organizing marriage practices which protect the paternity of others. Other feminists challenged the idea of motherhood as an instinctive need of women (Macintyre 1976). This also challenged the idea of motherhood as female fulfilment (Spender 1980: 54) and the necessity of the patriarchal nuclear family (Comer 1974; Barrett and McIntosh 1982). Motherhood had to be seen as historically variable in terms of ideas, experience and social relationships, rather than as uniformly natural.

These developments in feminist theory proved threatening to women whose political consciousness was low, and who had no other personal identity than that of wife, home-maker and mother. Motherhood thus proved a paradoxical institution to define as oppressive, since motherhood was also women's peculiar power of creation and nurturance which was denied to men. Some American radical feminists of the 1970s developed a quite different and distinct theme of women's special closeness to nature (Jaggar 1983: 95) and celebrated the creative potential of women's natural powers. Motherhood was then seen as a special capacity of women. The task of feminism became that of 'extending the feminine sphere until it becomes coterminous with the human totality' (Maroney 1986: 422).

Childcare

Since the 1970s feminists have begun to identify motherhood not only as female creativity or as an oppressive social construction, but also as a major area of unresolved contradiction, particularly in urban and industrial societies. The separation of home and workplace has created childcare as a serious but virtually unrecognized social problem. Since children have been ideologically defined as belonging to the home, that is, to the private, domestic, female sphere, they have also been defined as the practical, daily responsibility of women. Fathering a child refers to the single physical act of placing sperm where it can biologically unite with an ovum. Fatherhood is socially important for

71

providing the social identification for the child that ensues. Mothering a child refers to innumerable acts of caring, nurturing, guiding, and loving which extend over years. Mothers may be isolated, exhausted, depressed, impoverished, violent towards their children, or hooked on tranquillizers, but these are taken to be their private inadequacies rather than general social problems.

Women in urban areas or industrial societies are then faced with the personal, private problem of resolving a contradiction which cannot be resolved without major socio-economic transformation. If they have children they may be able to choose to remain in the home with them, supported by a man, or by the state, until the children can move independently into the public sphere. Some women are happy to do this, and for those cushioned by affluence, good housing, adequate means of transport, and access to leisure facilities, this period of their life may be personally rewarding.[3] Such women are vulnerable if their husbands leave them, removing their source of income, or when their children no longer need them, and they have no social place outside their empty home. Other women suffer from depression, isolation, or poverty in these circumstances. The stress of being isolated in a confined space in winter, alone with one or more energetic and demanding small children, with inadequate money for heating or outings, while trying to cope with endless domestic chores, has to be experienced to be believed. When money is also inadequate for food and clothing, and housing is sub-standard or lacking, women's ability to lavish multifaceted care on children as their personal dependants within the private sphere is mythical.

The need or choice to maintain some independence by working outside the home does not resolve the contradiction since it creates the problem of finding adequate childcare at a price low-paid women can afford, and still leaves the domestic labour to be done. (Again, more affluent women have fewer problems since they can pay less affluent women for childcare and domestic labour, but, as Currie (1986) shows, affluent mothers still experience their decision to work away from their children as conflict-ridden.) Women are torn and guilty at trying to operate conscientiously both at home and at work. Women suffer because of the lack of social recognition of childrearing as a social rather than as a private issue. In the worst situations, millions of children scavenge on the streets, getting by as best they can, or starve, because their mothers are unable to provide the most basic care.

Public childcare facilities in Britain are generally poor, but better childcare will not resolve the central contradiction of women taking responsibility for children and domestic labour, when home and work are physically separated (New and David 1985). Socialist societies, for example, have provided extensive childcare facilities, but still leave women with the problems of combining mothering with domestic labour and paid work (Bassnett 1986: 65ff.; Wolf 1985).

The notion of motherhood in industrial societies as contradictory is not one that can be generalized to all societies without appropriate qualifications. In rural areas where children are not confined to the home, and are surrounded by older children and relatives who can keep an eye on them, mothers may be less restricted. Where rural women can work with their children on their backs or nearby, the separation of home and work is not the same issue. This does not mean that life is easy for rural women, or that the institution of motherhood is not oppressive, but that motherhood cannot be treated as universally oppressive without the context and mechanisms of oppression being established in each case. The way in which responsibility for childcare is enmeshed in the economic dependence of women on men is a particular historical development, but one which is now very widespread.

Motherhood and childcare remain contradictory experiences for the majority of the world's women — an unparalleled experience of creativity, an area of limited control over their bodies for most, and a direct connection to economic and political subordination. Pregnancy and breastfeeding provide some restrictions on economic activity, but these natural functions cannot account for the social mechanisms by which women are very generally restricted to their roles as mothers or potential mothers or as motherly people, in relation to dominant males.

Reproductive technology

Shulamith Firestone made controversial proposals for women to take control of reproduction through technological means, and thus to liberate themselves from male dominance (Firestone 1979). This introduced an interest in reproductive technology early on in new-wave feminism. Although her political conclusions have been widely criticized (Rose and Hanmer 1976), Firestone saw that science offered far more than intervention in barriers to conception. It offered potential control of the whole reproductive process. Separating sexual intercourse from childbirth challenges the relationships between women and reproduction (Rowland 1987). In some respects these technical developments offered women choice (at least for the more affluent): the choice of preventing conception, the hope of motherhood for those whom nature had failed, the choice of selected and healthy offspring. Feminists were quick to point out, however, that these choices were still being made within the male-dominated, patriarchal social institutions of marriage and the family, and within patriarchal systems of state health care. Feminists have been paying increasing attention to the possibilities and the dangers of the ways in which reproductive technology has been developed, particularly in the west, but also elsewhere (Arditti *et al.* 1984; Corea 1985; Stanworth 1987).

The paradox for feminism is that while all women have been socially constituted as natural mothers, reproduction left to nature is far from perfect. Childbirth can be physically dangerous, not all women are physically able to bear children (even assuming adequate attention to women's general health and standard of living), and some foetuses are not physically fit to survive. Societies which demand that every woman should survive every labour, and that every foetus should be born alive and treated as viable, are going against nature. Human interventions in childbirth which enable more women to become mothers, and more mothers and foetuses to survive, have, therefore, been in women's interests as mothers (Berer 1986). They have a long history which predates more modern scientific interventions.

There are two main problems raised by the rapid development of scientific intervention into women's bodies. First, women have little if any control over this technology, which has been developed within male-dominated hierarchies in patriarchal societies. Stanworth (1987: 35) argues that it is not whether there should be intervention which is at issue, but whether we can create the conditions within which 'such technologies can be employed by women to shape the experience of reproduction according to their own definitions'. This raises the further problem of how such definitions can be expressed — how the full range of women's needs around the world, and across class, racial, and cultural divisions, can be known and acted on.

Second, little attention has been given to the extent to which women can have fulfilled and satisfying lives without necessarily becoming mothers. Where women expect themselves, and are under social pressure, to find motherhood their greatest fulfilment as proper women, infertility can be a terrible personal tragedy. McNeil and Scott (1986) point to motherhood as the main way in which women's identity is constructed, leaving not having children, whether through choice or lack of choice, as aberrant. Reproductive technology potentially increases women's choices over motherhood but realizing that potential will entail widespread political struggle.

Since motherhood itself is a site of women's oppression, control of reproduction has remained a site of struggle for power between the sexes. Hanmer and Allen (1980: 227) argue that reproductive engineering 'offers a vehicle for the final working out of the antagonism between women and men'. Feminists have also called for men to be involved in reproduction, through shared parenting, and through applications of scientific knowledge which subvert the oppression of women by men (O'Brien 1981). But any such scheme will require very radical social transformation in order to be effective.

Production and reproduction

What mothers actually do with their time has been one of the most dramatic revelations of feminism. Once feminists turned their attention to what women actually do, both inside and outside the domestic sphere, it became very clear that most women live lives of more or less unremitting toil. Although ridiculed at first (Mainardi 1980: 104), feminists established housework in capitalist societies as an area of unpaid labour to be given serious consideration. At first in empirical and historical studies (Oakley 1974; Malos 1980) and then in the much more abstract domestic labour debate taken up by marxist feminists, women's work in the domestic sphere was shown to be much more than private housework. It was revealed as work of social and economic importance, and shown to have a place in the systematic oppression of women (Kaluzynska 1980).

Feminists were then faced with yet another situation in which knowledge of the familiar, everyday world of women was inadequate because of the lack of concepts with which to comprehend it. Feminists used the marxist concepts of production and reproduction in an effort to include women's work in producing babies, hot dinners, clean shirts and emotional support, as well as their paid labour. While the conceptual separation of women's work into production and reproduction encouraged knowledge of women's work in both spheres, this dualism also created problems (Edholm *et al.* 1977; Ferguson and Folbre 1981).

The 1970s conception of reproduction was one of the more abstract and contentious areas of marxist feminism (influenced by the work of Althusser) as it was very difficult to specify in general how the ideology of sexual subordination interacted with the organization of production and reproduction. While marxist analysis should be applicable to any mode of production, and some feminists have taken up this point, marxist feminism has tended to concentrate particularly on common features of women's oppression in western capitalism. This has led to considerable problems with generalizations.

Clearly there cannot be one universal answer as to why women's work tends to be valued as less than men's that will always be valid in every historical situation, but marxist feminists did look for a general framework of explanation, and they did this sometimes at a very abstract level. Women were not only workers inside and outside the home, they also physically reproduced and reared the labour force of the future as mothers within families. Women helped to reproduce and sustain the social structures of capitalism. Marxist feminists then located women's oppression in the family, heterosexuality, and marriage, as did radical feminists, but also in the production system, and with reference to the activities of the state.

The concepts of production and reproduction established women as workers, but as workers on very different terms from men. Studies of work exposed the unequal sexual division of labour, both inside and outside the household, not as natural but, as with sexuality, violence, and motherhood, as having its own history and ideology. Questioning the dualism of the private and public domains led directly to the need to reconceptualize women's work, both at home and in the public sphere. The nature of the work allocated to women could not be separated from their general subordination to men. Feminists began to reassess concepts of work, and in particular of the idea that 'real work' took place outside the home in organized productive activity. Women's work at home in servicing the needs of the household and reproducing the labour required for production became visible.

Wages for housework

As a reaction to the revaluing of women's work in the private sphere, some radical feminists began to campaign for wages for housework (Federici 1975; Edmond and Fleming 1975). This was seen as a way of gaining value and independence for women's work in the private sphere. This view came at a time when increasing numbers of western women were taking paid work outside the home. It was quickly criticized for failing to address the relationship between women's domestic labour and the mode of production, specifically, the relationship between the work of the western housewife and the capitalist mode of production (Landes 1980). However, Phillips has pointed out (1987: 153) that wages for housework has different implications for working-class and for middle-class women, given their differences in earning potential. The international network of Black Women for Wages for Housework has also argued that finance could be found by cutting military expenditure (1988). The problems of women isolated in their own homes, with heavy workloads but without economic independence, remain. Women in Britain in the 1980s are confined not only by the care of small children and their low earning ability but, in greater numbers and for much longer periods than ever before, as carers for the elderly, chronically sick, mentally handicapped, and physically disabled. These women provide major social services in the invisibility of domestic privacy. As right-wing social policies bite deeper, the development of so-called community care, in place of public institutional care, will swell their numbers.

The domestic labour debate

The problem of how to conceptualize housework in capitalist societies where it was not productive labour in Marx's sense of the term (housewives produced things or services to be used, rather than things which produced surplus value) and where housewives were not exploited by employers (they did not receive a wage for their work which was less than the value of what they produced) led to the domestic labour debate (Benston 1970; Gardiner 1976; Hamilton and Barrett 1986). Part of this debate was a consideration of whether housework should be seen as some other mode of production which was articulated with the capitalist mode. In part, the domestic labour debate was a consideration of the usefulness of housework to capitalism. Since domestic labour cannot be a mode of production in a marxist sense, though, this argument changed the meaning of mode of production. This left the meaning of an articulation between capitalism and a domestic mode of production unclear.

Questions about domestic labour led to the conclusion that housework existed in the forms that it did because it served the needs of capitalism. Unfortunately this conclusion is logically flawed and takes no account of variations in forms of domestic labour, for example, those created by different migrant labour systems.[4] (The capitalist system can operate without housewives through the use of immigrant labourers living in dormitories at low levels of subsistence, but at the cost of losses in consumer spending.) These views were quickly criticized (Molyneux 1979). The position of the twentieth-century western housewife is much more clearly understood as a historically specific and highly contradictory phenomenon which has both advantages and disadvantages for the maintenance of capitalism.

The question of whether capitalism requires the subordination of women, or whether historically capitalism has facilitated the entrenchment of male dominance, remains disputed. Obviously this question cannot be resolved without some reference to the relations between the sexes at different historical periods and in different modes of production. Lewenhak (1980), for example, argues that women's status as workers has declined in recent history. The precise interrelations of production and reproduction, in any general terms which can be applied to different situations, remain elusive. But a considerable body of knowledge now exists on specific interrelationships of production, reproduction, and women's oppression (Afshar 1985; Mies 1986).

Women's work

Investigations of the role in production and reproduction of the western housewife clarified women's work elsewhere. In the third world and in some parts of the advanced capitalist societies, women were shown to be directly engaged in productive labour in the course of their domestic work. This has been shown particularly clearly in the case of African women but there is also overwhelming evidence from all other parts of the world to show women's contribution to food production, processing and distribution, care of livestock, craftwork, and community development (Slocum 1975; Rogers 1980; Bujra 1986; Roberts 1984). Once women were defined as workers, rather than as wives and mothers, the extent and variation of male dominance around the world became much easier to recognize. Social distinctions between men's work and women's work concealed divisions in access to land, knowledge, skills, and other resources, the control of labour, and rights to dispose of what was produced. By making women's labour (and in particular, women's unpaid labour) visible, feminists could show how this work had become devalued in relation to that of men, although not in any uniform or harmonious way.

A distinction between arguments which apply to all capitalist societies everywhere and those which are specific to particular capitalist societies at particular historical periods has not, however, always been carefully drawn. Marxist feminists also tended to treat women in capitalist society as if they are either full-time housewives or workers. This ignored the extent to which women juggle these contradictory areas of work throughout their working lives. Work on production and reproduction in the third world has brought home the need for much more careful qualification of generalizations (Redclift 1985). In the 1980s, more historically specific knowledge has been produced of the complex relationships women experience in the processes of production and reproduction, and in the relationship of these processes to the activities of the state (Elson and Pearson 1981; Balbo 1987).

The gendered structuring of capitalist labour markets ensured a sexual division of labour at work. Women became less valued as workers than men, had access to a more limited range of work. Men benefited from this situation and played a part in maintaining it (Cockburn 1983). Some marxist feminists argued that women were a reserve army of labour, available for work outside the household when insufficient men were available. The problem with this view is that women in advanced capitalist societies are a pool of cheap labour rather than a reserve army of labour in the sense intended by Marx (Bruegel 1979). Marx (1976: 781ff.) argued that it was an essential mechanism of the capitalist system that the industrial reserve army could be brought in when extra labour was needed, to prevent wage rises eating into profits. This labour could be dispatched again when the demand for labour fell. Women in advanced capitalist societies remain a contradictory form of cheap labour, since when they are not in paid work they still have to be maintained, and have rights to housing, health care, education, pensions, etc. Even though these rights are being rapidly eroded by Thatcherism in Britain in the 1980s, women's cheap or part-time labour rarely directly replaces men's more expensive or full-time labour because of the extent of gender segregation in the labour market. This argument also needs specific qualification in different parts of the world depending on the structure of labour markets, and women's rights to maintenance from the state.

Women's work is oppressive with respect to their levels of pay and conditions of work. There is a limited choice of work available for women. They lack access to skills, and male activities in the home and the workplace ensure that women do not leave the domestic sphere without a struggle (Burman 1979; Cockburn 1983; Westwood 1984). Work, status and rewards became linked to the relative power of men and women in the home, and women's responsibility for children. The impact of technology on domestic labour then occurred in ways which have reinforced rather than relieved women's responsibility for domestic labour (Ravetz 1987).

Making women's oppression through work visible made the connections between production and reproduction plain, but left a number of problems in explanations of how and why these connections had come about, and how and why they vary. Nicholson (1987: 29) suggests that the separation of production and reproduction should be seen not as a characteristic of all societies, but as an historical development 'which led liberals to differentiate the family and the state and marxists to differentiate production and reproduction'. The inability of the marxist concept of production to take account of gender leaves feminism with the problem of explaining the different ways in which women's work is oppressive.

THE CONTRADICTIONS OF WOMEN'S OPPRESSION

Although feminists are not yet in agreement on how biology is to be taken into account in any understanding of women's oppression, they have made a very powerful case that women are very generally oppressed by men. The problem for feminism is that the forms that women's oppression takes are themselves contradictory.

Psychoanalysis and the contradictions of femininity

The problem of explaining motherhood and feminine identity without falling into the trap of biological reductionism has led to a link between feminism and psychoanalytic explanation. The issue of what use feminists might make of psychoanalytic thought cannot be easily summarized though, because feminists have taken up very different positions. While some key texts in this area, notably those by Kate Millett (1977), Juliet Mitchell (1974) and Nancy Chodorow (1978), have become popular, much of the debate over psychoanalysis developed at a level of intellectual impenetrability which has pushed it to the sidelines of popular feminist thought. This is unfortunate because recent debates in psychoanalysis have focused on key problems in feminist understanding of the oppression of women (Sayers 1986).

Nancy Chodorow (1978) asked new questions about the development of masculinity and femininity in the light of women's power and practices as mothers. Chodorow argued that the process of the infant becoming differentiated from the mother produced different personality construction in boys and girls because of the universal character of women's behaviour in mothering. As boys get older they have to cease to identify with the woman who mothers them and to identify with a largely absent father. Masculinity is then based on the rejection of femininity. Chodorow's American work differs from European feminist thought, however, in that it does not focus on the unconscious or use a concept of contradiction. As Rose (1983: 9) has commented, Chodorow assumes that the internalization of norms works, whereas the basic premise of psychoanalysis is that it does not. The unconscious reveals the 'failure' of identity. Whereas there is some ambiguity in feminism about the stability of gender identity, Chodorow seems to assume that femininity is fixed, since women's mothering is universal. Chodorow's work has probably had most appeal to those feminists who celebrate the positive difference of femininity from masculinity. Chodorow characterizes men as psychologically dependent and insecure, because of the way in which differentiation from the mother takes place, while women can achieve psychological security and a sense of self-esteem.

Chodorow did challenge existing conceptions of femininity, motherhood, and female sexuality, but other feminist uses of psychoanalytic thought have focused on the inherent contradictions of femininity and on the difficulty with which biological females (at least in modern western cultures) become socially 'normal' women. (Because psychoanalytic generalizations tend to be applied to people in general, it is often unclear in this literature how far conclusions are general, and how far they are specific to western cultures.)

Psychoanalysis became an issue for new-wave feminism initially through Kate Millett's attack on Freud, first published in 1969 (Millett 1977). Millett drew on ideas promoted by earlier writers to produce a fierce rejection of Freud. In Millett's view, Freud became an apologist for women's oppression rather than an observer and therapist in the midst of oppression. The development of subsequent feminist thought on psychoanalysis has depended largely on challenges to this interpretation of Freud. Moi, for example (1985: 27), has argued that

Millett's interpretation distorted Freud's meaning by treating Freud's work as unified and coherent, ignoring his cautions and revisions. Millett assumed that Freud could be dismissed as a biological essentialist for arguing that women's social subordination was a necessary consequence of the lack of a penis, and the working out of the Oedipus complex. This interpretation of Freud was influenced in part by the development of versions of psychoanalytic therapy, particularly in the United States, which sought to rectify the behaviour of those who deviated from the paths of supposedly normal development (Rubin 1975: 184). But the chief characteristic of this 1960s view of psychoanalysis is the absence of Freud's conception of the unconscious.

Millett's approach was challenged by interpretations of Freud which treated his work as revealing sexual ideology. These interpretations owed much to the impact of the French philosopher Althusser on marxist thinking in the 1960s and 1970s, and to the reinterpretation of Freud by the French psychoanalyst Lacan (1968). This approach to the study of femininity was made popular in English-speaking feminism by Juliet Mitchell (1974). Mitchell set out to make constructive use of Freud's insights for feminist politics. Mitchell drew on Althusser and Lacan in order to treat Freud's work as a scientific account of the development of femininity. She located Freudian feminism at the level of sexual ideology. In Mitchell's view, penis-envy was a characteristic of phallic culture rather than of little girls' personal observations of their physical lack. But, as Mitchell's critics have pointed out (Barrett 1980; Wilson 1981), this results in a feminist political strategy which is directed at changing ideology, rather than one which addresses the relationships between sexual ideology and material life.

Lacan's influence on feminism outside France was limited by the abstraction of the concepts he used. Interpretations of Lacan vary, but his work was seen as relevant to feminism in that it could help explain how women arrive at femininity and the contradictions in the construction of female sexual identity (Coward et al. 1978: 13). This allowed both for the possibility that sexual ideology could develop in contradiction to the needs of a mode of production (Coward et al. 1978) and also that femininity, far from being a natural course for women to take, is difficult for women to achieve (Rose 1983).

If Lacan's theory is taken to be situated at a very general level, then it cannot explain or take into account cultural differences in the achievement of sexual identity (Wilson 1981) nor the reasons why the phallus, rather than say the womb, is a socially privileged symbol. It may well be that all humans develop an unconscious through infants' struggles to separate themselves from their parents and to gain a separate identity which resolves or represses their infant sexual desires; it does not follow that these struggles always take the same form or the same cultural expression.

The impossibility of disentangling the significance of biological from cultural sexual differences when these are conceived in the value-laden terms of possession of/lack of a penis needs to be clearly stated. How many little boys get the chance of some cultural expression of the lack of a womb? How many little girls get the chance to relish the possession of both womb and clitoris? To a very great extent the existence and importance of penis-envy is taken for granted in the literature which leaves women with no concepts for thinking about their identity except those of lack and inferiority (Rubin 1975: 197). Feminists have argued that we need not take penis-envy and the Oedipus complex for granted, since though we may all have an unconscious, what is in the unconscious can vary. The entrenched sexism of psychoanalytic thought and therapeutic practice has made the political use of psychoanalytic insights an exceedingly problematic area for feminism.

Barrett (1980: 56) has argued that Mitchell took an 'unduly charitable' reading of Freud, in that she overlooked the sexist implications of Freud's work, in particular his treatment of masculinity as active and femininity as passive. Rose (1983: 9) argues, against Mitchell's critics, that psychoanalysis reveals women's resistance to their socially constructed feminine identity. While she agrees that criticisms of psychoanalysis are valid if it is used as universalistic theory of patriarchy (10) there are challenges to Freudian phallocentrism (in, for example, the work of Karen Horney and Melanie Klein) and there can be different conceptions of femininity. But it is still not clear that a general feminist political strategy can be derived from the centrality of contradiction that psychoanalysis identifies. This lack of a general strategy has become a critical political problem for feminism.

The discovery of the contradictions of feminine identity do not lead to any clear political strategies for women's liberation. Once the concept of contradiction was introduced, it proved something of a two-edged sword for feminism. The feminine roles into which western women were supposed to fit were exposed as cultural products, but arguments around the political significance of psychoanalytic thought for feminism imply that patriarchy, far from being a coherently oppressive, general system, is more realistically seen as complex and contradictory. Women's sexuality and their love and care for their supposed oppressors are central features. Freed slaves do not need their masters, but it can be argued that the majority of liberated women would need men.

Political lesbianism

New-wave feminism offered an unprecedented opportunity for women who felt oppressed and distorted by heterosexual norms and the conventions of femininity, marriage, and family life to 'come out' as lesbians with clearly defined common interests. These were common interests as women, rather than interests shared with homosexual men. Many prominent new-wave feminists publicly identified themselves as lesbian and drew on their personal experiences to make effective analyses of women's oppression. Feminism provided a framework within which lesbianism developed from a source of private, personal problems into a public, political issue (Ettorre 1980), although this was not without discrimination against lesbians within feminism (Bunch 1981: 68). New-wave feminism has received much of its initial revolutionary impetus from lesbian women, even though lesbianism does not provide feminism with a specific political position. While radical feminism has been most closely identified with lesbian interests and support, there are heterosexual radical feminists and lesbian marxist feminists. There are also lesbians who are not feminists. Feminism had the effect both of providing public political support for lesbian women as women and of challenging public harassment of lesbians, but it also produced some diversity in sexual and political definitions of lesbianism (Abbott and Love 1972; Clarke 1983; Rich 1983; Kitzinger 1987).

Most feminist theory on this issue, as on others, moved away from conceptions of sexuality as biologically fixed. Some confusion then developed in the literature as to how the biology of female sexuality can be taken into account. Increasing emphasis has been put on conceptions of lesbianism as socially constructed. The problem with seeing sexuality as socially constructed, though, is that this conception poses new problems rather than providing answers. As Seidler (1986: 117–18) has argued of the historical construction of human nature, the statement that human nature is socially constructed leaves no room 'to consider the *nature* of the historical formation of human nature'. The historical construction of lesbianism and of heterosexuality is central to any understanding of the oppression of women by men, but remains elusive. This lack of theoretical clarity has raised considerable political problems.

Lesbian feminists have been careful to specify that they are not attacking heterosexual women. On the contrary, they have sought common ground for unity and freedom between women. They have attacked heterosexuality as a social institution which forces women to form subordinated relationships with men, rather than heterosexual practices as such (Rich 1983). Rich acknowledges that not all heterosexual relationships are awful, but argues that women have no real power to determine the meaning and place of sexuality in their lives (1983: 167). Because lesbianism exposes the roots of male power in a society, it forms the basis of a struggle against patriarchy, and so has political implications for all women (Kitzinger 1987).

Some lesbian feminists have taken the view that heterosexuality is politically inappropriate for any women, regardless of their sexual orientation (Leeds Revolutionary Feminists 1981). Lesbianism is then defined not as a personal sexual orientation or identity, but as a political commitment to women (women-identified-women) which might or might not entail sexual activity. This political lesbianism is an attack on patriarchy and heterosexuality through its direct effect on male power over women. The woman-identified-woman sides with other women against male power. Rich (1983: 165) argues that 'woman-identification is a source of energy — a springhead of female power which is curtailed and wasted by the institution of heterosexuality'. Valeska (1981: 28) characterizes heterosexuality as a mandate that divides women through their allegiance to one man in the home and all men outside it, leaving lesbianism as a 'powerful political force' (31).

While total political separation from men has been a minority practice, and has attracted criticism of its biologically determinist logic, it has been a politically significant force in feminist movements. But, as Christine Collette (1987: 77) has noted, there are many husbands hidden in feminist closets — and surely many men who are not husbands (Spender 1986). The differences in the sexual-political identities of feminists have been a constant source of unease in a movement that has sought to build its politics on the basis of a shared state of sexual subordination. Differences of sexual politics have emerged not only between heterosexual and lesbian women, but also between radical and liberal lesbians (Kitzinger 1987). The women's movement has proved an 'intensely moral project' (95) in which there is a danger of the new moralism becoming as oppressive as the conventions of patriarchal society. Little space has been left for those who reject the available labels for sexual orientation.

Some tension remains between the nature of lesbian sexuality, which need not be politically feminist, and the nature of political lesbianism, which need not be sexual. The problems for feminism raised by women's sexual differences are taken up in chapter 7.

Power

While the power of men over women is the theme to which new-wave feminist analysis of women's oppression is addressed, there is surprisingly little feminist work directly on the analysis of power. Yet problems of how power is to be understood lie at the heart of feminism. The power of men over women is certainly shown to be widespread, and the basis of its legitimacy questioned, but the question of what this power is based on remains disputed. Landes (1978) argues that feminism makes the exclusion of women from power and decision-making visible, but that not all women are affected in the same manner. This is a theme which has perhaps been directly explored in political activity, novels and feminist science fiction rather than in the more theoretical production of feminist knowledge.

Since power was associated with the oppressiveness of patriarchal society, new-wave feminists embraced non-hierarchical organization. They looked for ways of sharing and co-operating and at new means of empowering women, rather than striving for power and position on male terms. There is, therefore, considerable confusion between the various strands of feminism on this issue. The movement of women into male-dominated occupations, and into positions of political power, for example, has been claimed by liberals as an advance for feminism. Radical feminists, however, explicitly rejected the idea that patriarchy could be challenged by competing with men on existing terms within patriarchal hierarchies. Rather, they looked at the ways in which patriarchal societies rendered women powerless, and at how feminism could lead to the empowerment of women in different terms.

There is no unified feminist theory of power, because liberal, radical and marxist feminists disagree, at least implicitly, over where power is located in society. While most feminists qualify their positions, liberals see power as diffused in some way through society, although not equally so. Radical feminists would generally locate male power in the structures and ideology of patriarchal society. Marxist feminists have a more contradictory and historical notion of male power being invested *both* in the organization of systems of production and in the structuring of gender relations, including perhaps men's physical advantages. These differences have prevented any resolution of feminist theories of oppression in terms of a common political strategy for liberation.

Radical feminist approaches to the issue of power have been primarily to turn away from aggressive and competitive western ideals of dominance to uncover women's feminine abilities of nurturing, caring, creating, sharing, and co-operating. This view challenges notions of government, political, community, and domestic organization which are dominant in the west and proposes new means of social organization which are not inherently hierarchical and oppressive.

Radical feminism also shows that men's power over women, and power exercised by women, cannot be separated from women's capacity for reproduction. The consequence of the strategy of eschewing power in patriarchal society, however, was to leave the problem of power insufficiently theorized and so inadequate in terms of effective political strategy. Feminist struggles against male power have made what Hartsock (1983a: 232) calls 'the vision of the oppressed group' visible. But she goes on to argue that while this reveals the one-sidedness of masculine conceptions of power as historical, cultural constructions of dominant groups (243–6), it does not explain the sexual division of labour which is what needs to be transformed. She points out (1) that feminists have concentrated more on women's oppression than on how male power over women is constructed and maintained.

The issue of power is a potentially divisive one for feminist struggles against oppression, since the power of women of different classes and races over each other remains problematic. Black or working-class women do not have the same capacity or choice for exercising feminine power in the United States or Britain as white or middle-class women do. A focus on power exposes the conflicting ideas of radical and marxist feminism while also showing that neither can do without the other (Landes 1978). Radical feminist conceptions of female empowerment need to be grounded in historical analysis of the organization of production, but marxist feminist analysis only differs from marxist analysis in that it takes radical feminist challenges into account. Studies of power point up the inherent contradictions in feminist theory and political practice. This is a problem which occurs in rather different ways in feminist approaches to peace and ecology.

Peace and ecology

Feminist exposure of male violence as a social problem has been chiefly concerned with violence directed towards women, or towards women and children. Questions of peace, war, and environmental destruction have only slowly been taken up as feminist issues, and new-wave feminism retained little knowledge of earlier women's struggles for peace (Liddington 1983). These questions indicate a central problem in feminist politics, of which there is some awareness in the literature (Assiter 1983). Peace, the safety of the individual, and care of our environment are not concerns which clearly reveal the specific oppression of women by men. Women, children and men face common dangers on the roads, from industrial accidents, agricultural disasters, environmental destruction, and from conventional and nuclear war. Women's active engagement in peace movements has, therefore, exposed a contradiction for feminist politics. If women share feminist political interests as women because they are all in various ways oppressed by men, or within male-dominated social institutions, then women's struggles should have political priority. Some feminists have been concerned that current peace movements do not take adequate account of feminist priorities (Wallsgrove 1983; Feminism and Non-violence Study Group 1983: 5). But struggles for women's health, housing, economic independence, and improved quality of life cannot logically be separated from struggles for pure air, clean water, and protection from greed and war. Struggles with men against common dangers cannot then clearly be separated from struggles for women. Women are left in the contradictory position that they need simultaneously to struggle both with men and against them. This, it seems, is the political contradiction at the heart of new-wave feminism.[5]

McNeil (1987) argues that in Britain the women's peace movement has been based on a challenge to the dominance of male reason and expertise. As Cohn (1987: 716) comments, the technical language of defence is gendered, so that women have to either learn it and so limit what they can say, or remain outside it. Women protesters at Greenham Common, and also elsewhere, have used images of spinning, twining wool around the perimeter fence of the American missile base.[6] Spinning (see Daly 1978) symbolizes women's abilities and knowledge, as opposed to the masculine logic and expertise which makes the use of nuclear weapons seem reasonable. The emphasis on women's capacity for motherhood, and on their intuitive knowledge, provides some basis for female unity but, as McNeil points out (42), only by obscuring the contradictions inherent in women's struggle for peace.

Feminist analysis indicates the connections between patriarchal mechanisms of male dominance, scientific rationality, capitalist accumulation, and the ethos of war, but feminism does not constitute a total social analysis. Feminists cannot, therefore, challenge oppression on every front as the oppression of women. Feminists can and do argue that the struggle against women's oppression entails struggles against other forms of oppression, but the broadening of struggle means making alliances with men and losing the focus on women. Issues of peace and ecology identify threats to human survival but, less obviously, specific sources of women's oppression. Nevertheless some feminists have taken up these problems as feminist issues (Thompson 1983), and the practical feminist politics in which they have engaged have received considerable (if generally unfavourable) publicity.

Women struggling for peace and for the environment as feminist issues have had to trace links between male power, dominance, hierarchy and reason, and the global threat to the survival of humanity and the natural world. Resistance against male domination reveals the necessity of struggling against all forms of violence and oppression. For feminists, eliminating war means more than getting rid of weapons, it means eliminating the root causes of war and violence which are enmeshed both in patriarchy and in modes of production (Feminism and Nonviolence Study Group 1983: 21). Women have begun to organize separately within the peace movement, notably in Britain against the missile base at Greenham Common, but also elsewhere in Britain and in many other countries. Women have taken up the issues of environmental pollution and destruction in the third world, the social causes of famine, and the neglect of women's role in food production, but these are not mainstream feminist causes.

Questions of peace and ecology tend to divide rather than unite women in practice. Saving the environment in the long term can imperil the economic survival in the short term of those who are destroying it. The cause of ecology exposes the conflicts of class, racial, and national interest which exist between women. In the name of women's rights, women have fought for the right to join armies on the same terms as men. More conventionally, women are brought into the military to service the male establishment or to help produce weapons as low-paid workers. Women contribute to militarism and to actual conflicts in ways which support mechanisms of male dominance, and the rationality of war and destruction.

In Britain feminists have had a limited impact on specific conflicts, notably against the patriotic fervour of the Falklands war and in Northern Ireland. For British women the violent conflict in Northern Ireland epitomizes the contradictions of feminist politics. There have been feminist developments in Northern Ireland in which Protestant and Catholic women have overcome considerable practical difficulties to recognize their common interests as women and to campaign against their oppression by men. But feminists have also organized along sectarian lines, and there are only limited links between English and Northern Irish activists. Contradictions for feminism remain (Fairweather *et al.* 1984; Jennings 1985). Loughran (1986) argues that feminists in Northern Ireland remain divided over the relevance of the national question to the liberation of women, and are caught up in the divisions of class and sectarianism. Loughran (77) ends on a question: 'Do contradictory situations like Northern Ireland leave feminists with no choice but to develop separate strategies, and if so does this not show the weaknesses of feminism?' It is this pervasive contradiction which remains to be addressed in all areas of feminist thought and political strategy.

Difference and division

The case made by new-wave feminism that women are very generally oppressed by men is overwhelming. While feminism may be very generally ridiculed, misinterpreted, dismissed, or ignored, there has been no concerted effort by men to rebut the argument that women are oppressed. Feminist attempts to establish this case certainly come up against men's intransigence in attending to the issue, since most men have a great deal to lose and little understanding of what they might gain. Feminists have also had difficulty, though, in making their case to women. An immediate problem for the success of feminist politics is women's lack of unity in oppression. The question of how far differences between women constitute real divisions of interest remains unclear. It is to this problem that the next three chapters are addressed.

DIVISIONS BETWEEN WOMEN — INTO THE IMPASSE

INTRODUCTION
TO PART TWO

As soon as the part men played in oppressing women was established, the conception of women as generally oppressed was shown to be problematic. Feminism faced serious divisions. Taking the variety of women's situations and experiences into account is not a simple matter of adding on those which had been omitted. Understanding the full range of women's lives has entailed looking not only at women's oppression by men, but also at women's solidarity with men, and at women's oppression by women.

The diversity of ways in which women are oppressed was not altogether overlooked by new-wave feminists. A careful reading of 1970s radical feminism will reveal many instances where authors acknowledge that women's experiences are variable in terms of race, ethnicity, class, and culture and admit that these issues need to be addressed. Anthologies, particularly those published in the 1980s, did include contributions by a variety of women. But the most influential radical feminist texts did not follow up the implications of these variations for feminism as an international political movement. As a result they did not take adequately into account the power relationships which can exist between women. These divisions were treated as subordinate to women's common interests as women. Feminists writing in the 1980s have made renewed efforts to take the differences between women into account, but the problems of how to recognize and act on diversity have led feminism into contradictory elaborations of oppression, rather than to a common political focus on liberation.

Barrett (1987) notes the new concern within feminism in the 1980s to recognize the differences between women, as well as the differences between women and men. She says (29):

This new politics recognizing the idea of difference within the category of woman, is radically challenging to conventional feminist arguments. This is because it is attempting to deconstruct the very historical identity on which feminist politics has traditionally been based.

The questioning of the meaning of 'woman' has come primarily from women's experiences of divisions between us, such as those of class, race, religion, and sexuality. Barrett identifies this sense of difference (33) as commonsensical, pragmatic, and rooted in women's experience. She seems to be arguing that this conception of difference is a limited one because it leads to a feminist politics based on women's experience that is inadequately theorized. It is hard to see, however, that those feminists who have raised the problems of material, cultural, and power divisions between women are arguing that these divisions are only knowable through the sharing of women's personal experience. All these divisions are sufficiently theorized for us to argue that women's common interests as women are effectively divided, whether women consciously experience divisiveness or not. It is the growing recognition within feminism of the material differences of power and interest between women which makes feminism as a general theory of the common oppression of women so problematic.

We can at least approach the problem of differences between women critically, and with an awareness of the problems involved. It is certainly not in men's interests that women should recognize a common cause with other women as against men. There are varied patriarchal pressures in different societies towards women's conscious identification with family, home, heterosexuality, husband, motherhood, service, obedience, submission, and the cultural and religious legitimation of these virtues. The future of feminism looks dim if feminism's political base is eroded to the limited sum of common interest as members of the female sex which remains. Not surprisingly, some authors have begun to write in terms of disillusionment or depression about the women's movement. The point of my argument in this section is that this depression can be lifted if we are more realistic about feminism's contradictions. By identifying women's interests as rooted in shared oppression, new-wave feminism constructed an impossible political task of transforming the entire world on the basis of a partial theory of oppression. Feminism as a theory of women's shared oppression has paradoxically encouraged the elaboration of the varieties of oppression which women suffer.

In Part Two, I present the problems of treating feminist knowledge as a theory of shared oppression. In chapters 5, 6, and 7, I set out to justify the argument that any attempt to characterize the relations between men and women as those of oppression must come up against the contradictory situation that women also exploit, oppress, and discriminate against each other. I have not, however, considered differences between women based on age or disability. While these are crucial areas of oppression for many women, they take different forms in different cultures, and so are difficult to generalize about. They are also forms of difference which could be transformed by changes in consciousness. Leaving them out does not mean that they are unimportant, or that feminists need not consider what to do about them.

Feminists have long recognized the need to take account of class divisions between women. The problems raised by class differences are considered in chapter 5. The further complications of nationality, ethnicity, and racism have been raised through criticism of new-wave feminism, and these are reviewed in chapter 6. The personal and painful ways in which women's interests become differentiated through culture and ideology are discussed in chapter 7. In chapter 7 I also deal with the political difficulties raised by the ways in which feminists have tried to make sense of women's sexual differences. These chapters show that women's situations not only differ, but that at least some of these differences constitute material divisions of interest — interests which cannot be changed simply by changing people's consciousness. Many women share their most vital interests with some men rather than with all women. The development of feminism as a theory of the oppression of women is then a limited exercise which ends in an impasse.

Chapter Five

WOMEN AGAINST WOMEN — CLASS, WORK, POWER

The question of whether women are always and everywhere oppressed as women continues to raise very difficult problems of explanation,
and continues to divide feminists. Feminist work in producing
knowledge of women's oppression led to the uncovering of the diversity
of ways in which women experience oppression, and women's power
over each other. New-wave feminists often acknowledged this problem,
but had no clear means of dealing with it. Once the class relations
between women are taken into account, 'women's dream of unity'
as Dorothy Smith has put it (1983: 40) 'is almost certainly illusory'.
Social class creates both divisions between women in the course of our
daily lives and also divisions between feminists in their interpretations
of where women's political interests lie.

Variations in the situations of women in different social classes, in
the work that women do, and in the power they hold over others
become particularly significant in evaluating the assertion that women
are everywhere oppressed by men. Once it is argued that women are
not always oppressed by men, or not as badly oppressed in some places
or at some times as in others, then specific explanations are needed
of why there should be such difference or variation. If women's
oppression by men is something which needs to be established and
explained, rather than something which can be taken as universal, then
we need to be much clearer about the implications of class divisions
for feminism.

WOMEN AND CLASS ANALYSIS

Feminist studies of the relations between gender and class have tended
to concentrate primarily on class relations in capitalist societies, since it

96

is these relationships which now need to be changed. But divisions of class, work, and power between women have a long history. Without reviewing every place and period preceding capitalism, the growing volume of historical research shows the gulf between those women who toiled and those who did not. Everywhere that cities developed, privileged women benefited from the labour of subordinates, however socially circumscribed their own lives.

It is a useful corrective to generalizations about pre-capitalism to remember that women's lives constitute half the experience of humankind since the beginnings of the human race. General statements about the relations between women need to be well qualified in relation to the places, times, and cultures covered. The relations between women and between men and women, as well as between the dominant and the subordinate classes, varied considerably between the various empires of the Mayas, the Incas, the Japanese, the Chinese, other South-East Asians, the Arabs, the Ottomans, the Moguls, the Romans, and many others, as well as between these and the enormous variety of simpler societies.

The argument that the populations of industrial societies are divided into social classes has taken different forms in western thought. Marxists, in spite of the many divisions between them, generally see classes as analytical categories. These are used to identify the different parts played by historical groups in the way each society's system of production is organized. Marxists agree that once the organization of production is dominated by capitalism then two main classes will have appeared: workers, who sell their labour power to produce goods worth more than they receive in wages, and the capitalists who expropriate this surplus value, and live by accumulating capital.[1] Marxists are much less in agreement over the parts played by other classes and parts of classes which co-exist with these: the unemployed, farmers, peasants, small shopkeepers, workers in the service sector, white-collar employees, the military, and professional and managerial groups. That is, they disagree over the groups whose positions in relation to the dominant (capitalist or bourgeois) and the subordinate (working or proletarian) classes can vary considerably over time and between different societies.

There is also disagreement over how to interpret the enormous changes in production and in the relationships between classes since the nineteenth century. Classes are not static or merely economic categories. Relations within and between classes are mediated by ideology and politics and are constantly contested. The point of class analysis, however, is to analyse how particular production systems work, to see which groups dominate and control each production system, and which groups are dominated and exploited. Once this analysis is clear, strategies can be developed for the subordinate classes to struggle to change the system.

Other theories of class have become primarily classification systems for ranking people according to their social status and lifestyle. Such analyses try to combine multiple indices of status, such as education, income, housing type, and personal prestige, or to amalgamate these by using classifications of occupations. While people may be quite unaware that they have class interests in a marxist sense, they are usually acutely conscious of nuances of status and prestige, of what constitutes a dead-end job, a nice neighbourhood, marrying beneath you, or a better income. Any discussion of women and class divisions, then, needs to clarify the notion of class that is being used. In this chapter, class is used in a marxist sense. The question of how other social differences are experienced by women is taken up in chapters 6 and 7.

Both marxist class analysis and other social theories of social and occupational stratification have conventionally left women out. In advanced capitalist and socialist societies the place of women in relation to men poses particular problems for class analysis. If women do not spend a lifetime in paid employment, enterprise, or trade, they have a clear place of their own neither in the production system nor in the occupational system. In order to avoid the need to specify the complex interrelations of class and gender, marxists and liberals alike have tended to identify women's social positions and class interests with those of their fathers or husbands. In the third world, peasant household production is treated as production by men with help from their wives and children.

As Ortiz (1985) has noted, the specificity of women's class positions has been ignored, and their position in the household seen as outside class. New-wave feminism decisively challenged this assumption that women are the passive dependants of their men, and that women share class interests with their men. There is now a growing body of feminist knowledge on the extremely complicated interrelations between class and gender. These show that class analyses cannot sensibly ignore women, and that the difficulties of establishing the relationship between class and gender are not insuperable (Crompton and Mann 1986; Abbott and Sapsford 1987).

WOMEN AND MARXIST CLASS ANALYSIS

In nineteenth-century Europe, pressure for women's rights to education, suffrage, and legal equality clarified the difference of interests between bourgeois and proletarian women. By the nineteenth century bourgeois women might have inherited wealth of their own, but they were still socially dependent on, and had their resources and their bodies controlled by, their husbands or fathers. They lacked productive roles and had very little control over the reproduction of social life. These women had domestic servants, but were themselves confined to the domestic sphere, leaving the public world of work and politics almost exclusively to men. Working-class women also lacked legal and other rights over their own lives but, through poverty, were very generally forced out to work, often with their children.

In Britain this gulf between women developed unevenly after first commercial agriculture and then industrialization reduced working women to the status of sub-humans, suitable for very long hours of manual labour in fields, factories, mines, sweatshops, and on the streets. The physical separation of home and work created a new situation for bourgeois women. They had not previously been isolated and without productive functions in their homes (Pinchbeck 1981). Their social and legal freedoms were increasingly curtailed as they became passive symbols of male affluence. Marxist women began to argue that women's interests were so deeply divided by their class membership that they could not unite together to improve the lot of women *vis-à-vis* men.

There was, in this view, virtually no common basis for unified action between destitute, working-class and bourgeois women (although of course there were numerous intermediate groups of women: small shopkeepers and traders, teachers and governesses, craftswomen, skilled employees, and upper domestic servants, whose positions were less clear-cut). The only common experiences were probably those of male violence in the home. While violence was undoubtedly widespread, campaigns against it had a limited impact. Working women's struggles in nineteenth-century Britain were for the shorter working day, better conditions of work, higher wages, and unionization, and to keep off the poor law or out of the workhouse. They struggled to provide their children with food, against dirt and disease, and for better housing.

Bourgeois women's struggles have remained more widely known

99

than those of working women. Ladies responded very quickly, although in small numbers, to the growing restrictions of bourgeois life, fighting for education, the vote, rights to own property, rights to control their own income, custody of their children, divorce, contraception, and employment.

The difference between the goals of working-class and of bourgeois women was clearly differentiated by German socialists and liberals. Clara Zetkin argued that bourgeois and proletarian women stood in different relations to capitalism. Bourgeois women did not want to live like dolls in a doll's house, so in order to achieve a more satisfying life they had to fight bourgeois men to gain their rights. Proletarian women, on the other hand, had no separate women's goals to fight for. They were oppressed as wives and mothers, but changing this would still leave them oppressed by capitalism. If women were granted political equality, they would still be divided by class (Draper and Lipow 1976: 197). Zetkin then took a marxist rather than a marxist feminist view: 'our task is to enrol the modern proletarian woman in the class struggle. We have no separate tasks for agitation among women' (198). Louise Kautsky argued that working women got no benefit from the campaigns of bourgeois feminism: 'they can be unmoved spectators to the war of the sexes in the upper class' (219). Eleanor Marx saw more clearly than her father that working women's lives were worse than those of working men. She described women as proletarians at work and household slaves at home, but women's issues were still class issues. 'We are not women arrayed in struggle against men, but workers who are in struggle against the exploiters' (226).

These views are based on observations and experiences of the gulf between the life of the frustrated ladies of the bourgeoisie whose lives were physically comfortable but hedged around with the restrictions of a narrow and idealized feminine role, and the struggles for survival by the overburdened women workers, who could not afford the luxury of a struggle for equal rights. (Then as now it was difficult to get working women to attend political meetings because of their domestic responsibilities.)

Since the nineteenth century, the massive expansion of capitalism, the consequences of technological change, and the very unequal distribution of the world's resources have transformed western women's lives. The two great classes of capitalism are much harder to identify, and the intermediate classes of service, technical, and professional and managerial workers have expanded and diversified.

Bourgeois women in many parts of the world have won most of their battles for legal equality, and working women have shared in their achievements of rights to vote, education, health care, and property ownership. Employed women in the west are more likely to be in white-collar or service jobs than in factories, and bourgeois women are likely to work for wages for at least some part of their lives. We cannot then generalize about the impact of class divisions on women without taking these changes into account.

The nineteenth-century arguments clarified the differences between liberal women's movements which fought for equal rights with men, and socialist women's movements which fought (in different ways) for the overthrow of capitalism. These arguments also clarify problems within feminism today. Many third-world, black and working-class critics have argued that the goals of radical feminism appear to them as the goals of bourgeois struggle — that is, as geared to the 'freedoms' demanded by relatively privileged, western, middle-class women who already have gains on the political, legal, educational, health, and employment fronts which are denied to many other women. The struggle that remains for these privileged women is the struggle against the domination of men in patriarchal societies, against male violence and over the control of women's bodies. The political priorities of working-class and peasant women appear very different from those of women who do not share their conditions of poverty or exploita-tion. They have struggles which they share with working-class and peasant men, rather than with all other women (Latin American and Caribbean Women's Collective 1980; Afshar 1985; Mies 1986).

WOMEN AS A SEX-CLASS

The initial radical feminist response to the marxist incorporation of women into class analysis was to assert that far from sharing class posi-tions or interests with men, women *were* a class. The idea of women as a sex-class (Millett 1977; Firestone 1979) identified oppressed women as having common interests against men, since men had common interests in dominating women. In the sex-class system, men benefited from patriarchal beliefs and practices which ensured that women serviced their needs, raised their children and were excluded from political and economic power. Christine Delphy (1974) differed from many radical feminists in arguing that sex-classes existed alongside social classes in the marxist sense, but she still maintained that in order to be liberated, women had to develop consciousness of their interests as a class, and to struggle against men and against the organization of patriarchy.

The idea of women as a class, sharing common interests in opposition to men as a class, does raise problems for feminism. This radical feminist view draws on marxist notions of class interest and struggle, but gives them rather different meanings. The point of class struggle in marxist terms is for the subordinate, exploited class to obliterate the dominant class and so to create a production system that does not depend on their own exploitation, the ultimate goal being a system of production which does not depend on exploitation at all. The point of sex-class struggle is not so clearly to obliterate men. While individual capitalists could physically survive a socialist revolution, given a change of heart and a loss of private property, it is less clear on what terms individual men would survive sex-class revolution. But as long as women are looked upon as a sex-class, then the differences between women are not seen as of prime importance, as they have common class interests which unite them against men. Gender is seen as more fundamental than class in the organization of women's oppression.

Some radical feminist groups did take up the idea of class struggle as overthrowing men, and did proceed logically to take a physically aggressive stance towards men (e.g. SCUM, the Society for Cutting Up Men), but these tended to be small, localized or relatively short-lived. Larger and more enduring radical groups have developed various strategies for separating their lives from those of men, and even, in extreme cases, from those of their own sons. The long-term implications of separation as a feminist political strategy are potentially very divisive, which makes a clear understanding of the nature of women's class interests an urgent necessity for feminism.

Whether men are regarded as ultimately reformable or as essentially different, once women are taken to be a sex-class then men, rather than the production system, are the main enemy (Delphy 1974). Women's antagonistic class interests have less political and personal priority than our common interests as women. Women's oppression by men provides us with a common political basis for unity and struggle. Radical feminists who take this line do not necessarily deny significant class divisions between women, but they argue that it is the gender struggle to which feminist politics must first be addressed. The argument in this chapter, that women's common interests in struggling against gender oppression are divided by their class interests, then draws on a marxist feminist line of reasoning, and constitutes an argument against a generalized assertion of women as a sex-class. I have not pursued this argument in a destructive spirit, but to try to clarify the enormous complexity of the divisions which exist between women, alongside the divisions between women and men. The theoretical split within feminism over this issue constitutes a serious impediment to an effective feminist politics.

WOMEN, CLASS, AND WORK

Attempts to see both gender and class as oppressive of women showed problems both with marxist class analysis and with conceptions of women as a sex-class. The way in which divisions between women can be conceptualized has been clarified, however, by feminist studies of the range of work that women do. Once the variety of women's work is observed and is reconstructed from the past, the complexities of social divisions between women become more visible. But these divisions are both within and between classes. Once systems of production are examined in particular instances, then variations in women's work can be more clearly seen. Women cannot be understood simply as members of social classes. The particular places occupied by different categories of women in capitalist and in other societies have to be conceptualized for the first time. Marxist class analysis has had to be modified by new conceptions of women's work relationships and women's power both inside and outside class relationships. When women's work is made visible, it becomes clear not only that women's work tends to be devalued in relation to men's work, but also that women are in different working relationships to each other. Women have different work positions even though women cannot always be clearly identified as having independent class positions. Even Rosa Luxemburg scolded her servants (Nettl 1969: 9).

It does not seem useful to invent a new mode of production as a way of understanding women's work relationships. The relations between class positions and work need to be clarified. The clearest way in which women can be seen to be divided by class is when some women are able to own or control productive resources while other women who lack such resources work for them. Throughout history few women have been in such positions, except as wives. Where women have controlled resources this has usually been in family businesses or trade, or where women have had rights to land use which enabled them to grow their own food and to maintain their children. In pre-capitalist Europe, women generally played active economic roles but had little control over the productive labour of others. With the rise of capitalism bringing individual businesses, and turning land into a commodity to be bought or sold, women have had more opportunity to become employers, or to control labour from managerial positions. Women who own capital and who directly employ labour other than on a casual basis, or on behalf of men, certainly exist, but they remain a tiny minority.

If we simply apply class analysis to women, the results are confusing. We can certainly amass evidence that there are women workers who sell their labour power like working men, and who receive wages which are less than the value of what they produce. Relatively few women at any one time, however, have been engaged in productive industrial labour (as opposed to agriculture, services, or trade). In the west, most women who work for wages or salaries now do so in the service sector, in catering, cleaning, clerical, and lower professional and managerial posts, particularly in health, education, and welfare services. Dorothy Smith (1983) has argued that capitalism has turned all women's work into personal service, making any class analysis of women problematic. Privileged western women are less likely to be bourgeois themselves than to be in salaried employment which affords them pecuniary, social, and health advantages, or to be married to men in such positions. Housework in industrial societies does not have any direct relationship to the system of social class in a marxist sense, but it is the interrelations of gender and class under capitalism which have given those who do the housework their dependent social positions. We can argue that women observably stand in varying relations to the way in which the production system is organized, but not in any one distinctively female way that has been identified in general.

The argument that women are now divided by class is, then, an argument that women, in a world dominated by international capitalism, do stand in different relationships to the capitalist mode of production. Some are worked to death, some are directly exploited, some are much less clearly exploited, and some clearly benefit at the expense of other women. Feminists have pointed out, however, the limitations of marxist class analysis when historically women's work has become so highly segregated from men's, and the domestic domain so ideologically separated from public life (Sassoon 1987).

An additional source of confusion has been the tendency of

marxist feminists to abandon Marx's concept of contradiction. Feminists have simply followed major schools of marxism in this respect. Apart from Gramsci and Mao Dzedung, most prominent marxists have made little use of this concept which is fundamental to any effective political application of marxism. This has meant that rather than appreciating the *contradictory and specific* ways in which the class positions of women develop together with capitalism (Lown 1983), there has been a tendency to look for *harmonious* ways in which *women's oppression in general* fits with *capitalism in general*.

A marxist analysis of social class is not an adequate means of grasping the divisions between women because marxist analysis does not comprehend the contradictory place of women in capitalism, where they straddle the supposedly separated worlds of the home and the labour market. Feminists have shown the connections between the public and private domains in, for example, the areas of male violence towards women, motherhood, and sexuality. Criticisms of class analysis led to identification of the connections between women's work at home and in the labour market; the connections between family life, women's work, and state intervention (Delphy and Leonard 1986; Balbo 1987). Beechey (1978) pointed out that Marx fails to give an analysis of female wage labour which shows how women's work is integrated with analysis of the labour process, *and* with analysis of the family. It is these factors together which can define the specificity of the position of female wage labour (Redclift 1985). If we look again at the relationships between class and gender, we can see that women's positions tend to differ from those of men. For women, far more than for men, domestic and kinship relationships structure and condition common experiences which cut across class, although in variable ways. At the same time, class cuts across domestic labour and women's work outside the home in ways which divide women from each other.

These connections and disconnections are not yet adequately theorized, as there are a number of different approaches to the problem of how to conceptualize a general relationship between classes in capitalist societies and the general dominance of men over women, but the connections are increasingly well documented (Herzog 1980; Hunt 1980; Phizacklea 1983). The greatest division of interests between women in the west today is perhaps between women who work or who are married to men who work, and women whose labour is not required in paid employment or women who are caring for dependants, and who are thus forced to depend on the state for their subsistence —

the unemployed, single mothers, and old age pensioners. The poor in Britain, as in America and other European nations, are increasingly female (Glendinning and Millar 1987).

The position of the dependent middle-class housewife with money to spend on herself and her children and that of the single mother living on social security are hardly comparable. In Britain, the increasingly punitive stance of the Conservative government in the 1980s towards social security 'scroungers' has pressurized single women living on social security to choose between absolute celibacy, without male visitors, or to accept a situation in which their social security money could be paid to a man who supposedly supports them in return for sexual intercourse. The degree of abuse to which this arrangement is open has no real parallel in the lives of middle-class or independently employed women (Campbell 1984). While men can benefit from this system at the expense of women, women taxpayers have also benefited from the savings made in social security payments and state expenditure generally, which have been increasingly returned as tax cuts.

Class analysis does not allow us to understand the extent of the material differences of interest which have developed between women. We also need to look at women's work relationships more generally, and at the power of some women over others. There are limited areas of work where some women directly exploit others (as opposed to receiving the general benefits of cheap goods and services), but there are some areas of social life where direct and personal relations of exploitation do exist. To see this relationship we need to look not just at production, but at the interconnected area of the reproduction of social life.

DOMESTIC SERVICE

Through much of history a minority of privileged women have had their needs met through services provided by subordinate, servile, or enslaved women. They have had their hair combed, their food prepared, their babies breastfed, their clothes put on them, their houses cleaned, and their whims danced to. While the majority of women have always been far from reaching these heights, domestic service in a variety of forms has been and still is widespread. Although Marx was aware of the army of domestic servants which maintained the comfort of the Victorian bourgeoisie, servants only rendered services or made things for the home, they did not produce things to be bought or sold, and so were marginal to the operation of the capitalist mode of production. In order to play any part in class struggle, they would have to identify with the interests of the productive workers on whose labour power the capitalist system ultimately depends. A capitalist system can operate without any domestic servants, albeit at some domestic disadvantage to bourgeois women, but it cannot operate without a force of workers who make the goods from which profits are made.

In the 1970s, marxist feminists took up the issue of how domestic work could be understood within the general operation of the capitalist mode of production. The domestic labour debate (see chapter 4) and more recent work exploring the links between gender and class generally assumed that domestic labour (household work to provide food, cleanliness, and childcare) was work done by the oppressed housewife. While this work has ensured that women's labour in the home, which was previously overlooked, is now taken into account in any understanding of capitalism, it has been widely assumed that domestic service is a thing of the past.

In Britain, the uniformed domestic staffs of the pre-war years have virtually disappeared, and middle-class women have had to learn to cook, care for children, and keep house since the Second World War. The great majority of women take responsibility for the household's domestic labour, generally with some 'help' from husbands, cohabitees, and children. They rely on domestic appliances or buy commercial services from launderettes, window cleaners, and dry cleaners. They can use products such as drip-dry clothes and frozen and prepared food to reduce their labour, but they still do much more than is necessary for the survival of a healthy workforce (e.g. ironing) and work long hours compared with men (Oakley 1974; Burman 1979; Malos 1980). Where housewives have sufficient resources to pay others to do this work, or where women go out to work for salaries which can cover the cost of replacing some of this labour, there is a strong incentive to pay for domestic service. Paradoxically, women's successes in achieving educational and occupational parity with men have enabled a growing minority of successful women to buy cheap domestic services from more disadvantaged women.

The extent to which domestic service still exists remains unknown and largely unregulated. In Britain, America, and parts of Europe, for example, it can take the form of cleaning women paid for a few hours a week, childminders who come to the house, au pairs, or

107

house servants recruited directly from the areas of high unemployment, the third world, or from 'immigrant labour'. As increasing numbers of women return to work after having children, or remain in work, many are directly dependent on the personal services of other women. Where this dependence is on family labour, or state nurseries, or where poorly paid working women pay poorly paid childminders to take children into their own homes, working relationships between women are unclear. But where women with careers, businesses, inherited wealth, or wealthy husbands can afford the private domestic labour of others, women clearly stand in contradictory relations to each other, and do not have the same interests in the transformation of society.

There are variations between European societies depending on, for example, types of middle-class housing; cultural values concerning motherhood, caring, and housework; school hours; the availability of cheap labour; and the availability of alternative forms of employment for women. There are some points at which the opening up of opportunities for emigration for the poor, or a diminution in income differentials between middle-class and domestic workers, will rapidly remove the possibility of domestic servants from all but the wealthiest. But it is also possible to tap new sources of cheap labour, for example by employing the dependants of immigrant labour, or by importing domestic labour directly from the third world.

In the third world, the rise of capitalist agriculture has meant that the rapidly growing rural populations cannot be absorbed into agricultural production. Poverty and destitution on the land leads to an abundance of cheap labour in many areas, and domestic service is widespread. Servants are not necessarily women, since much depends on pre-capitalist cultures and economies, or on colonial traditions, but once domestic service is established, women will be brought into service, and will work directly for other women. Middle-class women in the third world can often employ impoverished or dispossessed peasants for little more than their subsistence. Those who cannot afford cash wages may be able to draw on a pool of impoverished relatives or women forced off the land, who will do domestic work in return for their keep. Whitehead (1984: 10) has pointed to the widespread exploitation of the labour of junior or dependent young women by more senior women in many parts of Africa. Even where third world women are much worse off than European and American women in terms of standard of living, they may still be able to keep a servant. Indeed where middle-class, third-world women work as lawyers, doctors, teachers, nurses, secretaries, etc., without domestic machinery, with interrupted supplies of water and electricity, and without convenience foods, the pressure to pay for domestic service is very strong. Even in communist China there are reports that some urban grandmothers have begun to hire village girls to relieve them of the childcare and domestic tasks which they are expected to do for the household so that their daughters-in-law can go out to work. With increasing recognition that women cannot be drawn further into production without reducing their tasks of domestic labour and caring for children and the elderly, the employment of domestic servants in large cities has become increasingly formalized (Croll 1986).

The status and bargaining power of domestic servants and dependants vary widely, with little in common between the uniformed New York or London nanny with her own car and self-contained quarters and the undernourished teenage peasant sleeping on the kitchen floor in a Latin American city. But domestic service indicates the existence of a category of women who directly control the labour of other women. Women employers of servants may themselves be wholly dependent on their husbands or fathers for the resources to pay for domestic labour, but they still exercise power as employers. The lack of control by servan's over their own lives ensures that domestic workers and their mistresses stand in very different relations to the way in which social reproduction is organized (Cock 1980; Gaitskell *et al.* 1983; Collins 1985). As Carby has argued (1982: 218), where black women labour for white families, the concept of reproduction is called into question.

This work relationship between women within the domestic sphere has no clear place in class analysis, and it does not seem either necessary or useful to try to squeeze this relationship into categories of class analysis. It seems much more useful to look at the complex operations of the capitalist system in its particular historical forms, and at the *connections* between the systems of production and reproduction, however contradictory these may be. In contrast to class relations rooted in the capitalist mode of production, domestic service can be a volatile category, with different groups moving in and out of domestic service over relatively short periods of time. Servants can move into productive labour, becoming clearly working-class. Middle-class women left without servants may have to move back into the home, disappearing from class analysis. Since the bourgeoisie can use unpaid family labour if necessary, capitalism can survive without servants.

Ghandy and Chaudhry (1984) argue that in Nagpur in India, housewives directly exploit their women servants and yet the institution of domestic service is used to avoid changing the existing sexual division of labour.

Rather than hypothesizing a separate domestic mode of production, or some general relationship between capitalist class and domestic service, the varied relationships between women employers and their women servants can be seen as historically specific aspects of the inter-relations of production and reproduction. These specific working relations need to be taken into account in any understanding of the relations between gender and class. We can then recognize women employers and women servants as entering into a contradictory relationship between categories of very differently subordinated women.

THE INTERNATIONALIZATION OF PRODUCTION AND WOMEN'S WORK

Domestic service indicates something of the complexity of women's work relationships under capitalism. The way in which the capitalist production is organized is not always indifferent to the sex or age of the worker, because historically capitalist societies have simultaneously developed patriarchal institutions and ideologies. Some women live materially privileged lives under capitalism, and can struggle against men's patriarchal privilege. Other women are exploited, maimed, or left to starve within the same system. They may be exploited alongside men, they may be simultaneously exploited by men. Where state regulation is lacking, and workers' organizations are weak, employers will still allow workers to be killed, disabled, or simply worked to death in the interests of capital accumulation. Industrial injuries, occupational diseases, unregulated homeworking, and sweatshop conditions are widely accepted as facts of life in the west, but they are not equally experienced by men or by women. But the worst excesses of unregulated employment probably now take place in the third world, where the abundance of cheap labour and weakness of state control allow many employers to be particularly careless of workers' well-being.

There might not seem at first sight to be any direct relationship between the lives of the divided women of the western world and the varied lives of women in the third world. Such relationships can only be seen to exist if we conceive of capitalism as a world system. The internationalization of production has two main aspects. In agriculture, the third world has been very rapidly transformed, through the intervention of western powers and international agencies. Countries which formerly depended largely on small producers growing their own subsistence, with some taxable or exchangeable surplus, are now dominated by cash crops exported largely to the west. Where women who previously grew their own food now grow coffee, cotton, sugar, fruit, grain, or other crops to sell abroad, they are wholly dependent on international pricing mechanisms which are beyond their control. They must sell their cash crops for what they can get, and must depend on these diminishing proceeds to buy food, clothing, education, new seeds, fertilizer, pesticides, etc. Where cash crops are defined as men's work, or land is taken over for large-scale production, women farmers may be reduced to subsistence, may be forced off the land or may become unable to feed their children. Meanwhile western women can benefit from imported cash crops, and remain largely ignorant of their conditions of production.

In industry, critical areas of production are now controlled by multinational corporations which are dedicated to the accumulation of capital, and thus to profitability. These companies no longer have national allegiances. Once production is dominated by these giant companies, the manufacture of many kinds of easily transportable products can be switched from place to place in search of cheap labour and resources. On the one hand the relatively wealthy peoples of the west benefit from cheap clothes, food, and raw materials, but on the other, western workers can lose whole industries over very short periods to the more highly exploited workers of the third world.

Women of the west can benefit directly from the labour of third-world women working very long hours in very poor working and living conditions. But at the same time, working-class women around the world are brought into direct competition for work, exacerbating the already high unemployment rates in the west. Workers in different areas derive very varied benefits (or the lack of benefits) from the productivity and profitability of capitalist production. Workers are enabled by their employers and by state intervention to undercut each other, and to shift employment and production between different parts of the world in ways which benefit management and investors, but which benefit some workers at the expense of others.

While capitalism operates as a world system, classes emerge at the level of production, and this has implications for the work available to women. The Japanese working class has not, for example, developed in the same way as the British working class. The Japanese system of large firms with stable workforces which receives so much publicity in the west is supported by a complementary system of casual labour which is laid off when demand is low, and by a system of subcontracting many production processes to small family firms. In these firms, pay is low, working conditions poor, and employment insecure. This is a system which has given Japanese production immense power and flexibility and left workers weak and divided. The wives of men employed in the largest Japanese firms stand in a different relation to the production system than the women employed on piecework in family firms. This is a relationship that has some similarities to that between bourgeois and working women in the nineteenth century, even though Japanese bourgeois housewives are primarily wives of salaried or professional workers.

Any discussion of the divisions between women rooted in class and work must, therefore, take into account the specific and variable power relationships between women in different parts of the world, and in different positions in particular capitalist systems. The relations between western and third-world women cannot be understood in general as one oppressive relationship in which men oppress women, or as one relationship between western and third-world women. Women's lives, for example as Saudi Arabian princesses, as British 'immigrant' public toilet cleaners, as African peasants, as Wall Street executives, as Appalachian miners, as Turkish bank managers, as Guatemalan plantation workers, as white South African housewives, or as Filipino servants, indicate some of the complexities of the inter-relations of class, work, and gender which carry different dimensions of oppression. Women's lives are affected by class and work relation-ships in ways that give some women power over others, in which some women benefit from the exploitation of others and in which women have different interests.

THE CONTRADICTIONS OF CLASS AND WORK
IN WOMEN'S OPPRESSION

The claim that women's common sisterhood as women is subverted by class differences is not one that can easily be established. Some clear class differences can be documented for some women. But a focus on women's work relationships emphasizes the specificity of women's places in capitalism, and the connections between the public and the private domains of work. Analysis of the interrelations of class and work can show that women have developed contradictory interests in production and reproduction. Women in different working situations do stand in different relationships to each other. Some women do have power over others.

Just because women's oppression exists under capitalism, though, it cannot be assumed that it can be explained as a product of capitalism. The class differences between women remain confused, because concepts of class are not tailored to women's experience. But if feminists reassert that class may be a less significant factor in dividing women than has been argued here, a case has to be made for treating the material differences of class and work as less than those of gender. Robin Morgan (1984: 19) argues that 'class analysis is at best incomplete and at worst divisive of women . . . invented by patriarchy to divide and conquer'. Her solution, supported by contributors from every part of the world, is to emphasize women's attempt to build bridges between groups of women divided by class, race, ethnicity, and other forms of oppression.

Mistress and maid may indeed try to join hands, as Marjorie Agosin (1984: 142) imagines of a transformed Chile, but I would argue that they have very different interests in doing so. While both may be subordinated by men, this subordination is mediated by class and work interests. Mattelart (1980: 282) describes bourgeois Chilean women arriving for right-wing political demonstrations against Allende in their cars, 'often accompanied by their maids'. In a discussion of women's position in Brazil, written in the late 1960s, Saffioti (1978) argues that any transformation of women's situation depends on tackling class as well as gender, including the class divisions within feminist movements. Chen (1986) says of women in Bangladesh that women of different classes experience different degrees and types of patriarchal control. She concludes that 'production and kinship systems in rural Bangladesh should be analysed not only in terms of *purdah* and patriarchy, but also in terms of class variables and should be seen as remaining in a dynamic not a static situation' (221).

The problem remains of how far women's common interests are cut across by their variable class and work relationships. If we are to come to any conclusion about whether or not women are divided by class and work, in ways which subvert their common oppression as women, the recognition of the development of contradictions in

113

women's histories is essential. If patriarchy is universal, or if men and women are simply biologically different, then class and work divisions between women assume limited significance. If, however, social divisions are made by people in the course of their daily lives, they can be changed by people choosing to act collectively, with a common strategy for change. These divisions between women then become extremely significant in inhibiting collective political action.

One way of connecting feminist theory with the possibility of political practice is through the notion of standpoint. Nancy Hartsock proposed a concept of a feminist standpoint (as opposed to a women's point of view or perspective). Hartsock's version (1983b: 285) is rooted in the marxist distinction between essence and appearance. She envisages a feminist standpoint as rooted in women's essential material life. The oppression which shapes women's lives gives them the basis for a different political theory from that of men. By taking a feminist standpoint, women can reveal the real relationships between people which are mystified by patriarchal ideology. Women can see that they are not naturally feminine in the ways that male-dominated cultures have defined them. They are not naturally inferior to men. The feminist standpoint, by clarifying the mechanisms of oppression, can point the way to liberation.

This conception of feminist standpoint, however, leaves class differences between women as problematic. Maureen Cain (1986: 260–1) has developed the notion by suggesting that women have one standpoint as women and another as members of a social class. These standpoints are not compatible because neither is reducible to the other.

> It is not the case that the class structure is in some way more fundamental than the sex gender structure or vice versa. These identifiable patterns of intransitive[2] relationships appear to have a separate existence and effects, and while they always produce these effects through an articulation with each other, and while their specific forms in a given social order are constituted each by and in relation to the other, none the less they can be distinguished and neither has primacy. Therefore a standpoint in one structure is not the same as a standpoint in another.

This conception of two standpoints, neither of which is always more fundamental than the other, does seem to offer some hope of resolving the political problem within feminism posed by women's class and work relationships. Rather than feminists facing a general theoretical problem of whether women in general are primarily oppressed by their class or primarily by their gender, we can define instead specific political problems of how to build effective alliances between women's differing standpoints: between women's variable class and work interests and their gender interests. What is not clear at present is exactly how this can be done.

Power differences rooted in class and work relationships between women have been clearly identified by feminists. If women have opposing class and work interests, they cannot share a common interest in changing society, since their oppression as women can be consistent with powers and privileges shared with men. Marxist feminists have rejected the view that women's oppression is simply reducible to class (that is, that it can be explained as class oppression) but they also reject the view that women's class differences are reducible to patriarchy (that is, that they can be explained as aspects of men's power). If working women want to struggle alongside men for socialist change, then bourgeois and salaried women stand to lose their class privileges: their social position, their standard of living, their inherited wealth, and their servants.

This political problem of women's power over each other as a divisive issue is not, however, confined to class and work. Divisions between women are also rooted in nationalism, ethnicity, and race, and these are considered in chapter 6.

Chapter Six

WOMEN AGAINST WOMEN — NATIONALITY, ETHNICITY, RACE

Class and work have divided women in ways that may be unclear to them, but within classes, as well as across classes, there are divisions of race, ethnicity, and nationality that more obviously structure women's lives. Marx pointed out in 1870 how English workers had been duped into seeing their Irish fellow workers not only as competitors for jobs who lowered wages, but also as their inferiors. The Irish immigrants in return saw their fellow English workers as the stupid tools of English rule in Ireland (Marx and Engels 1955: 237). Little has changed in this respect since 1870. English workers are much less aware of their common interests with other British workers than they are of the differences between 'English' workers and people identified by their appearance, language, or customs as 'immigrants'. Marx argued that proletarians had very different interests from those of the ruling class in maintaining the capitalist system of production. All workers, despite the divisions between them, had common interests as workers. The divisions within the working class helped to mystify their common oppression as workers.

The comparable argument that all women share common interests as women, and that apparent divisions between them of nationality, ethnicity, and race simply mystify these common interests, is much less clear. Criticisms of new-wave feminism's theory of women's common interests have come from women variously identified as black, women of colour, third-world, Indian, Muslim, Latina, and others. These critics, either explicitly or implicitly, reject the notion of national, ethnic, and racial divisions between women as some form of false consciousness. The argument that women share common interests arising from our oppression by men, but are prevented from perceiving them because of the power of patriarchal ideology, is countered with

116

the argument that women from dominant nations, racial, and ethnic groups not only play a part in the oppression of women of subordinate groups, but also benefit from the continuation of such subordination. Although these arguments vary somewhat in the issues on which they focus, they constitute a direct and powerful challenge to the idea of a common sisterhood in oppression as a basis for a common women's struggle.

New-wave feminism brought the gulfs between women sharply into focus through women's powerful reactions to the original conception of universal sisterhood. These passionate and often personal accounts of the divisions between women are also addressed more generally to liberal, radical, and marxist feminists. Becoming visible as a specific minority (Carmen *et al.* 1984), acknowledging racism as a personal responsibility (Pence 1982), or exploring the specificity of one's position in relation to racial and ethnic divisions (Cameron 1983) are personal and painful processes. Criticisms of feminist conceptions of women's oppression have come from women's direct experiences of feminists' intolerance or ignorance, from pain, frustration, and disillusion that have made some women feel that feminism excludes them. Much of this literature is very sad to read because of the range of women's sufferings, and the extent of personal pain that is revealed (Davenport 1983; Bryan *et al.* 1985). These women's experiences have identified problems both with the feminist argument that women in general are oppressed as women, and with the view that this form of oppression is more fundamental than any other form.

Within this emotional turmoil, feminism has to look for ways of taking all women's contradictory identities and experiences adequately into account, which is a task that had never previously been attempted. The immense problems involved can be considered by looking at the divisions between women of nationality, ethnicity, and race.

NATIONALITY

It is not easy to define women by nationality, since the idea of 'nation' is itself disputed. Definitions vary, at least in part, because experiences and histories of nationality vary.

Nationality can divide women on the basis of birth and citizenship. It can specify our civil rights, or the lack of such rights. Nationalist ideologies allocate to women, as to men, allies and enemies in cases of international conflicts. Feminist conceptions of Iraqi and Iranian women, or of Israeli and Palestinian women, or of Northern Irish and other British women as all suffering from male domination can be supported from observations of women's lot in these nations, with the oppression of Iranian women appearing particularly severe under the Khomeini regime (Tabari and Yeganeh 1982; Afkhami 1984). In the experience of the vast majority of women in these nations, however, their oppression as women may be much less immediate than the economic and military struggles in which they and their families are engaged. Nationalism is a source of opposing interests between women of different nations, however arbitrary national boundaries and conceptions may be.

It could be argued that, as with class, nationalism and international conflicts only divide people because they do not understand that they do have interests in common. In this case, Iranian and Iraqi women do have common interests in ending war by asserting their common sisterhood. While this may be true in theory, it is unlikely that many women drawn into such bitter conflicts will see struggle against sexual oppression as their political priority. The arguments of western women who favour the dismantling of nuclear weapons are countered by those of women who see the defence of their nation as threatened. Nationalism is very powerful as an ideology and as part of people's self-identity. In defence of a feminist theory of oppression, we could argue that nationality structures women's experiences and perceptions of where our intersts lie, but need not divide women if common interests could be defined and recognized. Feminism is a means of conceiving the common interests of women but, as people, feminists are generally identified with nations in ways which actively inhibit the realization of common interests. The ways in which feminist conceptions of international solidarity have interacted with national loyalties and national liberation struggles have received relatively little attention (Jaywardena 1986).

ETHNICITY

Ethnicity is more difficult to define than nationality and in some cases overlaps with definitions of nationality. It can be taken as largely a question of how smaller groups define themselves defensively, or are defined as different, in relation to larger, dominant groups. I have not attempted to evaluate the numerous definitions of ethnicity and nationality which have been produced by social scientists. For the purposes of this chapter, the terms are used fairly loosely to indicate powerful sources of division between women, without specifying exactly how boundaries may be drawn. This leaves open such questions as, for example, whether the Basques, or the Kurds, constitute nations or ethnic groups. The enormous historical variation in structures and ideologies of nationality and ethnicity around the world make any brief general overview or classification of limited practical use. These peoples, with their own histories, cultures, and languages, and many others around the world, identify themselves as oppressed and restricted by the larger nations which surround and dominate them. Ethnic group is a very loose conception based on various differences of origin — language, culture, religion, territory — where small groups are subordinated by larger ones. Virtually no modern nation is without its minorities, and minority-nation relations are rarely harmonious.

In societies without centralized states, ethnic differences can remain just differences. The definition of an ethnic group, however, generally denotes not just difference but some level of political, cultural, or economic inferiority. These power differences between groups arise in specific circumstances. For example, subordinate ethnic groups arise where conquered, nomadic, or other peoples are absorbed into larger political units (for example, Amerindians, Native Americans, Australian Aborigines, Basques, Kurds, Sri Lankan Tamils, Lapps, and Gypsies). More commonly since the rise of capitalism, ethnic minorities within larger nations are a legacy of capital's insatiable demand for cheap labour. This has drawn millions of peasants out of household production and into wage-labour in capitalist societies (sometimes with the added incentive of forced labour, taxes imposed on subsistence cultivators, or religious persecution).

Efforts to conceptualize ethnic differences between women need, therefore, to start from the assumption that ethnicity is not just a means of preserving cultural difference, or defining boundaries between groups. It is also a means of structuring power relations between groups. By defining other races or ethnic groups as inferior (as lower in the evolutionary scale, beyond the religious pale, or as like children rather than adults), their labour power could reasonably be demanded. Once this situation had been established, it became very difficult to change the meaning of ethnic identity. The meaning and experience of ethnic difference is, therefore, historically variable, but these differences are often active sites of struggle and resistance.

119

Wherever women are divided by ethnicity, our common oppression as women is cut across not only by differences of class and nationality, but also by ethnic differentials in privilege and access to power (Phizacklea 1983). Anthias and Yuval-Davis (1983: 62) go further than this in arguing that every feminist struggle has a specifically ethnic (as well as class) context. Ethnic divisions also entail cultural identities within each group which can be distinctive in terms of, for example, language, religion, kinship structures, dress, or diet. It is problematic for women in deciding where our interests lie to evaluate our often contradictory national, ethnic, and racial identities. The problem for feminism is that these are identities which we share with men of our own groups, rather than with all women.

RACE

The question of how people are divided by race is perhaps the most difficult of the three terms to define, since it is arguably the most painful of the divisions, and thus the most mystified. I use mystified here to mean that the idea and practice of taking physical racial differences to be socially significant work to the advantage of the dominant race and to the disadvantage of the subordinate race(s). It is then in the interests of the dominant race to ensure that the issue of what racial difference is 'really' about will not be made clear. This is the difference between arguing that people of African origin were enslaved by Europeans because they were naturally inferior, and arguing that people of African origin were enslaved because they were socially designated as inferior and that this designation was maintained and reproduced by slave-owning societies.

Race is in origin a biological category, but one that is widely misused as such. It has some basis in scientific observation of genetic differences, but the social practice of racial difference cannot be understood in terms of physical difference. All extant human beings belong to the same race, *homo sapiens*, but over time this race has become physically differentiated in ways which have become socially meaningful in distinguishing between social groups. There is no agreement on how many sub-races or species exist, or on how far these can be genetically identified. Whatever system of classification is used, not every individual will be classifiable. Some scholars argue that races cannot be identified at all, since exact boundaries around distinct physical types cannot be drawn (Lieberman 1970). Our 'scientific' knowledge

120

of racial difference and its significance, then, has to be seen as a product of western thought. More specifically, it is the product of western thought at a time of colonial and imperial expansion.

When people use racial categories in socially discriminatory ways, they draw on popular understandings of scientific categories uncritically. Discriminatory labels thus come into use as if they were objective and static categories. The popular use of the term white, for example, does not indicate a distinctive physical species. White is, therefore, a very specific historical category used to identify certain peoples of European origin who have been in political and economic positions to dominate peoples of generally different physical appearance. In areas where whites have at particular periods of history dominated other racial groups, for example, Afro-Americans and Amerindians, the white group is itself a social rather than a strictly biological category.

Race, as identified by criteria of physical appearance, is only socially significant when racial groups are unequal. Since all racial categories merge into each other and all sub-species interbreed, it is easier to classify simplified stereotypes than the complex physical variety of individuals that can actually be found (as the South African state has found, when parents and children, or sisters and brothers, have been split by different racial labels being applied to members of the same family). The racial categories which divide women from each other, then, are not physical differences which can be transcended by sisterhood, they are the active categories of scientifically legitimated racism.

Women are not divided by biological racial categories, but by the consequences of racism as historically specific systems of domination, discrimination, and exploitation. Racism identifies specific groups as racial groups within a hierarchy of racial superiority and inferiority. Within this hierarchy, the dominant racial group exercises power in order to discriminate against subordinate groups (and more dominant groups against the less dominant). Discrimination is then practised in such areas as employment, housing, education, health and welfare, law, and physical safety.

Gilroy (1987: 3) has pointed to the need for a concept of race formation, to indicate that political struggles determine which definitions of race prevail at any one time. Obviously there are physical differences of hair, skin colour, and physical shape which we use as (more or less obvious) clues in identifying others, and these are real differences.

Children can be socialized into awareness of extremely subtle physical differences in identifying subordinate categories. But these physical differences are simply used to distinguish between superior and inferior and, unlike differences of class, nationality, and ethnicity, they have no clear boundaries. But they cannot usually be concealed or fully compensated for by wealth or education.

ETHNICITY AND RACISM

Ethnicity takes on particular meanings when social life is structured by racism. Anthias and Yuval-Davis (1983) have been criticized (Kazi 1986) for arguing that black feminists, by concentrating on racism, render women's ethnicity invisible. But since all advanced capitalist societies are racially and ethnically mixed, ethnicity is an ambiguous category intermeshed in various and shifting ways with class, race, and nationality. Where nations are divided by race, as in Britain and the United States, ethnicity will cut across class, and will subdivide racial categories. Some ethnic groups will then be identified as superior to others within racial categories, leading to complex hierarchies of subordination and domination at all levels of society.

The ways in which people have become subordinated are also somewhat variable. European Jews, for example, were forced into limited economic roles by anti-semitism in pre-capitalist Europe. Since Jewish identity is itself neither wholly physical, cultural, religious, or ethnic, the category of Jewishness is cut across by nationality, class, and ethnicity. The relations beween Jewish and gentile women in the Soviet Union are very different from those between Israeli women and Palestinian Arab women. In the case of Europe's Gypsies, there is a long history of hostility between the nomads and the settled peoples. Nomads are generally treated as outside civilized society, once their demands for transit space conflict with the needs — or desires — of the settled population. Feminists in Britain have shown no great public solidarity with Gypsy women, although the levels of harassment which Gypsy women (and men) now endure as they are increasingly deprived of legal campsites is reaching unprecedented levels. Where ethnic groups such as Gypsies react defensively to the hostility of the larger society, it can be very difficult for women to make any positive contacts with each other across group boundaries (Okely 1975).

The implicit racism of the versions of feminism which swept Europe and America in the 1970s was a historical product of the specific racism

122

of these cultures. Other imperial powers — the Japanese, the Ottoman, the Arab — have been explicitly racist in somewhat different ways. Socialist societies have not transcended racism and discrimination against ethnic minorities. Most groups define themselves as superior to outsiders. But the racism which has characterized recent western feminism has been given a specific character by its development in expanding capitalist powers, and by the scientific and moral justifications provided for it.

DO DEFINITIONS MATTER?

Racial and ethnic definitions do matter because they do much to hide the real differences between groups, but they are also clues to changes in the relations between groups. There cannot be correct definitions provided by social theory if labelling each other is part of an ongoing struggle for power, self-respect, and personal identity. In the post-war period, with the spread of independence to the former colonies and the restructuring of world capitalism into international, rather than national or imperial, systems of production, overt racism has been reduced at the level of official discourse. Changes in the official vocabulary used in Britain and America, however, have had a very limited impact on the common sense of racism which persists in popular racist beliefs and practices.

Identifying women as members of racial and ethnic groups is a delicate business. The 'acceptable' labels of public discourse in racist societies exist alongside the intentionally abusive terms which are in everyday use. There may be some doubt in Britain as to whether it is currently correct to address people as 'black' rather than as 'Asian' or 'coloured' or 'Afro-Caribbean'. There is similar doubt over whether to say 'mixed-race' rather than 'black' or 'half-caste'. But everyone will know who to address as 'black bastard', 'paki shit', 'nignog', 'yid', 'mick', 'immigrant'. Women are the focus of particularly explicit sexual terms of abuse. The important point for the purposes of this chapter is not so much to establish what are the 'correct' political definitions for any category of women, but to clarify women's divergent interests in what lies beneath the shifting labels which are used to conceal racism.

The question of being defined by physical appearance is socially significant for women on the grounds that appearance leads to differences in the experiences of racist discrimination, domination and physical danger. Racist stereotypes, and their consequences in educational, health, and welfare provision, are not experienced by white women.

Women of mixed race, or those whose origins lie in the Indian sub-continent or South-East Asia, are divided by culture, language, ethnicity, and class, but they are not perceived as inferior in exactly the same way as those of African appearance. In Britain, these differences have been used to discriminate between those of more African and those of more European appearance (so that Asians and Indo-Caribbeans are treated differently from Afro-Caribbeans), and also between lighter and darker European types (so that northern Euro-peans are treated differently from Mediterranean Europeans). Women with pale skins and bridged noses do not *experience* racism in the same way that those of African appearance do, particularly when they are middle-class (Cameron 1983). These differences have led to political problems in defining who is black, for example at 'black only' meetings. In practice, black activists have been faced with the same problems as the South African state in deciding politically salient racial categories on the basis of physical appearance. In both cases the problem arises because people of different physical appearance are treated differently.

Definitions matter because racist categories and definitions derive from the ideas of dominant groups. It is in the interests of dominant groups to stress the divisions among those whom they dominate. Colonial cultures, therefore, were very sensitive to gradations of hier-archy among subordinated groups. It is only when the system of categorizing racial difference is exposed as a system of racism that it is possible for women in the subordinated racial and ethnic groups to 'see' their common interests in challenging racist categorization. But these are common interests shared with men. The conception of being black or a member of an ethnic minority in western society has had to be politically constructed as a working definition for those engaged in a common struggle against racism.

When the abstract conception of sisterhood in oppression is confronted with the experiences of women of diverse national, ethnic, and racial categories, feminism as a theory of women's common oppression seemed to have little to offer black, ethnic-minority, and third-world women.

BLACK CRITICISMS OF WHITE FEMINISM[1]

Black and third-world criticisms of new-wave feminism identify the assumption of common sisterhood in white feminism as rooted in a narrow version of western experience. These critics challenge new-wave feminist conceptions of women's oppression by arguing that women's domination by men, although very general, is not the only form of oppression that exists. Privileged white, western women are unusual in that sexism is the main form of oppression that they experience.

These criticisms of new-wave feminism were conceived within the historically specific conditions of the expansion of European domination into much of the rest of the world. Black, white, and other women have, therefore, different histories with respect to slavery, forced labour, enforced migration, plantation and indentured labour, colonialism, imperial conquest, and genocide. Individual women may not know their own histories (and it is a product of the colonial domination of culture that such histories should not be known), but these histories have helped to shape the present structure of our societies. They have led to cultural conceptions of white as superior and black as inferior, and the legitimation of racist beliefs and practices. Black critics of new-wave feminism locate this wave of feminism within white western culture. This culture takes white experience and values to be normal. It takes racial and ethnic hierarchies for granted and does not acknowledge its inherent racism.

The upsurge of radical feminism that swept across the world in the 1960s and 1970s was seen as contradictory in holding a conception of female oppression as a common condition, while focusing on specific demands for personal autonomy which came mainly from educated, white, western women. It provoked mounting criticism from women who felt that their own lives had been overlooked (Davis 1982; hooks 1982, 1984; Hull *et al.* 1982; Moraga and Anzaldua 1983; Hussein 1984). These criticisms express the pain and outrage of women whose lives, work, struggles, and suffering had been rendered invisible not only by the categories of thought available in male-dominated society, but also by the language and concepts of new-wave feminism. More than this, these critics claim that far from being sisters, white women, women of the imperial nations, and women generally in advanced capitalist societies benefited from, or engaged in, the exploitation of black women, ethnic-minority women, third-world women, and

125

peasant women. Where women can employ servants, wear cheap clothes produced by sweated labour, or eat food produced from cash crops at the expense of food grown for peasant families' own consumption, then exploitation and advantage cut across sisterhood. White Australian women, for example, can own and inherit land from which Aboriginal women have been dispossessed (Sykes 1984: 68). Where nations incorporate racist evaluations into their culture, their legislation, and their education, health, and welfare services, then white women benefit at the expense of black and ethnic-minority women. Several black authors have pointed out that life is less healthy and less safe if you are black (Cameron 1983; Lorde 1983).

From the perspective of the third world, the divisions between women are much more obvious than any common condition. In addition to the divisions of class, race, ethnicity, and nationality, there are three main sources of difference. First, new-wave feminism was not only produced by women in relatively affluent societies, but in those societies which have dominated and divided the third world between them in the course of the expansion of capitalism. Imperial and colonial relationships have shaped the experience of third-world women in ways which have benefited western women.

Second, third-world nations are frequently nations constructed from the power struggles of the colonial period, or from conquered kingdoms and declining empires. Few such nations have much homogeneity in terms of language, culture, ethnicity, or religion. Within these nations, ethnic and racial differences could be exploited and emphasized by the colonizing power. This leaves women in the twentieth century experienced in differences between women, rather than united as women.

A third problem lies in the gulf between poverty and wealth in many third-world societies. The poorest die of hunger, malnutrition, and water-borne disease, while the wealthiest live in luxury. The incorporation of the third world into the world capitalist system has transformed agricultural production in a very short period of time, without being able to absorb dispossessed rural populations into productive employment. The contrasting situations of affluent and educated urban women with the women of the peasantry, the sharecroppers, the shanty towns and the streets are very marked. It is much less clear that women can share common interests than has sometimes seemed the case in the west. In part these are differences of class, but there are also hierarchical, racial, religious, regional, and ethnic divisions, particularly where colonial or imperial powers favoured some groups over others in terms of access to education, political power, and economic development.

It could be argued that women of all nations, ethnic groups, and races still share a common struggle against oppression, since all are still subordinated as women and subject to sexual oppression and male violence. But it is not clear how sexual oppression can effectively unite women whose lives, work, life expectancy, and children's futures are structured by the hierarchies of racism, ethnicity, or nationalism. Sykes (1984: 69) comments:

> Black women, despite their sexual oppression, are correct in their belief that oppression is greater on the question of race, that along race lines white women participate with white men in creating this oppression, and that the division of the black community along sex lines can only weaken our already unenviable position and may, in fact, spell doom to all of our black people.

Power differences between women both within and between nations are so great that even apparently similar struggles against men can in practice be very different. Another black Australian, Eve Fesl (1984: 110) also emphasizes white women's role in racist oppression. 'If one were to measure oppression . . . we would see white women being greater oppressors of black women than black men ever have been.'

New-wave feminism is then seen not only as offering a very limited vision of liberation which does not address the main forms of oppression experienced by other women, but also as actively or passively colluding in these forms of oppression. Fesl quotes an Australian example where the women's refuge in Alice Springs was taken over by white 'battered wives' in order to keep out equally battered black women (Fesl 1984: 115). Women cannot stand together against men's oppression if we stand in different power relationships to one another. As Carby (1982) has argued, the way in which societies such as Britain are structured by racism creates power relationships between black and white women which have their roots in colonial relationships. The struggles of feminists who have to contend personally with racism as well as with the oppression rooted in class and gender are not the same as those of (middle-class) white feminists who need only struggle against domination by men. Theories of oppression need to be general if they are to form a basis for transforming societies, but any general theory must be able to take account of the diversity of women's experiences of oppression and the parts that women play in oppressing others.

The problem for feminism is that if a view of the universality of women's oppression by men is replaced by a view of the specificity of the forms of oppression experienced by different classes, races, and ethnic groups of women, then it is not clear that anything of feminism remains. Some black critics have made this point, and do not see feminism as relevant to the struggles that they share with black men. Others, though, have taken the view that male domination is still a real element in their oppression, even if not always the most immediate problem. Rather than seeing nothing for black women in feminism, they have urged white feminists to see racism as a problem for white women, as one which diminishes our humanity (Davenport 1983; Moschkovich 1983; Welch 1984). In this view feminists need to redefine conceptions of liberation so that the liberation of all women from all forms of domination can be envisaged (Smith 1983; Brixton Black Women's Group 1984). This point is qualified by the stipulation that those who are suffering should be able to define their own priorities for transformation, rather than have these specified for them (Carby 1982).

Black and third-world assertions of the divisions between women then serve to redefine feminism as a theory and practice which conceptualizes the intermeshed oppressions of class, race, ethnicity, and gender as unacceptable, and redefines women's liberation as part of a struggle against all these forms of oppression. Not all black and third-world critics make all these points, but the body of criticism which has come from black and ethnic-minority women in North America and Europe, and from women in the third world, is forcing a reconceptualization of feminist theory and practice in which women's differing experiences of oppression become central.

This point has been developed more specifically in the case of black, ethnic-minority, and third-world lesbians, who are dependent on other women for support, but who also encounter racism and discrimination from women in making their specificity visible (Carmen *et al.* 1984; Zehra 1987). Ngahuia Te Awekotuku, a Maori lesbian, identifies racism as a disease of feminism which must be dealt with, but argues (1984: 120) that 'sexism is the primary offence against humanity.' Yet she also sees her position as contradictory and adds (121) 'frequently, the contradictions of my life are harrowing.' Black women, women in

128

the third world, and ethnic-minority women experience racism in ways that white women do not. The experience of both white and black women, therefore, has to be seen as specific in ways that cut across our common interests as women.

THE SPECIFICITY OF RACE AND ETHNICITY — WOMEN'S EXPERIENCES

The question of how far nationality, ethnicity, and race really divide women remains a controversial one in feminism. Male violence, male control of sexuality and reproduction, and patriarchal ideology remain problems for most women. But the contradictions of black women's lives place them in specific positions which differ from those of white women. The Combahee River Collective (1983: 215) argued that feminism can threaten black women, by undermining their common struggle against racism with black men, but they also comment (214) that 'no one before has ever examined the multilayered texture of Black women's lives.' The universality of new-wave feminism provoked a response from black women that has encouraged such examinations. The specificity of different women's experiences which has been uncovered makes it difficult to generalize about the ways in which nationality, ethnicity, and race cut across class and gender.

Criticisms of the racism of new-wave feminism are complicated by the historical fact that the radical feminism of the 1960s and 1970s was propagated primarily by women who were not only white, but apparently relatively highly educated and middle-class (in culture if not always in terms of standard of living). The anger of their critics is, therefore, directed at this class privilege as well as at the unconsciousness of racial advantage. Other criticisms focus on particular areas of women's lives where black and white women in the same society have different experiences. The contrasts are particularly sharp between impoverished black women and white women with their own careers. Although black members of the business and professional classes and the impoverished, homeless, and destitute whites of the 1980s need to be taken into account, racism defines an area of difference within these groups. Some of the problems of the specificity of women's experience can be seen by considering Britain in the 1980s.

129

RACISM AND WOMEN IN BRITAIN

In Britain, black and ethnic-minority women disproportionately occupy the lowest occupational strata, particularly those below the level of the unionized working class. Black and ethnic-minority women are over-represented in sweatshops, in homeworking, in cleaning, and in repetitive factory work, although there are white women here too. Recent feminist texts have made visible some aspects of the lives of women where women bear the 'triple burden' of class, race/ethnicity, and gender (Phizacklea 1983; Westwood 1984). It is the added dimension of race and ethnicity that distinguishes the experiences of these women from those of white workers.

The history of colonialism makes little impact in British schools, so the racist character of the immigration legislation which has grown up in the post-war period is considerably mystified. 'Immigrants' are seen as unreasonably flooding in to swamp a country and a culture which does not need them and has scarce resources to offer them. They are seen as competing for jobs and housing, lowering the quality of state education, and introducing dirt and disease, drugs, and street violence. Deportation or repatriation are then logical solutions to the problem. If colonial history is put in its proper place, however, the 'immigration problem' can be seen as the consequence of a long history of using colonial subjects as a source of cheap and flexible labour. Deliberately imported to meet the labour needs of the post-war boom, recession in the 1970s found them with rights of residence which they were never supposed to take up. Restrictive immigration legislation here, and colonial economic policies there, had the contradictory consequence of turning migrant labourers into a settled British labour force, but with continuing ties of kinship and economic obligations elsewhere. Because these workers brought with them the racial categories of colonialism, they were established as inferior groups, with the generation born here barred by racism from equality with their peers. Where passing as white is physically impossible, or culturally undesirable, then men and women in any given category will have interests in common with each other which they do not share with those of the same sex in other categories.

Where feminists have identified the patriarchal nuclear family as a major source, or the major source, of women's oppression (Barrett and McIntosh 1982), black women have argued that the understanding of the family has been limited to white experience (Carby 1982;

hooks 1984). What has happened to family and household structures has become extremely complex (Bhabha *et al.* 1985). Black women do not necessarily argue that all is well with the family in Britain; various forms of oppression undoubtedly exist (Wilson 1984). Critics do not deny that the family can be the site of male violence to women. The family can be the site of incest and other forms of child abuse, and of depression, and the physical isolation of women. Theories of patriarchy which see only oppression in the family, however, miss other experiences of kinship.

Black and ethnic-minority women's roots very generally go back to slavery, colonialism, or migrant labour. British culture which propagates the idealized, monogamous, nuclear family as the desired form has also legitimated the destruction of families for those who are constituted as cheap labour. Slave families in the American states were deliberately split up, and children born into captivity were sold away from their mothers (Lerner 1973). British colonial policies, which fostered migrant labour, institutionalized the separation of family members, and encouraged prostitution for men with money but without sexual partners and for women left without income. Black and ethnic-minority struggles have been to unite separated families and to preserve family forms which differ from that of the idealized nuclear family. Black struggles for the right to a family life are not adequately accounted for in new-wave feminist theory (Ladner 1976; Bhabha *et al.* 1985). Kinship as a source of strength and support for women needs to be reconsidered.

The institutionalization of racism has consequences for the provision of health services and for women's control of their own bodies. In Britain the national health service is now dependent on the labour of black women in the worst paid and least skilled positions, but this labour does not ensure that black and white women have equal access to the means of good health. It is difficult to disentangle race from class and ethnicity in looking at this area, but black critics of feminism have established that being black gives women worse access to health care (Bryan *et al.* 1985; Sheffield Black Women's Group 1984; Torkington 1984). This is another area in which black and white women can see different priorities for struggle.

Even more pointed are women's different experiences of contraception and abortion. White women's struggles for the right to abortion is contrasted with black women's struggles against the use of abortion, sterilization, and contraception to limit the reproduction of black populations. It was the white women's call in the 1970s for abortion on demand that aroused much of the hostility of black critics who could not see that this demand bore much relevance to their own needs and experiences. I will return to this divisive issue in chapter 7.

There are other areas of British social life which could also be reviewed here, such as housing, education, the law, relations with the police, mental illness, state welfare programmes, and control of sexuality, where considerable variation could be found in the experiences of women of different racial, ethnic, and national groups, as well as between women of different social classes. In all these situations, it could be argued that women have more interests in common with men of the same group than they do with women of different groups. The difference in the experience of black, white, and other women in relation to these issues constitutes further evidence for the specificity of women's experiences of racial and ethnic differences, and leaves feminism as a theory of women's common oppression in doubt.

The points outlined above have been taken to cover the main grounds on which British black and ethnic-minority women have argued that their histories and present lives incorporate experiences of oppression, subordination, resistance, and struggle in which they share interests with black men (or men of their ethnic or third-world groups). Although it is generally acknowledged that all women do suffer sexist oppression too, there is no very clear way in practice that the interrelations of class, gender, race, ethnicity, and nationalism in Britain can be disentangled. This body of criticism raises serious problems for feminism as a general theory of women's oppression, and so for the efficacy of feminist strategies and struggles. Women cannot set themselves common goals for transforming society if they have only limited interests in common.

THE SPECIFICITY OF RACE AND ETHNICITY — THEORETICAL PROBLEMS

Feminism cannot specify women's common interests in confronting racism effectively if there is no clear analysis as to what racism is, and what factors in society create and maintain different forms of racism. There are obvious links in our present societies between the rise and expansion of capitalism and the institutionalization of racism in its present forms. If the racism which divides women from each other is to be clearly understood, then we need to turn to theory to explain it.

There is plenty of evidence to show that racism is a bitter, painful, and destructive form of humiliation and discrimination that diminishes those who exercise it and the individuals, societies, and cultures that legitimate it. Since there are no genetic grounds for any one human sub-species to claim natural superiority over others, racism is integrated into other historically specific struggles for power and domination. Women as well as men have come to benefit from the domination and exploitation of other groups. But racism cannot be explained piecemeal by adding together the sum of these histories. Some general theory is needed in order to make sense of specific cases. Theory is also needed to connect struggles against racial, ethnic, or national difference with the liberation of women.

The main theoretical approaches either explain racism in terms of something else, that is, they are reductionist, or they explain race as a source of social division in its own right, that is, as autonomous. The reductionist argument is reductionist in the sense that it reduces the explanation of racist oppression to the prior existence of some other form of oppression. That is, racism can be explained in some way as a product of biology or of production systems. Theories of autonomy are ones in which racism is seen as being an independent form of oppression, in the sense that it cannot simply be explained either as a consequence of natural differences or as a consequence of, for example, the rise of capitalism. It needs a separate explanation of its own.

It is difficult to support either of these positions convincingly with observations because of the level of abstraction involved, and the philosophical problems of such arguments. It is, however, politically very important for the future of women that a correct analysis is made. Otherwise women's struggles for solidarity with each other and for the general transformation of our societies will be misdirected and ineffective. If racism is a product of class or some other source of oppression, then it is the class or other form of oppression that needs to be tackled directly, rather than racism. If racism is an independent system of oppression, then it is racism that must be tackled, alongside the other forms of domination experienced by women.

The argument that racism is reducible to class is comparable to the argument presented in chapter 2 that women's oppression can be reduced to biology, or the argument in chapter 5 that it is ultimately reducible to class oppression. The reductionist view takes the way in which each system of production is organized to be the ultimate determinant of the forms of oppression that are maintained and reproduced in any society. In addition to the general limitations of reductionist argument, accounts of racism need to take contradiction into account. Black women are not uniformly oppressed and they can have contradictory interests in which race, class, ethnicity, and nationality cut across each other. A middle-class, black American woman who can have a career and employ a cleaning woman may experience the social impact of racism but she is not in the same structural position as an unemployed Bangladeshi woman worker in Britain who is treated by the state as dependent on her husband even if he is refused entry to Britain. In the west, black women are disadvantaged by racism in relation to white women, but black is not a static or universal category of disadvantage that transcends all other sources of social difference which determine the quality of people's lives.

The reduction of racism to class oppression begs the question of why the operation of the capitalist mode of production should need racism. Where societies are most overtly racist, as for example in South Africa, the decision to make racism structurally essential is contradictory for capital and for the state. Racism defines black people as cheap labour and divides the working class, but it also makes exploitation explicit and demystifies the relationship between labour and capital, which is politically destabilizing. South African racism, violently enforced by the state, compels blacks and migrant labourers to provide cheap labour, but at enormous social and political costs for the reproduction of capital. Class analysis cannot explain the contradictions of South African racism for different categories of women, or the differing implications for women's lives between this form of racism and racism in, for example, Britain, the United States, or Japan.

An additional reason for arguing that racism is not reducible to class oppression is the difference between class oppression and racial oppression in the degree of violence involved. In early capitalism, when productivity could only be increased by workers working longer hours, and cheap labour was abundant, then workers were killed or maimed by their labour, but this is a limited strategy for capital as sooner or later workers will be used up and productivity will decline. Capital had to develop other means of increasing productivity, largely through changes in technology. Racism, on the other hand, can lead to extermination and genocide, and frequently has done, where those of a conquered race or ethnic group are unwilling or unable to act as cheap labour, or are surplus to immediate labour requirements. The facts of lynching divide black and white American women in a way that is not reducible to class.

The argument for treating racism as an independent form of oppression seems the strongest option politically. The problem with this position lies in the difficulty of specifying the exact origins of racism. But while the origins of racism remain obscure, the reality of racism in the world today is overwhelming and this is the immediate issue for divided feminists.

My own feeling is that racism differs in nature from class oppression, but is not ultimately explicable in terms of other factors, and its origins will remain obscure. It has been so closely intertwined throughout history with other forms of domination in variable ways in different situations that we will probably never be able to establish its autonomy in any certain way (Brittan and Maynard 1984; Gilroy 1987). This means that I am politically prejudiced in favour of tackling racism as an independent form of domination and oppression. Although there are problems with the theoretical claims for autonomy, it seems more urgent to tackle racism directly, and risk the error that this struggle is really only part of a wider struggle against capitalism, than to tackle other issues and risk the error that racism will remain untouched. We cannot, however, treat racism as if it were unconnected to other social processes, structures, and ideas.

Feminism is left with the very practical problem of how to identify the interconnections between the various forms of oppression which both unite and divide women, and unite and divide men. Cain's argument that women have different standpoints as women and as members of classes (Cain 1986, see chapter 5) can perhaps be extended to take in the further standpoint of race and ethnicity. This extension to the notion of standpoint would need very careful qualification because of the theoretical difficulties of establishing the basis of such a standpoint. But it can be argued that there is some basis, in that women experience the benefits and consequences of racism differently. Rather than searching for one relationship between class, race, and gender in general, feminists need to identify specific grounds for building alliances between women's different standpoints, including that of racial difference. Barbara Smith has said (Smith and Smith 1983: 126):

What *I* really feel is radical is trying to make coalitions with people who are different from you. I feel it is radical to be dealing with race and sex and class and sexual identity all at one time. I think *that* is really radical because it has never been done before.

Black and third-world critics of white feminism have shown how limited white women's understanding can be of the realities of racism when comprehension of the part they play in racist society is simply beyond their own experience. This issue demonstrates the methodological problem of theorizing a feminist standpoint rooted in women's experiences of oppression *via-à-vis* men. If white feminists behave in racist ways, without having any conception of racism, the knowledge produced from a feminist standpoint will continue to exclude any conception of the prevalence of racism in all western women's lives. Flax (1983: 321) notes that a feminist standpoint should be sensitive to race divisions, but does not indicate how such sensitivity could be put into practice. A feminist standpoint, then, is not at present an adequate basis for taking account of the divisions of class and race between women.

Black feminists have confronted white feminists with the racism of liberal, radical, and marxist feminist theories of recent years. The overwhelming evidence of the power dimension in racial, ethnic, and national divisions between women cannot be adequately reviewed in the space of one chapter, but the problems raised here need to be taken into account in deciding whether feminism can transcend the divisions of racism. The future of feminism as an effective international movement depends on establishing much more clearly whether the oppression of women from the standpoint of gender constitutes an interest which can unite women across the divisions of class, race, ethnicity, and nationality.

We need the image of the bridge to survive

It is doubtful if the new-wave writers who have been most heavily criticized for the racism of their universalistic theory would put their arguments in the same form today, in the light of the criticisms made of them. But there are still bitter divisions between women on the issue of racial and ethnic difference. In her rather depressed foreword to the second edition of *This Bridge Called My Back* (Moraga

136

and Anzaldua 1983), Cherrie Moraga considers the many obstacles still in the way of an international feminist movement. She concludes that we still need the image of a bridge between women in order to survive.

Constructing bridges between women of different classes, races, ethnic groups, and nations means finding political strategies for overcoming racism and ethnic and national differences within feminism. Black critics have argued that just as gender oppression cannot change until men recognize its existence, so racist oppression cannot change until whites recognize their own part in racism and take action against racist ideas and practices. Beyond the general recognition of racism in white dominated societies, women need to recognize the specific oppressions of class, race, ethnicity, national liberation struggles, and gender which structure women's lives. This means white women confronting racism at every level, from personal slight through discriminatory practices to physical violence, as *their* problem (Pence 1982).

Where women's consciousness of racism is limited, this is very hard to achieve. Just as there are plenty of men who think that they have reconstructed themselves as the 'new man' on the basis of a little extra help with shopping and childcare, so there must be many white women who have very limited notions of what confronting our own racism means in practice. There is a great deal of political work here for white women to do. Otherwise the burden is thrown back on black and ethnic-minority women to take on the whole burden of dealing with white racism.

Feminism also needs space for black women to define their own situations. 'Our objection to reductionism then, is not simply to make an academic point. Rather it is to allow the oppressed some kind of say in the way their oppression is theorised' (Brittan and Maynard 1984: 210). We need to conceptualize racism as intrinsic to all western experience in order to observe the many specific relationships in which women experience the divisions of gender, class, and race. We cannot begin even to imagine how we might construct new bridges between women if women themselves lack critical consciousness of where we stand in relation to the divisions between us.

Chapter Seven

WOMEN AGAINST WOMEN — CULTURE, IDEOLOGY, SEXUALITY

While women can lack any awareness of class, and may fail to acknowledge racism, they are generally very much aware of numerous other divisions which structure and colour their daily lives. Culture, ideology, and sexuality are critical areas in the relations between women. They are all problematic areas in social theory which are dealt with in extensive literatures of their own. I cannot attempt to review them here as they are all disputed terms that have been given different meanings within different theoretical discourses. I have used them to help identify further divisions between women which constitute problems for feminism. I have not tried to evaluate the usefulness of the concepts in any extensive way but have indicated the particular meanings that I am drawing on.

The ways in which women are divided by their cultures and by sexual difference, and the ways in which these differences are constituted ideologically, are particularly important when we come to think about how to change societies for the better. Sources of division between women such as class and racism cannot be tackled without also taking account both of how women are divided by beliefs, customs, religion, and sexuality and also of where these divisive ideas derive their power from. Feminists have had the extremely difficult task of trying to explain how women, who are divided in so many respects, can develop common political interests in struggling against oppression.

There are a number of problems in deciding how to approach these areas of difference. In some situations differences between women are apparent, but women only appear to be divided because they fail to recognize their common interests beneath apparent differences. There is a fine line between these situations and other cases where women are more clearly divided by opposing material interests — where women have conflicting interests in maintaining existing social arrangements. The recognition of difference is often difficult to establish, since women do have interests in common as well as interests which divide them.

In addition to the possibility that some differences are more divisive than others, and are complicated by women's consciousness, or lack of consciousness, of divisions between them, there is the problem that divisions between women may appear differently when viewed from different cultures. In particular, western views of what constitute desirable forms of freedom and autonomy for an individual, which have informed feminism, may not be recognized or valued by women in other cultures. This raises the problem of how far feminism has, or can, develop a view of women's oppression which transcends cultural divisions.

A further source of confusion lies in women's ability to generate ideas of what is good and better. Since women have throughout recent history been subordinated to men in most societies of the world, women's access to ideas, education, and independent thought has been restricted, mediated, or controlled largely by men. In looking at women's ideas of what they have in common and of what divides them, we need to ask how far male ideological dominance limits women's conceptions of their common interests with other women. I do not wish to imply that women are not capable of specifying their own needs. There is ample evidence from all over the world that women can and do struggle for themselves and for each other, but women are still subject to forces of conservatism and religious obedience in many areas which favour men and effectively divide women from each other. In this chapter I argue that culture, ideology, and sexuality are sources of divisions between women which have created enormous problems for feminist politics.

CULTURE

There is no one definition of culture which encompasses the great variety of ways in which this term has been used either in popular usage or by intellectuals. In social theory, the term culture was developed to indicate the boundaries of the knowledge, beliefs, and customs peculiar to particular communities. More recently, the revival of marxist thought, particularly in the 1970s, has led to the development of much more critical conceptions of culture, and to the differentiation between culture and ideology. I take culture loosely to refer to what people in any given society know and believe. This is what Gramsci (1971) called the 'common sense' of ordinary people's traditional conceptions of the world, although this term needs some qualification. While the complex and highly theoretical debates which ensued need not concern us here, the fact that different women take for granted different cultural assumptions about, for example, freedom, sexual expression, kinship obligations, and personal autonomy is an issue for feminism as an international movement.

Feminism was largely conceived within western cultures during the period in which capitalism came to dominate and transform not only the economies but also the cultures of other societies. Women with secondary education over much of the world have now been educated in broadly similar ways. They often share languages (i.e. the languages of colonialism, such as English, French, Spanish, between which translation is not problematic). This means they can read the same literature and communicate with each other directly. At this level feminism can spread fairly easily (although it does not necessarily do so) because a number of cultural assumptions are shared, and communication is based on these common assumptions. Criticisms of feminism have arisen where women have questioned the extent to which such assumptions are common among the majority of women. In complex societies there is no uniformity of belief, although ideas of homogeneity may be propagated through state education and the mass media. The lack of uniformity is much more obvious, however, to those whose beliefs and customs differ from those of the dominant ideology, or the supposedly uniform. The spread of new-wave feminism to those whose only knowledge is the common sense of their own local cultures has made the cultural location of new-wave feminism a problem for many women. While Gramsci (1971: 323) has argued that we are all philosophers in that we have languages, common-sense notions of the world, and beliefs, superstitions, opinions, and religions, he pointed out that we do not all have any critical or conscious awareness of why we know and believe what we take for granted.

Feminism is a critical form of consciousness. It enables us to make sense of existing social arrangements as patriarchal. Feminism, therefore, is critical of existing ideas, beliefs, customs, and practices, including scientific and religious knowledge. This can pose problems for women who are not conscious of being oppressed, and who do not question their own beliefs or the authorities who uphold these beliefs.

140

When the Pope speaks out against feminism, he exposes contradictions for feminists who are also Roman Catholics. Feminism requires critical re-evaluation not only of religious beliefs, but also of kinship obligations, sexual practices, scientific knowledge, the nature of femininity, and the obligation of women to serve the needs of men. This kind of critical approach is perhaps easier for women with education, who are familiar with the existence of a range of beliefs beyond their own localities, than for uneducated women familiar only with local beliefs and customs. But feminists should not make the mistake of confusing lack of formal education with lack of intelligence or of the capacity to know what women want. There are now very few areas of the world where even isolated, rural women are not aware of the existence of other beliefs and practices threatening the survival of their own.[1]

There is also very considerable resistance to feminism by western women who do not want to abandon their familiar beliefs, and who feel that they have much to lose when marriage, family, religion, and heterosexuality are threatened. Feminism, rather than uniting women of different cultures, has become a source of divisions between women. It challenges the foundations of women's cultural identities as 'proper' feminine women. This again raises the problem of false consciousness. It is not always clear how far cultural divisions between women are problems of failure to develop a critical consciousness of our common interests, and how far women have essential interests which do divide us. If western feminists demand change along similar lines for women all over the world, then they encounter the problem of cultural relativism.

Cultural relativism

recognizing diff. ♀'s
problems globally

2 WAYS

Third-world critics of western feminism have demanded reconsideration of the ways in which the nature and causes of women's oppression can be explained. The varied situations of third-world women raise issues which challenge the more generalizing new-wave feminist assumptions. First, there is the question of whether the oppression of women is really the same phenomenon wherever it is found, or whether each historically specific form of oppression needs to be identified and explained. Second, there is the political issue of whether all third-world women (and by implication, women everywhere) have to struggle against oppression in the same way, and for the same ends. Can women achieve full human dignity as people without destroying their varied cultural identities?

> Ironically, as their grandfathers colonised the Maori people as a whole, so do some feminists attempt to indoctrinate Maori women, disallowing cultural differences, challenging the struggles for land, culture, and language at a brother's side, silencing a unique contribution by seeing stunned muteness as implied agreement.
>
> (Te Awekotuku and Waring 1984: 487)

These problems need to be considered before feminist strategies for change can be worked out. They leave open the question of whether the politics of women's liberation can properly be viewed as general rather than as culturally specific. It is not clear how women could develop universal political practices if their oppression takes culturally specific forms, struggles, and solutions.

There is great difficulty in steering interpretations of these arguments between the trap of cultural relativism on the one hand, and the claim that there is only one feminist view of what oppression 'really' is on the other — that is, between the view that practices such as purdah, female circumcision, polygyny, and child marriage are not oppressive if they are not judged by western standards, since third-world women do not want western individualism, and the view that western women know that third-world women really are oppressed, even if the women themselves do not, because we have universal criteria of oppression which define such customs as purdah, female circumcision, polygyny, and child marriage as oppressive. Somehow feminists around the world have to find ways of steering solutions between these extreme positions. In practice, it is hard to distinguish between different kinds of relativism. Cultural relativism can only be analytically separated from moral relativism and claims to superiority of scientific knowledge. When we judge other cultures in practice, we tend to judge our own as morally better and also as superior in terms of knowledge of what is best.

It might seem that to resort to cultural relativism would be a simple way of letting feminists off the hook. No judgement need then be passed on the conditions of other women's lives. They could be accepted as neither better nor worse, but simply as different. This position, however, destroys the basis of feminism as an international, political movement. If the common nature of women's oppression does not give rise to a

142

common critical consciousness across cultures, then feminism has no basis for common political strategies. This dilemma is particularly clear in the case of female circumcision.

Female circumcision

It might seem that the issue of female circumcision is one that would simply unite women in opposition to these practices, but condemnation of female circumcision by western feminists has proved divisive. Western feminists have picked on clitoridectomy and infibulation as specific ways in which women are oppressed. Cutting off the clitoris severely reduces women's sexual pleasure, while retaining their ability to breed children. Infibulation is a much more drastic way of ensuring that only the husband has sexual access to his wife regardless of the consequences to the woman's well-being.[2] I use the term female circumcision to refer to these practices, others prefer the more expressive term genital mutilation. Circumcision invites us to try to clarify the cultural and ideological meanings which are embedded in the common sense of these practices, before developing strategies for changing them. Circumcision is practised and insisted on by women as well as men, in spite of the many physical and psychological injuries that can follow. This is not to underestimate the extent of the mutilation of women that does in fact take place or the resistance of young women to circumcision.

There is no doubt that female circumcision causes loss of sexual pleasure, mental distress, and ill-health to women, and that it enforces men's control of women's sexuality (el Saadawi 1980). But Muslim and African women have raised strong objections to the wholesale condemnation of these practices by western feminists, and notably to the analysis used by Mary Daly (1978). These objections arise because of the difficulty of separating female circumcision from other aspects of, for example, Arab and African cultures which have been threatened by colonialism and the development of capitalism on a world scale. If outsiders condemn female circumcision, they stand in judgement on a culture and its people. If Muslim women pick out female circumcision as a particular focus of complaint, they are also in danger of attacking the whole of their culture and their place in it, including their religion.[3]

Even at this point of the crudest physical assault on women's bodies and sexuality, where it might seem that women could find some basis of unity, women can be divided by cultural identity and their differing situations in relation to historically dominant cultures. There is a need to distinguish, then, between *cultural relativism*, which leaves each culture as acceptable on its own terms, and offers women no common ground between them, and *respect for each other's cultures*, which leaves us able to understand, evaluate, compare, and choose, but without a need to condone indiscriminately. It is doubtful that any feminist could condone clitoridectomy and infibulation as in any way meeting women's interests.

> Every woman is, or ought to be, concerned about sexual
> mutilation practised on the body of another, whoever she may
> be. But it remains for the excised and infibulated women
> themselves, being opposed to these practices and aware of their
> harmful consequences, to say publicly that they want an end to
> these ancestral customs; and to translate their words into
> action in their daily lives.
>
> (Thiam 1986: 85)

Thiam's view raises practical problems about effective ways of connecting feminist theory and practice. Action against circumcision can be defined by the women who have been circumcised, or who are under an obligation to have their daughters or others circumcised. But it is feminist theory which defines circumcision as a mechanism of patriarchy which should be opposed.

Nahid Toubia, who qualified as Sudan's first woman surgeon, defines female circumcision as a form of subjugation, since it is a means of removing women's sexuality while retaining their reproductive functions (Toubia 1985). But she argues that it is a form of subjugation which needs to be seen in its appropriate totality. Circumcision can only be understood in its connections to social, political, and sexual oppression in each society where it occurs. The modernization of a society can simply ensure more hygienic conditions of circumcision without any real social change. Toubia points out that circumcision cannot be tackled effectively without tackling the whole issue of women's subordination. Where there have been real changes in women's social position, as in Egypt, or a rise in political consciousness, as in Eritrea, then changes in circumcision practices have followed.

Western feminists have tended to see Islamic societies as generally oppressive of women, rather than recognizing the struggles within Islam, and the intermeshing of religious legitimation with economic, national, class, and women's struggles. They have come under increasing criticism for this attitude (Eisenstein 1984: 142). In her account of Sudanese women's struggles for change, Badri (1984: 656) comments on a Sudanese women's project working against female circumcision, but in her list of suggestions for 'feminist foreign aid' to Sudanese women, she asks primarily for financial support and for assistance with training local women to carry out this and other development tasks.

While Arab and other Muslim women undoubtedly suffer oppression as women, this is not necessarily the same form of oppression as that experienced by women elsewhere (and there are considerable variations between Islamic societies). The concept of being Arab, like the concept of being black, has had to be politically constructed as a basis for shared struggles in the aftermath of colonialism and the spread of capitalism (Hussein 1984; Mernissi 1985). El Saadawi (1980) has argued that female circumcision is part of a system by which men control women's sexuality, but is also linked to economic interests in land, through the necessity of establishing paternity. Struggles against the oppression of women then become complicated by women's class situations, and by the contradictory situations in which colonizing powers defined what constituted women's liberation, making any advance in this direction a concession to western cultural dominance.

Female circumcision challenges cross-cultural generalizations on the oppression of women. Such generalizations cannot adequately take into account the complex and contradictory ways in which relations between men and women (and so between women and women) vary and develop in different societies. These relations are also interconnected with other social divisions that fracture women's common interests in struggling against oppression. Women in Muslim societies are also divided by class, ethnicity, nationality, and sectarianism in ways which set women against each other. While we can all ask why, how, and when relations between the sexes have become oppressive to women, and what forms such oppression takes, the answers to these questions are not self-evident. They must be identified and empirically established in each case, which is obviously a massive task. Reconsideration of cultural differences opens the way to arguing that while the sexual politics of oppression may be shared to a considerable degree, this sharing is no simple matter. The politics of liberation needs to respect cultural variation while also recognizing oppressive aspects of different cultures. Western feminists need to attend to third-world women's criticisms of individualism and sexual freedom.

The problems of the cultural diversity of women's experience cannot, then, be fully understood simply as cultural differences. Some conception of ideology is needed to enable us to see where the power of ideas is located in each society. Where women do share (whether consciously or not) common interests as women, they must share these in relation to some form of subordination of women by men, or to social structures and processes in which men's interests are dominant.

IDEOLOGY AND MALE IDEOLOGICAL DOMINANCE

Ideology is if anything an even more problematic term than culture. 'Ideology is perhaps one of the most equivocal and elusive concepts one can find in the social sciences' (Larrain 1979: 13). My excuse for making use of it here is that it can help to explain why women do not necessarily see whether or not their interests are shared with other women, and why women resist feminism. The use of the concept is limited, however, to the extent that women cannot be treated as a class. Ideology can be used loosely to refer to particular sets of ideas such as nationalism. It is particularly useful here in Marx's sense of ideas which act to conceal key contradictions in any society, and ideas which work in the interest of the dominant class. In this sense ideology is distinguished from knowledge. Whereas ideology mystifies people's understandings of the societies they live in, knowledge reveals the essential social, political, and economic structures and relationships which really constitute society.

Marxist interpretations of ideology have developed and clashed over time. At the risk of considerable oversimplification, it can be said that the main contribution of marxist thought has been to develop the concept of ideology as a means of seeing how dominant classes can propagate particular representations of material reality which work in their own interests (although this is by no means the only use of ideology in marxist thought). This view was developed by Althusser (1969, 1971) who emphasized the connections between ideology and people's material conditions of existence. In this view, conceptualizing people's lack of awareness of shared interests as false consciousness is inadequate, because shared interests involve essential, material interests too. Ideology is not then simply false or erroneous knowledge, but is a way of representing the social world so that the contradictions of interest in the production system are concealed. Ideology, then,

[handwritten margin note: IDEOLOGY IS USED TO SEE the simul- arities between & culturally]

146

generally hinders members of subordinate classes from discovering where their real interests lie. Ideology is not so all-powerful, however, that it cannot ever be penetrated. Marxism is a form of knowledge which enables people to find out how production systems really work, and to whose advantage.

There seems an obvious parallel here between marxist demystification of bourgeois ideology and feminist demystification of patriarchal ideology. Feminist knowledge enables people to identify patriarchal ideas as patriarchal, and to find out how patriarchal systems work and to whose advantage. Patriarchal ideology will necessarily present women's subordination to men as natural, desirable, and legitimate. It will also emphasize the divisions between women. But women's consciousness of the differences of interest which separate them from other women are not simply false if women do (as I have argued in chapters 5 and 6) have different essential interests. Both marxist and feminist forms of knowledge seem to me to be needed if we are to have a full understanding of the ideologies we live with.

This conception of ideology allows us to see that cultures are not simply autonomous sets of ideas that people happen to believe in. The dominant ideas of what is normal, natural, and desirable are closely linked with the interests of those who exercise power (although this is often in incoherent, contested, and contradictory ways). Ideologies are then intermeshed *both* with the way in which production systems are organized *and* with the operation of male-dominated sex/gender relations. This is why we need a concept of patriarchal ideology. The meaning of ideology has been debated at very general levels of abstraction, yet the concept is only useful for practical feminist politics if the connections between ideas and the exercise of power can be specified. While it is easy to assert that the ruling ideas in a society are the ideas of the ruling class or of the dominant gender, it is much harder to demonstrate that this is so, let alone how and why this is so. Marxist conceptions of ideology cannot then simply be applied to women's struggles without qualification. The concept of patriarchal ideology is not a self-evident term, but one which needs to be historically situated and accounted for. Male dominance over women at the level of ideas is a problem which needs to be explained.

New-wave feminism initially conceptualized patriarchal ideology as a general characteristic of societies through history, but ideology is not a static phenomenon. Ideologies are historically variable. If patriarchal ideologies are discovered in different situations, then not

147

only the differences but also the *similarities* need explaining. They cannot simply be taken for granted. Ideologies which mystify women about the extent to which they share interests with other women do have much in common with each other. But there are also considerable variations, and we know very little about these variations. Any assumption that patriarchy must be universal will need adequate qualification and investigation if it is to have any explanatory value.

Familial ideology

Ideologies, in the sense used above, can be identified as particular sets of ideas which shape the way in which most people make sense of their social world. In capitalist society the 'work ethic' makes it seem normal, natural, and desirable that workers should work for wages which are less than the value of what they produce. Other ideas, which have been termed 'familial ideology', contribute to women's consciousness of divisions between them in two ways.[4] First, household and kinship structures can be experienced not only as what is in existence at present, but also as what is natural, normal, and desirable everywhere (Beechey 1985).

This view, which legitimates specific family and household forms as normal and right, has had profound effects on women's lives. It defines them as belonging to the domestic sphere for most of their lives. It has also had an enormous impact on colonized cultures, since through mission and colonial government education policies the monogamous nuclear family was presented as natural, prestigious, and desirable. Once this set of ideas about the nature of family life is entrenched, it not only promotes and legitimates one form, but it blinds us to the complex history of kinship and household structures, and prevents us from seeing the range of family forms and households which do exist. The consequences are considerable for those who do not conform to the stereotypically 'good' family, particularly, in Britain, those affected by state welfare provision and by immigration legislation. Second, familial ideology, by legitimating the social location of women within the domestic sphere, encourages women to give their loyalty to their own family and kinship groups rather than to public organizations, and undermines recognition of common interests with other women (Whitehead 1984: 9). The prospects for a shared consciousness as women are diminished by the structure and ideology of domestic organization (Bujra 1978).

148

Feminist thought has had the effect of revealing women's common interests by exposing much of western knowledge of family life and beliefs about the family as ideological. Women confined to the home are women controlled by men. Women's determined efforts to break out of the domestic domain, and the wealth of evidence that working-class and peasant women have rarely been fully confined, have challenged ideas of what is normal, natural, and desirable. Familial ideology can also divide women from each other because it defines the normal and the abnormal. In Britain it defines itinerant, 'immigrant' and single-parent family structures as deviant, thus exacerbating the divisiveness of racist and sexist ideas. Feminism has had little impact on these divisions.

Ideology is a particular problem for feminism. The ideas of western feminists developed within the capitalist cultures which dominate the rest of the world. Feminism is a critical form of consciousness which seeks to expose the essential relations which lie beneath the ideological appearances of patriarchy and capitalism. But feminists are only human, and we can only think about our problems and their solutions within the categories of thought available within our cultures. Feminism can divide women when feminist demands for separation from men, individual freedom and transformation of the family are seen as changes which benefit the west, obscure the contradictions between the situations of western and third-world women, or take no account of the value of other women's cultures. Where differences between cultures are defined by religion, the problems for feminism are exacerbated.

Religion

There is no agreed definition within feminism, or in social science more generally, of religion and I have not attempted to establish a definitive conception of religion here. Western common sense defines religion fairly narrowly in the image of Judaism, Islam, and Christianity. In the east, and in smaller societies which have retained spiritual respect for nature, the ways in which people order their lives by their beliefs is very variable. In defining religion, feminism needs to remain open-minded on the ways in which spiritual experience and relations with nature are conceived.

Religion is one of the most immediate, and often violent, ways in which women experience divisions from each other. Children are socialized into particular religions, sects, or cults which actively discourage them from adhering to, or marrying into, any other. Millions have died over the centuries for their religious affiliations. The nature of religious divisions, however, can be hard to identify, as religions develop within different societies. Divisions between Protestant and Catholic women, for example, are not the same divisions in Northern Ireland, Uganda, and Brazil. Their religious divisions are differently intermeshed with the historical development of class divisions and struggles, patriarchal ideology, conquest from outside and the development of state power. In Brazil, there are divisions between Roman Catholics aligned with the interests of the state, and those aligned with the poor and dispossessed. The violent conflict between Protestants and Catholics in Northern Ireland cannot be understood without a grasp of the English conquest of Ireland, the class origins of the two religious groups, and the denominational basis of state education. In Uganda, the intermeshing of religion and politics has a long history leading to battles in the nineteenth century between the French mission Catholics and the English mission Protestants, and the subsequent development of politico-religious affiliation through economic inequalities, education, and party politics.

Major world religions still demand from women not only obedience and service to gods but also to men. Fundamentalist Islam has produced its own feminists, for example Melika Salihbegovic, whose version of women's freedom under Islam is 'if a woman is a believer, then she will want to follow the Koran, and obey her husband' (Toynbee 1988).[5] This view of oppression and freedom is not only incompatible with that of western culture, but also with those of more liberal Muslim feminists. Religious divisions hold back the development of feminism as an international movement.

New-wave feminist texts often pay little attention to religion except to identify particular religions as sources of patriarchal ideology and practice. The Middle Eastern religions, Judaism, Christianity, and Islam, together with Hinduism, explicitly favour men and value women primarily as mothers and wives. Western radical feminists in the 1970s tended to view religion primarily as patriarchal ideology regardless of the different forms in which it appeared. 'All of the so-called religions legitimating patriarchy are mere sects subsumed under its vast umbrella/canopy. They are essentially similar despite the variations' (Daly 1978: 39).

Patriarchal religions were seen as having little to offer women

150

except the pressure to submit to the needs and desires of men. Robin Morgan (1984: 28) describes contributors to *Sisterhood is Global* as having made 'what may be the most fiery indictment of organised religion ever to sear its way across paper'. Other feminist writers have explored the possibility that earlier phases of these belief systems were more favourable towards women, and that feminine symbolism was eventually suppressed (Pagels 1983), but in general their oppressiveness is taken for granted.

Marxist feminists have followed Marx in treating Christianity and Judaism as ideological. They have largely ignored other religions. This stance has been sharply criticized by Fahmy-Eid and Laurin-Frenette in their comparison of the family in Quebec and France. They argue that marxists have ignored the variability of the parts played by the church in different societies. In Roman Catholic societies, the church can retain control of schools, hospitals and social services which elsewhere have been taken over by the state. The church can also influence family life through the mediation of women (Fahmy-Eid and Laurin-Frenette 1986). The impact on women's lives is therefore variable and dynamic.

The problem with dismissing religion as patriarchal ideology is that we are then in danger of overlooking the range of ideas, beliefs, practices, and institutions which constitute religion. Even if all religions were found to be working in the interests of men against women, there are still tremendous variations in beliefs and organization within each religion. These vary from fundamentalist sects which specify details of personal life to vague affiliation and participation in occasional rituals. Some fundamentalist sects monopolize state power, as in post-revolutionary Iran, others are marginal to social life, as are the Protestant Amish or the Hasidic Jews in America.

New-wave feminists have tended to have little interest in religion. Yet religion can be the dominant factor in the personal identity and cultural location of millions of women around the world. If religion is one of the most important and immediate factors which enables a woman to know who she is, and to give meaning to her life, an international feminist movement cannot afford to ignore religion. It can be a major force in uniting women into groups which then separate women from each other. In Northern Ireland, where women are politically compelled to identify themselves as either Protestant or Catholic, feminist activity has rarely been able to transcend these divisions. As Loughran (1986: 77) comments, 'Feminists are caught in division. They organise on opposite sides of the sectarian divide with mutually exclusive strategies.'

It might be argued with more power than in the case of class and race that religion is a form of false consciousness. It conceals patriarchal power relations. It conceals the extent to which the spiritual is entwined with economic and political organization. Women who obey religious authorities have then failed to recognize their essential sisterhood beneath the apparent differences of belief and practice. It is not clear, though, what are the material differences between the spiritual situations of women of different religions. The problem with the false consciousness argument is that it sets up the atheist or agnostic western feminist as a superior knower (see Smith 1979: 158). If religion is false consciousness then it must be established that there are no gods, there is no spiritual relationship with nature. While this may seem unproblematic to most western feminists, as it is to most marxists, it is less clear to many others, and to women whose cultural identity is integral to their religious identity (Chester 1984: 287).

Some Muslim feminists in recent years have made it clear that they regard Islam today as oppressive towards women, but they reject western feminists' condemnations of Islam. This stance has led them to the extraordinarily difficult task of trying to develop historically specific explanations of the development of women's oppression within Islamic societies (Hussein and Radwan 1984; Stowasser 1984). These writers do not deny the oppressive character of Islam today: 'the Islamic position on women along with the Islamic position on other social questions, became an instrument for the perpetuation of the general dominance of the Arab ruling classes' (Salman 1978: 29). Muslim feminists, however, have distinguished between Islam and male dominance. They have looked for the liberation of women within a purified Islam and are rewriting Muslim history. This development has been criticized by others. Tabari (1982: 18–19) sees the scope for reform within Islam as very limited. She argues that even the most reformist interpretations of Islam are barriers to women's real emancipation. This is because Islam is not just a religion, but also a political system.

A similar process of trying to struggle for women within religions is also occurring, however, among religious feminists in India (Dietrich 1986). There are also struggles within Judaism and Christianity which attempt to distinguish between men's patriarchal appropriation of religion and a purer version of the religion which can be purged of patriarchy (although these efforts often lead to schism rather than unity).

Organized religions can also develop splits between those at the top who exercise power and are closely linked with the state, and the mass of ordinary people who struggle to survive. The development of liberation theology in Latin America, and the active role played by some nuns and priests alongside peasants in resisting state violence, is a case in point. Dietrich (1986) notes, however, that liberation theology has as yet no feminist dimension.

Religion, then, constitutes a problem for feminism. Some religions are more oppressive of women than others, but to dismiss all religion as patriarchal ideology is to oversimplify the complexity of women's situations. The argument that religious ideologies and patriarchal church institutions should be swept away and replaced (if at all) with separate female spiritual ideas and practices needs careful qualification in the light of other differences between women. Religions may diminish women and legitimate their subordination to men, but they can also meet other needs for self-respect, spirituality, identity, and purpose which feminism should challenge with caution.

Obviously religions that preach the intrinsic inferiority of women or use state power against women are incompatible with feminism, but religious beliefs do not exist in a vacuum. Religious institutions develop and adapt over the years, but are always closely intermeshed with other social institutions, particularly kinship, education, and the state. Religion, with other social institutions, helps to construct the meaning of motherhood, childrearing, crime and the extent to which all people in a society are valued and respected. Religions cannot then be seen as passive ideologies which simply reflect capitalism or men's power. Religious ideas, practices, and institutions actively, though in contradictory ways, shape women's lives, identities, and sense of worth, and so legitimate and accentuate divisions between women.

The problem for feminism is that of how to develop a critical awareness of the religions which divide women that:

1 identifies the oppressive character of the specific ways in which the various religions have been integrated into social, political, and economic life;
2 clarifies the extent to which different religions legitimate men's dominance;
3 recognizes and respects the intermeshing of religion and cultural identity.

Apart from the oversimplified general solution of instructing other women to abandon all religious beliefs and practices, new-wave feminism has no clear resolution of these problems. Yet obviously most women will want to continue to celebrate birth and death, at least, with some shared practices, and to believe in some meaning to life. Only extreme poverty, or the extreme individualism of western life, leaves these occasions unmarked, and life as meaningless.

Perhaps as a first step it is enough for feminists to try to agree upon what constitutes oppression within religion and to develop diverse strategies of struggle against it appropriate to each situation. We need to be aware not only of the tremendous variation between different religious beliefs and institutions, but also of their variability and adaptability. Outside the major religions there is great variation in the content of people's beliefs and in relations between beliefs and the quality of women's lives. As Kader has argued (1984: 160), 'it might be best to study what aspects of religion women practise, and what aspects of it they think are of importance to their lives . . . .' Without such information feminism remains confused. Wherever women are oppressed, religions are integrated into oppressive social practices which feminists would not condone. At the same time, the potential cultural and spiritual value of religions to women is contradicted by the divisiveness of religion for women.

SEXUALITY

Sexuality has been so important in new-wave feminism, and so effective in the demystification of masculine knowledge of women's lives, that it may seem odd that I have come to it last. I have not left consideration of sexuality as a source of division between women until the last because it is the least important factor. I have come to sexuality last because:

1 it has been the *most* salient factor for many western feminist theorists in conceptualizing in general the power of men over women;

2 it was the basis of the new-wave feminist argument that women as women shared a common oppression by men;

3 it can only be properly considered as a common basis of oppression after consideration of the material divisions between women.

Sexual behaviour and beliefs need to be understood as social activity which is mediated by class and racism, is constructed within cultures, and is itself ideological. While people do share a genetic inheritance, and so have some common physical characteristics as males or females, we are socially constituted as human beings in ways that differentiate us from each other. Our sexual behaviour is learned within different societies and also within divided societies.

New-wave feminists argue that sexuality is not private. it is a political issue in the relations between women and men, the individual and the state, the acceptable and the criminal. It has been a strength of feminist theory to reveal the existence of sexual politics, the extent of male control over women's bodies, and the prevalence of male sexual violence. The feminist case for recognizing a broad spectrum of male violence towards women as a major social problem has been over-whelming. Through women's struggles it has changed public thinking on rape, sexual assaults, and domestic violence (albeit slowly and partially) in many parts of the world. There have been problems, though, in moving feminist thinking on sexuality beyond male violence and the social construction of sexuality, towards more general consideration of women's sexual divisions and the possibilities of women's sexual power and sexual pleasure. Clark (1982: 31) comments, 'there is no subject on which feminists will wax more eloquent than sex and sexuality, but there is also no subject on which we hold more opposed, stubborn and opinionated views.'

Disagreements over the nature of women's sexuality, power in sexual relations, and the extent of women's rights to sexual freedom have led to deep and bitter divisions between feminist activists. These have become particularly explicit recently among feminist groups in Britain and the United States. Opening up sexual power and pleasure as key areas of new-wave feminist concern provoked objections from other women for whom sexual pleasure came low on their list of priorities in struggles against oppression. These arguments have been discussed in the preceding chapters, but they provide an essential framework for keeping sexuality in context as only one part of human experience. The amount of choice now open to some women to define, pursue, and create sexual pleasure for themselves and other women is perhaps unprecedented in world history, but it is a choice at present only for a minority.

Even the largely white feminist movement in the United States, where more unanimity might have been expected, has experienced not shared sisterhood in sex, but deep divisions — divisions in how women experience sexuality, what they know of sex, and what they regard as normal, acceptable, pleasurable, and permissible (Vance 1984). Feminists who were reasonably united on male roles in the sexual repression of women were bewildered by what form the sexual liberation of women could or should take. Vance (1984: 21) comments that:

> the quest for politically appropriate sexual behaviour has led to what Alice Nichols calls prescriptivism, the tendency to transform broad general principles like equality, autonomy, and self-determination into fairly specific and rigid standards to which all feminists are expected to conform.

Much of the recent American debate over sexuality (also the silences, the tears, the pain, and the exclusions) has been over the intolerance of prescriptivism which specified the lifestyle, dress, personal adornment, sexual practices, and living arrangements deemed adequately feminist. Members of feminist groups have proved capable of considerable intolerance towards other women.

Our knowledge of women's sexuality and of the essential difference between male and female sexuality is still limited. Since scientific knowledge on these issues has been mainly constructed by male scientists within a patriarchal conception of the female, the exact relationships between infantile experience, social structures, and adult sexual orientation, fantasy, and practices are far from clear. We cannot generalize across cultures about sexuality without qualification. Even if sexuality had remained close to our biology, making all human sexuality basically similar, centuries of cultural conditioning of infants together with individual resistance and variation cannnot be discounted. Feminism still lacks an adequate theory of sexuality. There are still disputes over how far sexuality is biologically given and over what is meant by the social construction of sexuality.

Even if sexuality is taken to be socially constructed, it is not agreed why it takes the forms that it does, or what part (if any) is played by essential biological differences. Foucault (1979) has influenced feminism through his argument that sexual desires are not biological essences but are constructed in historical discourses. Power and knowledge came together in sexuality. The problem with Foucault's position, though, is that it does not explain why women have so generally lost power in sexual relationships. These problems of explanation have divided feminists politically in ways that are extremely difficult to resolve.

156

I have taken three areas in which feminist concern with aspects of sexuality, power, and the control of women's bodies has shown up divisions between women: women's rights to abortion; the division between lesbianism and in heterosexuality; and sexual desire and freedom in pornography and in lesbian sado-masochism. My discussion of the latter is confined to American and British sources because of the difficulty of generalizing from limited knowledge across cultures. This restriction does not imply that the underlying arguments are irrelevant elsewhere, but that they would need careful qualification and investigation in each case.

Abortion

The absolute right of pregnant women to choose freely whether or not to abort their unborn children was one of the rallying cries of early new-wave feminism. Abortion quickly proved both an emotive and a very divisive issue. Feminist campaigns politicized women's lack of control over abortion, and over reproduction more generally. They stimulated struggles for the liberalizing of abortion laws in a number of countries, with varying degrees of success. But they also stimulated active opposition from women and men, as well as protests from women for whom a more important concern was safeguarding the lives of their unborn children (Sykes 1984; Bryan *et al.* 1985).

> Abortion is not an isolated event in women's lives. . . . As women we all share a lack of control over our own bodies especially in terms of when and if we want children. But we experience that lack of control in different ways, and it is not only through abortion that control over our reproduction is felt.
>
> (NAC 1984: 238)[6]

Abortion raises the issue of who has power over women's bodies, and how such power can be legitimated. But it also raises a moral issue of the foetus's right to life, and a technical issue of the exact age at which a foetus can be expected to survive outside the womb (an age which has decreased significantly in the west since the 1970s).

Right-wing public opinion has been mobilized to protect the foetus, but right-wing campaigns ignore the power relations within which abortions and births take place. Efforts by right-wing women to oppose abortion rights reassert an idealized image of the family, without acknowledging the power relations within such families (Campbell 1987). They stress every pregnant female's duty to carry every new life to term. Anti-abortion groups at times seem to suggest that unwilling mothers should be compelled to breed, but then hand over unwanted babies to the infertile. There is some recognition that unwilling mothers do have problems, but there are no solutions when the right of the foetus to a life of any quality is accorded primacy over its mother's right to life of a specific quality. David Alton, the British member of parliament whose private member's bill sought to restrict women's access to abortion as a step towards total abolition, has publicly offered such unwilling mothers 'love', but there is no indication as to what use such love would be in practice.

Abortion also brings into question the rights and responsibilities of fathers of unborn children, humane and religious definitions of when human life begins, and the power dimension of the sexual relations in which women become pregnant. There is little evidence that women positively choose to kill their unborn children. It is rather the case that many women are left with impossible choices when they unwillingly become pregnant, of which abortion may be the least of the evils available to them (Rich 1980: 265ff.).

In her bitter attack on new-wave feminists for their rejection of Roman Catholic opposition to abortion, McMillan (1982) argues that feminists' demands for abortion express a rejection of our animal nature. The abortion 'death wish', she argues, comes from feminist attempts to separate sex and procreation. The feminist alternatives to abortion should be, in McMillan's view, to use natural means of contraception (specifically, the Billings method), to refrain from sexual intercourse when conception is likely, and to accept any inadvertent pregnancies that ensue. McMillan does mention (although without being specific) that men would have to share responsibility for sexual restraint, and that support for women with unwanted pregnancies would be required. But it is precisely the lack of these conditions which makes abortion such an urgent issue for many women. Sexual abstinence would have to be widespread, or even total, for women with poor health or poor living conditions, and for carriers of genetic disorders. Alongside abstinence we would need a vast programme of re-education for men, in societies which currently legitimate men's sexual access to and power over women. Practical, emotional, and financial support for women with unwanted children would be needed round the clock and for years on end.

McMillan's chosen solution of treating sex and reproduction as a natural unity ignores the social circumstances of many women's lives today. We may retain our animal natures but we are also constituted within cultures. Where knowledge and resources for contraception exist, sex and reproduction *have* become separated, giving women a potential for reproductive choice unknown in previous societies.[7] Women have very unequal powers of realizing potential choices. The separation of sex and reproduction has created both opportunities and disadvantages for women, with no clear political line for feminists to tread on every issue.

The problem of how to provide support directly to unwilling mothers (as opposed to abortion, infanticide, adoption, or state childcare) remains unresolved. Feminists have had relatively little to say on this issue, since contraception and abortion have seemed more direct solutions. Nevertheless, unwilling motherhood is a complex and contradictory issue, with many women ambivalent on what to do, or on what they have done. Feminists need to begin to consider what forms support for privatized mothers could and should take. This is clearly an area where women need to specify their varied needs and interests, including how far these conflict with the needs of their children. A woman with an unwanted pregnancy has very little time for decision-making.

The exuberance of western pro-abortion campaigns has also had to be qualified by differences in experiences of motherhood and child health. There are tremendous variations around the world in social and economic sources of support for mothers. Demands for abortion rights have come chiefly from societies where rape is prevalent, childrearing is extremely expensive, severely handicapped infants survive, children are unproductive, and women lack extended families within which childcare can be shared. In these societies, motherhood can entail physical isolation in the home, loss of independence, subordination to male needs, difficulty in engaging in paid work, and a drop in living standards. These are also societies with high standards of health care and low infant mortality rates.

In many third-world societies, the demand for abortion may also be high, particularly for the raped and those in cities. But it may be lower for other women in the same society. This point is somewhat oversimplified as the demand for abortion can also vary with changes in attitudes towards education, differential costs of marrying off sons and daughters, changes in the economic value of children, and so on.

Pro-abortion campaigns have mainly highlighted the specificity of white, western experience, the contradictions between a woman's right to control of her body and the foetus's right to life. They have also exposed differences in women's experiences of racism, female infanticide, and genocide. Black women have stated their need for the right *not* to be pressured into abortions, sterilization or unsafe means of contraception such as Depo-Provera (OWAAD 1981).

If the 'correct' feminist view is not simply and without qualification to be pro-abortion on demand for all who demand it, can there be a general feminist view of abortion rights? The case may be much stronger for western women struggling to raise children largely on their own than for Indian women pressured into destroying their daughters, or for Amazonian or Aboriginal women with collective experiences of genocide. It is also possible for women's situations to change over short periods of time. Where peasant women lose their access to land, or begin to value education, children as assets are suddenly converted into children as dependants, particularly where families have to migrate to urban areas. An additional pregnancy can become a financial crisis. Tension remains here, as in other areas of social life, between individual rights to choose a course of action and collective interests which impose limits on individual freedom (Petchesky 1986).

The argument that abortion is not the same issue for all women does not, however, mean that the control of abortion does not affect all women. Lewis (1987) uses a review of Petchesky (1986) to point to the links emerging between attacks on legal abortion in Britain and America, and struggles over the issues of contraception for minors, sex education in schools, and control of artificial reproduction. Lewis (1987: 10) summarizes Petchesky's position to argue that 'abortion is part of a much larger ideological struggle in which the meanings of family, motherhood and young women's sexuality are contested'.

Women's choices remain restricted, primarily because legal contraception and abortions are controlled within hierarchical, male-dominated medical institutions. (In Britain this leads, through a cumbersome process of referral, to late hospital abortions, rather than to early vacuum extractions.) Where these institutions are also dominated by one class and racial group, and ideology conceals where power lies, different groups of women will be in rather different positions with regard to access to abortion and pressures to be aborted against their will. Effective contraception is obviously more desirable than abortion for the sake of women's health, the allocation of resources, and the welfare of the foetus. Where contraception is lacking, expensive, ineffective, or forbidden by men or religion, demands for abortion will persist and means to abortion or infanticide will be found.

A single feminist strategy may not cover all eventualities as long as the control of abortion remains in male hands. Allowing women to control abortion decision-making would certainly bring greater self determination to some women, but it still leaves the problem of the power differentials between women of different classes, races, and ethnic groups. Abortion on demand cannot be a unifying feminist strategy without radical social transformation of other areas of human life. A general political strategy of achieving more choice for women would entail empowering some women to have abortions or easier abortions, and empowering others to refuse to have them.

Lesbianism and heterosexuality

Feminist support for the rights of lesbians to have a public existence has encouraged lesbians to 'come out' around the world. In many parts of the world it is still too dangerous to do this, or information is so restricted that the concept of lesbianism is not available to most women. Working-class lesbians in the west may have much more difficulty in expressing their sexual orientation than middle-class women (Dixon 1983: 145). In other parts of the world, cultural concepts of sexuality do not classify lesbianism and heterosexuality in comparable ways to those which have developed in the west since the seventeenth century. Lesbianism, however, has been a significant factor in uniting women, in at least some respects, across cultural, racial, and class boundaries, even though this unit remains to some extent contradictory (Combahee River Collective 1983; Carmen *et al.* 1984; Te Awekotuku 1984; Zehra 1987). At the same time the nature of the similarities and differences between heterosexual and lesbian sexuality has remained far from clear.

Lesbian feminists exposed sexual difference between women by making their oppression as lesbians public. The lesbian feminist case against institutionalized heterosexuality, however, has proved divisive (although this effect was not intended) since most women remain self-identified as heterosexual. While it might be argued that this is yet another case of false consciousness, of women failing to question their sexual orientation critically, the problem could also be posed as one of insufficient consideration of the potential of more fulfilling

161

heterosexual relations in transformed societies (Tsoulis 1987).

The possibility of political lesbianism (taken in its broadest sense to mean political identification with women rather than with men, as opposed to a narrower definition of sexual orientation) creates a potential basis for unity between all women. But the demands by some lesbian feminists that all women should forgo heterosexuality and separate themselves from men has raised obvious problems for those who regard themselves as heterosexual, and thus for feminism. Political lesbianism does not necessarily require sexual relationships between women, but it does entail an absence of sexual relationships with men. This leaves women who regard themselves as heterosexual without sexual relationships. If heterosexuality is defined as a patriarchal social institution in which men are able to impose their demands on women, rather than as a natural female selection, then heterosexual women should be able to change their social behaviour and become political lesbians. If this is the case, though, lesbianism could also be seen as a social institution which could eventually be changed in favour of a more balanced construction of heterosexuality — a view which is not generally proposed by political lesbians. Once heterosexuality has been condemned by feminists as an institution which serves to shore up patriarchy, it is difficult for feminists to argue for the pleasure of sexual relationships with men without appearing to condone male power over all women. But what might be separatism with sexual fulfilment for lesbians could be separation with celibacy for other women, a political platform which has a limited appeal.

The problem of how far biological considerations enter into explanations of sexual orientation and identity remains a theoretically contradictory and politically explosive area of feminism. The links between lesbian interests and feminist politics have been explored, although not without contention, but the question of why some women are lesbians and some are not is barely raised. As the various resolutions of this question are potentially extremely divisive of feminist politics, it is not one that has taken a central place in most of feminist thought. The merging of notions of lesbianism as a sexual identity for some women, or for some women some of the time, and lesbianism as a political identity for all women, further obscured this point. The whole question of how sexual identities are constructed and connected remains an area of feminism which needs to be further developed. We need to be much more critical of the sexual categories available to us in western cultures.

If we allow for the variable interaction of several causal factors we would also allow for different kinds of normal sexual identity and practice, and for historical and cultural variations in these patterns. If we took account of more complexity and contradiction in accounts of human sexual development it might be possible to understand sexual identity and choice using less rigid categories of sexual identity and sexual practices than the western categories of homosexuality, heterosexuality, and bisexuality. Feminist politics has given importance to the problem of how to allow people freedom to be themselves without oppressing others, whatever their sexual identity or however this identity was arrived at. But the nature of this freedom has become confused in attempts to define the construction of female sexuality in patriarchal societies as uniformly oppressive.

The current structure of western heterosexuality is oppressive for women, but the alternative of political lesbianism for all is also constraining. A problem with lesbian politics as feminist politics is, as Bonnie Zimmerman has argued (1984: 675–6), that:

> no adequate politics can be drawn from the experience of one segment of the community alone . . . Women of color, in particular, have pointed out that the notion of lesbian nation or lesbian tribalism is a white woman's dream and that an effective lesbian politics will have to be based on diversity and multiplicity.

Until the mid-1980s, there was very little public defence by feminists of heterosexual choice and pleasure, but plenty of undercurrents running through practical feminist politics (Abbott and Love 1972; LLOG 1984). The understandable reluctance of many feminists to air sexual-political differences in public meant that a serious flaw in feminist political strategy was given insufficient critical attention. Where sexual differences have proved divisive, attacks have been by women on each other, rather than on the problems of a political strategy derived from an inadequately explored notion of the social construction of sexuality.

In the most extreme versions of political lesbian separatism, a few feminists have suggested that men's oppression of women is so inevitably biologically determined that women should separate themselves not only from male sexual partners but also, eventually and painfully, from their sons, who are doomed to be their mothers' oppressors (Goodenough and Dogsbody 1984). This fatalistic argument is the logical conclusion of the biological determinist version of political lesbianism. It is one aspect of revolutionary feminist politics in which separation from male oppressors is taken as the political solution for all women. This political stance exposes the lack of a feminist theory of sexuality (Ardill and O'Sullivan 1986: 37). The majority of feminists do not appear to be convinced by explicit biological determinism, and accept the need to struggle with our sons rather than against them. Rejection of separation from men, however, leaves feminism with the intractable problem of how patriarchal society can be transformed, when most women are willingly enmeshed in more or less oppressive relationships with men (Hamblin 1982). The practical problems of how to separate personal heterosexual acts from the patriarchal relationships of heterosexuality have not been resolved (Friedman and Sarah 1982: 214).

It is undeniable that heterosexual sexual relations remain a focus of the exercise of male power over women, the site of much male violence and female misery. It can still be argued, though, that heterosexuality is susceptible to change. If the social bases of oppression in society can be changed, and if sexuality is largely socially constructed, then heterosexual relations do not *have* to be expressions of male power over women. If this is not the case, then arguments against heterosexuality must be based on assumptions of biological determinism, that is, that whenever males and females have sexual relations, the males must dominate. Separatism has been of political importance to those women able to choose it, for whom it has provided much-needed relief from patriarchal relationships, but feminist strategy could be to reclaim sexuality for women, rather than to endorse separatism as a total solution for every women. Valeska (1981: 30) suggests that the thinking behind lesbian separatism should be seen as a partial theory of oppression, rather than as a full programme of change: 'To end separatism we must end the causes of it.'

The political problem for feminism is, as lesbian feminists have pointed out, that sexual relations cannot be separated from other human relationships. It is not so much the mechanics of sex which oppresses women. It is men's power in the economy, in political life, and in the family. Patriarchal ideas legitimate men's use of sexual relations as an extension of their social, economic, and political power. Heterosexuality needs to be purged of male constraints on female choices, and male silencing of women's desires. We need to train our minds and bodies in terms of active enclosure and a range of sexual activity, rather than solely in terms of male penetration as 'normal'

CULTURE, IDEOLOGY, SEXUALITY

sex. Sara Scott (1987) has commented on feminists' apparent failure to seize the opportunity provided by the AIDS panic to enter into public debates on the social construction of male and female sexuality, sexual responsibility, and sexual practices. Feminist transformation of sexual power relations should allow women to live normal lives without sexual activity, but need not entail women *having* to give up sex.

Feminists' problems in approaching sexual divisions remain somewhat mystified. The oppression of lesbians and of so-called sexual deviants remains a serious problem, and one that is addressed in new-wave feminist work. Women's discussions of their sexual differences have led to considerable conflicts between feminists during the 1970s. The lesbian critique of heterosexuality has opened up new debates about power and about feminist conceptions of human nature, but women remain divided rather than united by their sexual differences. The majority of women develop attachments not only to male sexual partners but also to fathers, grandfathers, uncles, brothers, sons, nephews, cousins, male neighbours, workmates, and friends. I am not suggesting that these are ideal or egalitarian relationships. Plainly any such connections can be oppressive, but these attachments do have potential human value. It is the sources and abuse of power in society that need to be challenged and changed, rather than solutions being sought in the severing of relationships. Lesbianism remains a major empowering force within feminism, but most women remain identified as heterosexual, and so emotionally committed to men in ways which pose a continuing contradiction for feminist politics.

Sexual freedom — pornography and lesbian sado-masochism

Pornography is another thorny area for feminism. Feminist analysis has been very powerful in exposing pornography as a means of maintaining male domination of women. The position exemplified in the work of Andrea Dworkin (1981: 226) maintains that pornography *is* violence against women, and connects men's consumption of pornographic literature, films, videos, and live shows to active male violence against women and to the way in which women are treated in patriarchal societies. Wilson (1983: 166), however, rejects this view and sees pornography as revealing 'the disintegration of male sexuality under the pressures of a commoditising, fetishising culture'. It is paradoxical that the issue of male violence, which seemed to offer feminists their clearest example of women's common oppression, has provoked one of the most bitter divisions within feminism in recent years.

The importance of pornography in western society has raised a number of problems for the continuing unity of feminist activists. First, women are extensively employed (or coerced) as models, actresses, strippers, hostesses, and prostitutes in the pornography industry. This means that feminist political action against the industry is also action against working women. These women are generally highly exploited, but the economic alternatives open to them are likely to be very limited.

Second, there are disagreements over the closeness of the connections between the pornography industry and male violence to women. There are two arguments here. One is the argument over whether or not women should be seen as passive victims of male violence. The other is a philosophical argument about how causes of action can be discovered, comparable to debates on the consequences of watching violence on television. Although no feminists condone male violence towards women, new-wave feminists are divided on the causal connections between male violence and other social factors and on how women can act as agents rather than as victims. These arguments are complicated because of the range of material which can be defined as pornographic. Some feminists would want to discriminate between thoroughly erotic images and literature which women can enjoy, and wholly violent images of women being sexually abused, tortured, and murdered, many of which are not legally pornographic.

Third, there is the problem that practical action against pornography is effectively action which restricts women's freedom as well as men's. This raises questions about feminists' political strategies for restricting individual and sexual freedom. These are arguments about censorship, and questions about the grounds on which any one group can decide what other groups should do, read, see, or hear.

These problems were given substance in the United States through the consequences of an attempt by Andrea Dworkin and Catherine MacKinnon to counter pornography zoning laws in Minnneapolis in 1983 (Kelly 1985). Disagreement developed between Dworkin, MacKinnon, and their supporters and another group, the Feminist Anti-Censorship Taskforce (FACT). Whereas Dworkin and Mac-Kinnon opposed pornography because they believed it actively harmed women, FACT opposed anti-pornography legislation because its members did not accept that pornography directly instigated male violence (MacKinnon and Hunter 1985). They were more concerned that legislation would restrict women's sexual freedom (Rubin 1984).

These disagreements had surfaced earlier in the conference organized in 1982 at the Barnard College Women's Center. (Papers from this conference, together with a brief account of the problems encountered, have been published as Vance (1984) with an emphasis on the pleasure as well as the danger in sexuality for women.) In this instance, a conference with the theme of 'Towards a politics of sexuality' was actively opposed by radical and anti-pornography women's groups who objected to platforms being given to proponents of 'anti-feminist sexuality' (Vance 1984: 451). The views of such groups were roundly condemned by one of the participants, Gayle Rubin (1984: 302) who was also a member of FACT. 'The anti-pornography movement and its avatars have claimed to speak for all feminism. Fortunately, they do not. Sexual liberation has been and continues to be a feminist goal.' Commenting on the proceedings and conflicts of this conference, Elizabeth Wilson points out that Gayle Rubin has 'come out' as a sado-masochist (Wilson 1986: 205) which gives her a very different stance towards pornography from the anti-pornography campaigners. The anti-pornography stance is taken to indicate an unwillingness to allow women to explore sexual differences in the pursuit of pleasure.

These public differences between feminists are a gift to the mass media which can seize the opportunity to diminish feminism. Yet they do indicate serious differences in perceptions of women's rights to sexual freedom and the nature of women's sexuality. They also point to the contradiction between the need to protect women from male violence and women's right to sexual expression. These contradictions have led to alliances between feminist anti-pornography campaigners and the New Right. Introducing a discussion on these divisions in *Signs*, Freedman and Thorne (1984) point out the range of unresolved questions on power, violence, pleasure, and fantasy in sexuality which lie behind the debate on sexual freedom.

Most feminist work on sexual violence has been on the violent character of male sexuality. Relatively little attention has been given as yet to violence in female sexuality (Bower 1986). Although freedom of sado-masochistic expression is a need expressed by a small minority of women, and many women will be ignorant of it or shocked by it, the defence by some feminists of this sexual 'perversion' does raise general issues for feminism. Sado-masochism, like pornography, raises questions of how much sexual freedom should be allowed when violence towards others is incorporated into sexuality, and whether there can be an agreed feminist line on degrees of sexual freedom which meet women's sexual needs. Just because women who are feminists need sado-masochist fantasies or practices, it does not necessarily follow that sado-masochistic violence against women, even in clearly consensual relationships, has to be justified *as* feminist.[8]

Lesbian sado-masochism is a complex issue for feminism. Feminism cannot be disengaged from concern with sexuality, because sexuality is at the root of relationships between men and women. Sexuality is also at issue in relationships between women and women, but the liberation of women does not clearly hinge on the transformation of sado-masochistic practices. Feminists' lives, however separately they may be lived, cannot be wholly divorced from the cultures which constrain our thinking, needs, and experiences. Western culture is so deeply imbued with power differences and the legitimation of sexual violence against women that it is hardly surprising if these forces persist in relations between women. In the west, sexuality has come to incorporate hostility and domination rather than intimacy and pleasure, involving fetishism and the dehumanizing of sexual objects; anything can become eroticized (Hartsock 1983a: 156–7). Lesbian sado-masochism has attracted feminist criticism because it is an eroticization of power relations between women derived from patriarchal models such as master/slave, Nazi/Jew (Bellos 1984; Egerton 1984).

It is hard for women whose fantasies lie in other directions to empathize with sado-masochists. But we all need to recognize the violence in women, which feminism has often been reluctant to do. Women do not generally terrorize men, but they are capable of violence, particularly towards themselves, towards their children, towards those defined as of lesser value, such as prisoners, subordinate races, and servants. Women take part in warfare, guerilla movements, torture, and resistance struggles, and are perfectly capable of killing others. Bower (1986: 52) draws on the work of Melanie Klein to argue that we should acknowledge the violence within us:

> A female sadism with women as its object — which exists in its own right — is hardly an attractive idea. It has been comfortable for us to identify and attack this unattractive aspect of ourselves in men. By projecting our aggression on to men we attempt to maintain an illusion of innocence.

168

Feminists need to be realistic about the kinds of contradictions which shape women's lives. The kinds of intolerance that try to enforce one sexuality on all women may make sense if women are seen as a unified group ranged against their male oppressors. Yet prescriptivism does not seem to make sense in a struggle for the liberation of many different women. We need critical debate, tolerance and self-awareness about our varied sexual practices. It is illusory, however, to expect unanimity on where lines on what constitutes permissible sexual pleasure should be drawn. Feminism should enhance honesty and respect for women in sexual encounters and promote the view that any freedom must be qualified. None of us can do exactly what we like to others without consideration for the other, but feminism has not developed a unified moral code. Women need to resist patriarchal state interventions in the control of female sexuality but the idea of an agreed feminist political line on sexuality immediately encounters the differences between women.

Relations between women in which sado-masochism is an element should be seen as contradictory rather than as automatically beyond the feminist pale. Janice Raymond has pointed out (1987: 40) that lesbian sexuality is not necessarily politically feminist. But if sexuality is removed from lesbianism, the meaning of lesbianism lacks content. Sado-masochists are not necessarily feminists just because they are lesbian. Where women have a critical feminist consciousness, and also favour sado-masochistic practices, they are caught in contradictory relationships.

Sado-masochism is at the extreme edge of women's contradictory engagement in patriarchal sexual relationships. Any sexual relations between women in which power is an element are contradictory, but so are the more 'normal' relationships between heterosexual women and men, or between women of different races or classes. Rather than attacking women for their sexual preferences, or confining all sexual activity to egalitarian relationships between similar women, feminism needs more effective political strategies for countering the power relationships and abuses of power which shape and legitimate sexual power struggles.

OPPRESSION AND LIBERATION

This chapter might seem to be unreasonably inconclusive. It has looked for clear boundaries, for places to draw feminist lines on where differences between women become divisive, and it has failed to find them. When the contradictions of culture, ideology, and sexuality are added to the sources of division between women considered in earlier chapters, women's experiences of oppression, power, and choice can be seen to be very generally variable and contradictory. Women's conceptions of liberation, desire, personal freedom, and the significance of sexual activity are difficult to disentangle from male ideological dominance and from forms of oppression shared with men. Feminist transformation requires a revolution in cultural consciousness and conceptions of which groups we belong to. How we define belonging depends not only on what issues we are conscious of, but also on which standpoints we are able to adopt.

The attempt to develop collective political practices from new-wave feminism's theory of the oppression of women has encountered so many divisions between women that no clear political strategy for change is likely to emerge. This is the predicament that feminism is plunged into by the universal generalizations of early new-wave feminism. If we lose our universal generalizations, because women's oppression is only in part and in contradictory ways a universal phenomenon, then we lose the political focus of feminism and no clear feminist political strategy can be specified. New-wave feminism as a theory of women's oppression has arrived at an impasse.

DIVISIONS BETWEEN WOMEN — OUT OF THE IMPASSE

INTRODUCTION
TO PART THREE

There is of course no way out of an impasse. An impasse is by definition a position from which there is no escape. The only way that
feminism can be extricated from the political difficulties of a theory
of universal oppression is by reconsidering the relationship between
feminist theory and feminist political strategy. The way out of this
particular impasse is not to get into it in the first place.

In practice, feminism as a theory of the general oppression of women
has stimulated recognition of the power of numerous differences and
divisions between us. We have had to face the extent to which women
(including feminists) are drawn into power relationships with other
women. The idea of a shared sisterhood in opposition to men can be
reasserted as the basis of feminist politics, but only by concentrating
on selected aspects of women's experience, and by ignoring power and
privilege in the relations between women. We all have interests as
women in relation to those of men, but these are not necessarily the
same interests. The search for a common condition of oppression
inevitably ends in the fragmentation of feminist politics. In Part Three,
I attempt to avoid this impasse by looking at the problems of how to
derive effective political strategies from feminism's contradictory theory
and from women's contradictory lives.

Chapter Eight

FEMINISM AND LIBERATION

Divisions between women constitute both the theoretical and the political contradictions of feminism. If we are to avoid becoming trapped into contradictory strategies by our contradictory interests, then feminist politics has somehow to take these contradictions into account, and to offer some hope of resolution. This task is so daunting that it tends to be dealt with piecemeal and pragmatically. Around the world, and in many different ways, groups of women get on with what they see as the most immediate job at hand. This may be helping to set up a women's refuge, deciding to leave a violent husband, confronting a rapacious landlord alongside male peasants, defying apartheid, initiating a network, learning to read, setting up women's health groups, campaigning for more women politicians and engineers, fighting for a clean water supply, challenging sexism in a trade union, starting a women's co-operative, claiming land rights, picketing sex shops, or many, many other struggles. These diverse practical strategies have achieved many improvements in the quality of women's lives, and indeed have saved many women's lives, but they are improvements which can leave the divisions between women largely untouched.

We cannot afford wholly to abandon a sense of sisterhood. Without it there can be no basis for a feminist politics. But if feminism is to be more than a series of piecemeal reforms within the boundaries of our differences, we need to be able to develop feminist strategies for achieving women's liberation which connect women's struggles together.

CAN THE MEANS OF ACHIEVING WOMEN'S LIBERATION BE SPECIFIED?

While the goal of feminism is still women's liberation from oppression by men, few feminist texts address the practical problems of exactly how to liberate divided women. Since feminism deliberately has no hierarchical political organization, there is no authoritative source of political strategy. There cannot be a feminist 'party line' specifying the correct action to be taken in achieving liberation, because there is no 'party' which could lay down such specifications. Once the notion of universal sisterhood is challenged, there is no obvious basis on which a feminist political line could be drawn without encountering divisions between women. This means that there are no agreed principles for deciding what will or will not achieve liberation.

Maria Mies (1986: 217ff.), untypically, does follow her analysis of women's oppression in the context of world capitalism by a careful attempt to specify practical actions to be taken, particularly by western women, to transform the bases of oppression. These include a women's consumer boycott of luxury goods, goods which promote sexism, and goods made by exploited third-world women, and demands to return the control of their production to the underdeveloped countries. The consequent reduction of standards of living in the west would relieve women of their economic dependence on men, since all women and men would have to work for survival. Mies recognizes the considerable problems with these strategies: those of the third-world women who would be likely to die of starvation during the economic and political upheavals involved and the competition for survival between exploited women workers in different parts of the world. There would also be the problems of childcare that would remain wherever home and work are separated. Most western women would have little incentive to comply with these strategies, since they have so much to lose.

If, on the other hand, we start politically from the contradictory ways in which women are oppressed, and leave different groups of women to define their own political priorities, then political fragmentation and divergence follow, which again leaves feminism without any clear political strategy. The consequent dilemmas are outlined by Anne Phillips (1987: 149ff.) when she indicates the problems for feminist politics in situations where gender and class pull women towards different strategies for change. She says (161):

I would love to end with a long list of imperatives: to set out,

175

for example, how feminists should relate to a labour movement under stress; what they should say when they call for higher wages for nursery workers and are reminded that some men are low paid too; what they should do when resource constraints seem to impose a choice between more aid to the Third World and more money to social services; how they should respond to women's desire to stay at home with their children without sacrificing the demands of a woman's right to work. But on these and all the other choices that confront us, easy answers are not the solution — confusion may be the reality we have to force ourselves to face.

It seems to be the case that neither prescribing specific political strategies nor simply acknowledging our contradictions in oppression provides a clearly feminist political programme. It is hardly surprising that so many feminists have been cautious about specifying the exact means to achieve liberation when the relationship between feminist analyses of oppression and feminist political practices is so contradictory. Feminists have expressed quite different political positions, ranging from Marlene Dixon's expulsion of 'lesbian chauvinists' from the Democratic Workers Party (Dixon 1983: 196) to Andrea Dworkin's view (1983: 35) that women's common struggle 'has the power to transform women who are enemies against one another into allies'. Barbara Omolade, writing as a black woman in America, has said (1980: 256), 'no other group can demand liberation for us, because in doing so they take away our own capacity to organise and speak for ourselves.'

Feminism can only develop means of evaluating possible political strategies when women develop shared conceptions of liberation. It is this absence of shared visions of liberation which separates Dixon's political strategy from Dworkin's, and which leaves Omolade separated from white American feminists. It is the absence of a theory of liberation which leaves feminism without common political principles. Mies acknowledges (1986: 232) that her proposals do not overcome all the divisions of interest between western and third-world women which she documents, while Phillips's acknowledgement of divisions leads her to a regretful acceptance of the lack of common goals. Once we turn to asking what it is that women are to be liberated *to*, our present lack of shared conceptions of liberation becomes clear.

LIBERATION AND WOMEN'S POWER

The liberation of women, however it is defined, has to rest upon some notion of the empowerment of women. By empowerment I do not mean simply making individual women more confident and assertive, or more at peace with themselves. The goal of allowing women to exercise collective power entails a critical questioning of the nature of power and of how it is held by some rather than others. This means questioning and struggling against women's power over women as well as men's general domination.

Political divisions between feminists are not then matters of consciousness or language which can be resolved by the adoption of a correct sexual politics or a different discourse. Feminism has raised more broadly than before the problem of how people can live together in complex societies, without oppressing one another. Starting from the politics of gender, the development of new-wave feminism has made it clear that the domination of men over women cannot be altogether separated from other forms of domination. The disunity of interests between women cannot be resolved without also resolving more general antagonisms which divide people. Women cannot develop common political strategies while they have contradictory interests in class, race, and culture.

The notion of women having contradictory interests is a means of indicating sets of interests which cannot both or all be met within the forms of social organization which give rise to them. Societies dominated by racist ideologies and with discriminatory practices cannot meet the needs of subordinate races or ethnic groups for freedom from domination while also meeting the needs of the dominating groups to dominate. Societies which legitimate men's power over women cannot satisfy women's interest in freedom from men and also men's interest in continued domination. In any resolution of such contradictions of interest, the dominant group will lose power and its associated benefits.

This assumption that women's liberation entails tackling not just men's domination of women but also other forms of power has caused political divisions among feminists. The alternative is to go back to the idea that as women we do have some interests in common. It was these interests to which new-wave feminism was originally addressed. The problem here is that feminist analyses of oppression have made it clear that women's liberation cannot be confined to women's

177

common interests as women. If feminists turn from the immense task of tackling all sources of oppression, and refocus their sights on the narrower task of the transformation of sexual politics, then the divisions between women could worsen as relationships between women and men begin to improve. For example, changing white, male captains of industry into more caring, sharing parents, sexual partners, and househusbands could just result in more of their wives and daughters joining them as captains of industry. Changing sexual relationships between women and men will not address racism between women, or the imbalance of political and economic power between western and third-world women. More young men in Britain today 'help' their wives in the home and share in childcare than did their fathers and especially their grandfathers, but this noticeable shift in behaviour has not affected relations between women of different races or classes.

Feminism is not a total social theory that can explain the connections between different forms of oppression. But the problem remains that the oppression of women is, in complex and contradictory ways, enmeshed in all the other forms of oppression that people have created. The conclusion that feminists should then address all forms of oppression, as many have suggested, however, comes up against the problem that feminism has no clear theory of other forms of oppression from which practical strategies could be drawn. Feminism is a partial social theory, but to exercise power women need a total political practice. Feminist energy needs to go into making the connections between gender and other forms of oppression.

Since women themselves hold power over other women, empowering women in general will mean some women losing their power over others. Power is not a zero sum game in which one person's gain has to be another person's loss, but where women are divided by class, by race, or by global inequalities, then the empowerment of subordinate women will mean that, for example, dominant, white, heterosexual, middle-class women will lose their superiority in relation to other categories of women. Putting the strategy of empowerment into practice raises uncomfortable problems for feminists.

THE PROBLEMS OF CONNECTING FEMINIST THEORY AND PRACTICE

The aim of empowering women indicates the need for feminism to address all forms of oppression, but it does not indicate how this may be done. There are a number of problems in linking feminist theory and practice, of which three are particularly problematic. First, the material divisions between us which have been discussed in Part Two mean that women develop views of liberation from different standpoints. We do not only have standpoints as women, but also as members of different classes. Peasant women, black women, black working-class women, and lesbian middle-class women, do not have identical interests in liberation. As long as women have different class standpoints on these critical issues, and remain divided by race, culture, and sexuality, there can be no agreement on what constitutes liberation.

Second, conceptions of liberation also depend on what views we take of the relations between different sources of power, such as those between modes of production and patriarchal sex/gender systems. The development of feminism has shown that 'women' cannot be treated as a unitary category, and so the interrelations of the sources of divisions between women must be identified. But feminism has shown the difficulty of disentangling the connections between different sources of power. We also need to identify and to clarify the ideologies which legitimate different forms of power. The ways in which modes of production interact with systems of patriarchal and racial domination are exceedingly complex and considerably mystified. As long as these connections remain confused, it is difficult for women to organize their political priorities.

Third, there is a split running right through the feminist movement over whether or not women and men in a transformed society will still be essentially different from each other. This split is at root a disagreement over the social and political significance of our biological natures as women and men. This is not simply a theoretical problem on which we can agree to differ. The question of whether women and men are essentially different by nature raises practical problems for how relations between women and men can be changed. Although biological reductionism has been extensively criticized within feminism, the problem of biological difference refuses to go away.

The problem of standpoint

In this chapter I cannot lay down a collective blueprint for a liberated humanity which can resolve feminism's contradictions, although it is

179

tempting to try. Feminist politics will necessarily be constrained by the limits of women's experiences and the power of patriarchal ideology, and by women's affection, caring, and guilt felt towards those they live with. Women with different experiences will not give all aspects of transformation equal priority, so it is impossible to transcend completely the limitations of my class and racial standpoints. I can only try to clarify the obstacles which still lie between feminist theory and liberatory political practice. While our standpoints certainly limit our visions of liberation, this does not mean that we cannot have useful visions.

If we were to shift the focus of feminism away from the dead end of our divisions towards our diverse visions of liberation, we would have more positive goals to struggle for. Our separate standpoints could then become the bases of alliances created between divided women (Cain 1986). We need to make the bases of our differing standpoints clear, so that we can look beneath patriarchal, capitalist, and religious ideologies to see the standpoints of other women.

A consequence of building alliances between women, however, is that tackling oppression on many fronts means also struggling against women; for example, against right-wing western women who collude with men in trying to drive women back into the family and out of public life, except as cheap labour (Dworkin 1983), but also against Muslim fundamentalists and others who have defined their own version of liberation in serving men and God (Salman 1978). Feminists who define political aims for women have been put in the position of telling women things they do not wish to hear, and pronouncing judgement on women's definitions of their own experience and needs (McArthur 1984).

The alternative, of allowing women to define their own political aims from separated standpoints, however, undermines any general feminist politics. If different groups of women define their own versions of liberation without reference to each other, then no feminist evaluation can be made of the incompatible visions of liberation proposed. Loach (1987: 32) has pointed to the danger of aiming at popular democratic alliances across our differences which could end up as a 'bland political pluralism'. Feminism loses its political force if it is dissipated into an uncritical acceptance of women's experiences.

Feminists have stressed the importance of silenced women being able to express their own experience which patriarchal cultures ignore or devalue. But women may value their own experience without realizing where the ideas on which their beliefs and values rest come from (Sassoon 1987: 19). To adapt Gramsci's terms, men can dominate women by both leading and dominating. Women consent to marry men, indeed are eager to do so, and to some extent they have their interests met within marriage. They can gain fulfilment as mothers, considerable control over children and the domestic economy, and an assured position in society as married women (Campbell 1987; Koonz 1987).

Patriarchy need not, then, be a wholly negative experience for women. It only becomes perceived as negative by women when the concealed power relations between men and women become apparent, that is, when women take a critical stance towards patriarchy by standing back and seeing how the whole system works, and in whose interests. It is only when women think coherently and critically about the organization of society that they can see how patriarchy constrains their lives and divides them from each other, and they can choose to resist. Such critical understanding is particularly difficult to develop collectively when women have been personally successful in public life, or when women are excluded from public life and have little social value except as wives and mothers.

Most women do not recognize or resist patriarchal ideology, although they may organize around specific issues in their own interests. Resistance to feminist demystification of patriarchal ideology is, therefore, likely in a number of situations. First, resistance can be entrenched where the clear gains that women draw from male dominance are taken to outweigh their perceptions of the disadvantages. This can be the case, for example, where affluent housewives have their own incomes, cars, time, and resources to pursue leisure and pleasurable activities and control their time, or to take up careers. At the other end of the social scale, women are unlikely to be critical of patriarchal ideas and arrangements where men are so socially and economically disadvantaged that women feel little if any worse off than men. Resistance to the feminist demystification of patriarchal ideology also occurs where feminism is seen as the imposition of a dominant culture threatening to the traditions and customs of subordinate groups. This has been the basis for much third-world resistance to western feminism as a form of cultural colonialism.

The standpoints from which women understand the future, then, are not easily brought together. Depending on how far women develop a critical consciousness of their political interests, some feminist issues will be urgent, some may be of low priority, some will come up against barriers of class or racial interest, religion, or culture. In some cases it will seem more urgent to struggle with men than against them. Nevertheless, feminism *can* perhaps specify general areas of transformation without which women cannot be liberated. The boundaries of the transformations necessary to women's liberation can be defined. These boundaries are shaped, first, by the goal of ultimate liberation which is implicit in feminism, that is, by the notion that women can potentially live as sexual, productive, and reproductive beings without being oppressed by men. Second, given this general notion of liberation, boundaries are shaped by the connections in actual societies between systems of sex/gender, production, and reproduction, that is, by the ways in which people develop sexual, social, economic, and political relationships.

The problem of interconnected sources of power

If women are to live in societies where men do not in general have power over them and, conversely, in which women do not in general have power over others, or particular categories of others (such as servants, or ethnic minorities), then the interconnected bases of power have to be changed. Power lies:

1 in the way in which systems of production are organized;
2 in the ways in which sexuality and gender are socially constructed;
3 in the way in which reproduction is organized;
4 in the ways in which social differences (such as those of race or caste) become ranked;
5 in the ideological legitimation of the relationships to which these forms of power give rise.

The question of how far these are independent systems of power, and how far power in any given society can be reduced to production or patriarchy, has been reviewed in earlier chapters, but remains unclear because of the complexity and social diversity of human history.

The institutions of marriage, kinship, and family, which are central to social organization and so to the oppression of women, are conditioned in complex ways by all these sources of power. Families, households, and kinship structures are integrated into the organization of production, of sexuality, of gendered work, and of reproduction.

They are notable locations of ideologies which confirm women's specialized inferiority to men, and which legitimate male violence to women. Ideas of social difference are recreated through restrictions on intermarriage and the social definition of kinship ties. Marriage and the family cannot then be changed without taking into account the interconnections of different forms of oppression in any given society. It is not family life as such that gives rise to women's oppression, but the oppressive features of production systems, patriarchal sexuality, men's control of reproduction, and patriarchal ideologies which give rise to male-dominated families. Women who value themselves as mothers, and who identify themselves by their place in the family, would be less threatened by feminism if these connections were made clear. Feminism needs to offer women more than the abolition of the only place in society which is theirs.

The processes by which different sources of power help to shape social institutions are not simple one-way processes in which material conditions determine everything else. Families may be sites of women's oppression, but they are also sites of resistance and struggle, where women can promote changes, as current divorce rates in Britain and the United States show. The rise in divorce in Britain in recent years has been facilitated by changes in the law, but cannot be fully explained by changes in legal or economic conditions. Women have become active agents in ending marriages largely because of their resistance to patriarchal ideology. They no longer feel that they have to accept their lot as wives. Lack of corresponding changes in the organization of sexuality, gender, employment, domestic labour, and childcare, however, mean that very many of these divorced women suffer emotionally, and are compelled to live in poverty when their marriages end. The rate of remarriage is high.

Impoverished Indian peasant women, however, have shown that struggles against men in the domestic sphere can be linked to economic struggles shared with men (Kishwar and Vanita 1984: 41; Mies 1986: 231). When, on the other hand, women have limited opportunities to exercise choice, and have no other space of their own except family and domestic life, they can become very vulnerable to subordination through the acceptance of right-wing, patriarchal practices which grant them this space (Afshar 1984).

Changes in power relationships within families will depend on challenges to systems of production, notably capitalism, but also to socialist systems which are organized into male-dominated hierarchies

(Bengelsdorf 1985). Transformation of production would have wide-reaching implications for women. Changes in production would mean changes in the nature of ownership, and in the economic dependence of women on men. These changes would affect the organization of domestic labour and childcare. Ultimately the social organization of kinship and household structures would have to be transformed, limiting male power over women and ending the legitimacy of male violence. Changes in production would need to be linked with changes in the power relationships between races and ethnic groups which are enmeshed in both capitalism and socialism.

To be effective, transformation of production would need to be accompanied by more direct transformation of power relationships between women and men. This would be a sexual revolution in which male and female sexuality and gender would have to be reconstructed. Transformation of sex and gender would lead to changes in control of reproduction, and so to the reconstruction of parenthood and childrearing and to the transformation of kinship and household structures. These changes would transform the place of emotion in social life, and also conceptions of what is social and what is personal. Rethinking our notions of collective harm and benefit (Alderson 1988) would also help to undermine the present legitimation of male violence towards women.

The problem of difference

Feminists have become divided on the problem of whether or not women and men are essentially different, and so will remain different in classless, post-patriarchal societies. The alternative is that women and men could be merged into a single transformed humanity, comprising both sexes, with either one androgynous, shared sexual identity or several different sexual identities. Carolyn Heilbrun (1980: 265) has argued that androgyny is 'a necessary stopping place on the road to feminism. We must not claim more for it . . .'. This makes androgyny a way of conceiving that people could break out of the 'prison of gender' (258), with a transitional period in which differences are reconstructed. In some final state of sexual indifference, men would no longer dominate, exploit, or oppress women.

Underlying this conflict of opinion is the unresolved problem of how far the biological differences between women and men are socially significant. This is an issue which has split feminists more fundamentally than perhaps any other, and one which has immediate implications for feminist political strategies. If men are biologically determined to dominate women, then the political prospects for women's liberation are not of an active process of struggle for change but of a passive retreat into separate enclaves within unchangeable patriarchal societies. The affinity between sociobiology and right-wing politics should make feminists sensitive to the political dangers of biological determinism (Rose with Rose 1987). If men are natural rapists, are women no more than natural wombs?

Few feminists defend biologically determinist arguments explicitly, but there is some political divergence between strands of radical feminism which would avoid engaging men in common struggles with women and other strands of feminism which take co-operation with men as essential to women's liberation. It is important for the future of feminism that these arguments are not used to exclude either biological determinists or socialist feminists from women's struggles. Nor should the painful processes of living in patriarchal societies which lead women to adopt separatist strategies be underestimated. But I would suggest that challenging the idea of an unchanging, essential femininity and an essential masculinity creates an active prospect for women's liberation which is otherwise lacking.

The problem with this challenge, though, is that while biological determinism has been extensively criticized at the level of feminist theory, when women come to consider what a reconstructed sexuality might be like in practice, the loss of femininity through the abolition of essential difference begins to appear unattractive. Naomi Schor (1987) argues that we really have very little idea of what might replace the sexual differences between men and women which exist now. The danger of having no difference between men and women would be that this might allow men to define the single or plural sexualities that would emerge. Schor suggests (1987: 110) that women's position in western society is somehow connected through 'a tangled skein of mediation' to our anatomical differences. These connections remain obscure, but she comments (109) that 'some of the most sophisti- cated feminist theoreticians' who are writing today are showing a growing resistance to the idea of a world without male/female sexual difference. Women's valuing of at least some aspects of femininity, then, shows some common ground between today's 'sophisticated theoreticians' and the biologically determinist, radical feminists of the 1970s. This convergence is as contradictory as any other aspect of the connections between feminist theory and practice.

It is not at all clear where this debate over essential sexual difference leaves feminist political strategy. If rejecting biological determinism means rejecting the positive aspects of womanhood which feminists have identified, then women's liberation has much to lose. Women then have no special claim to nurturance, co-operation, caring, creativity, and closeness to nature. But if these characteristics can all be incorporated into new sexual identities, learned and shared with men, then there is little to be lost. The contradictions of femininity which have been revealed by psychoanalysis indicate the difficulties of generalizing about difference. Again it is difficult to develop connected strategies for liberation when this issue of biology remains unresolved. It does seem much more hopeful, though, to expand the positive aspects of what is now feminine into new feminine and masculine identities, rather than to preserve our present femininity through separation from men. The political problem for the future is how to safeguard as much difference as women need from men, rather than to treat femininity and masculinity as unchanging.

IMAGINING THE FUTURE

The problem with developing safeguards to deal with difference is that it is not very clear what sort of societies feminist transformation would give rise to. Any attempt to specify exactly what should be done encounters both serious disagreements and the danger of utopianism. It is clear that there cannot be one view of what women would like or indeed of what they would need. It is also clear that any form of liberation will be enormously difficult to achieve. Nor can minimum rights be specified as a solution, such as the right to a source of income, health, education, or civil rights, because such a list does not challenge the power base of the male-dominated hierarchies within which such needs are now met. Transformation of production, particularly in advanced capitalist societies, has quite clearly revolutionary implications, since it entails the overthrow of capitalism. Feminism needs, then, to develop some relationship to socialist transformation, which is very far from the intentions of many feminists, let alone from the mass of women who are not feminists.

More than a hundred years of socialist endeavour have produced adaptations of patriarchy rather than liberation for women. The post-revolutionary societies which now exist are far from ideal communist societies, but they do demonstrate some of the contradictions for women that remain after a revolution. Maxine Molyneux has argued (1981: 175) that socialist societies, in spite of their many differences, have adopted very similar policies towards women. In the USSR, China, and Cuba, the labour of childcare and domestic tasks remains largely in the hands of women or is taken over by the state. There is little evidence of the freedom of choice hoped for by Marx and Engels (1968: 45). The state has early access to children for purposes of political socialization and to women's labour for purposes of national development. Although most women are far better off than in their pre-revolutionary situations, the reproduction of social life and the social relations between men and women have been adjusted rather than transformed (Wolf 1985).

One way of approaching the problem is to abandon Marx's conception of socialism in favour of a broader, humanist conception of liberation. This version of social democratic socialism might appear to show some way out of feminism's dilemma. If liberation from oppression can be equally addressed by all, regardless of class or material interests, then women do not so clearly have to struggle with men and against other women. They can struggle at an ideological level to win people round to their vision of more equal, just, and democratic societies. The divisions between women which now exist, however, indicate that this let-out is less than satisfactory as the basis for effective feminist political strategy. Ellen Meiksins Wood's attack on the new 'true' socialism of the 1980s (Wood 1986: 1) characterizes social democratic socialism as having lost its revolutionary zeal by excising 'class and class struggle from the socialist project'. Class and work relations between people still need to be transformed and still divide women. 'True' socialism does not provide the new 'fundamental and enduring bonds' (198) which social transformation requires.

Feminists have given very little attention to alternatives to male-view socialism. Women's liberation requires something very different from existing forms of socialism, since socialism accepts considerable harm to its opponents in the course of a revolution and afterwards. Ideally women's liberation is not aimed at men as a class enemy, but at the economic, social, and sexual structures which allow men to dominate women and to legitimate this domination. Men are to be reconstructed through the empowering of women rather than to be rendered helpless or destroyed.

Feminism's relationship to socialism also raises the problem of how to deal with the conflict between personal liberty and collective freedom. The divisions in feminism over pornography and lesbian sado-masochism show this conflict in acute forms. It would be naive to suppose that we can expect opposing factions always to reach sisterly agreement. Socialism offers no guidance on the avoidance of factionalism. Women's liberation needs, then, to connect a range of related goals and political priorities, rather than to impose a specific or western view of individual women's autonomy. We need much more practical ideas on how to balance these oppositions, and how to make alliances.

Having a range of related goals, rather than one goal which every woman can agree on, is not intended as another way of saying that liberation can be achieved by leaving different groups of women to define their own goals. I have argued above that the sum of separated actions cannot achieve liberation spontaneously. A range of related goals does not specify exactly what women should be doing to achieve liberatory change, and does not provide agreed principles by which women can judge between the competing claims of some women against other women or between privileged women and oppressed men. Looking towards liberation is a shift in the emphasis of feminist effort rather than a resolution of irreconcilable contradictions.

CAN WOMEN'S LIBERATION BE ACHIEVED?

Realistically, the prospects of concerted political action by women in general to transform the world are limited. The extent to which the power of men has become entrenched at every level, including that of women's consciousness, is formidable. The way in which capitalist labour markets have developed, together with landholding and property rights more generally, has left the great majority of women in the most powerless sectors and also separated from each other. While workers in factories or on plantations might well be able to see their common interests both against capital and against men, women in service industries and caring professions, in clerical work, in part-time work, in sweatshops and brothels, as housewives, or workers for their households on the land, will have their interests considerably mystified.

Being realistic, though, need not discourage us from trying. Any evaluation of feminist theory should leave us clearer as to how we take action against women's oppression and for women's liberation. While the personal is political, the politics of gender are limited by the divisions between women. Practical consideration of how women can

188

be liberated can encourage us to think through the connections between gender and other forms of oppression. Since feminism does not provide a political manifesto to guide individual actions, we are left with the task of connecting our actions with those of others, in the light of our views on liberation.

I have tried to explore the contradictions within feminism as a social theory and as a political practice to show more clearly the range of problems that women have to deal with, and to think around ways in which divided women can look towards liberation. If we take feminism personally, we can clarify for each other our visions of liberation, and compare them with those of other women. Until the convergence and divergence of our views of liberation are made clear, we cannot connect our practical political struggles together in ways that will achieve liberation. These visions of liberation will not be personal idiosyncrasies if they emerge from collectivities of women, and from women's critical consciousness of their experience. Building collectivities and clarifying the goals of liberation will also clarify the major divisions between women, such as those between separatist activists and those who feel they need to work with men.

The position of men in relation to women's liberation remains contradictory. But the interrelations of men's and women's interests should not mean that all women have to engage in all forms of struggle. It does mean that separatist and non-separatist struggles need to be connected, rather than either of them being declared outside feminism. It is these connections that we need to work on, rather than devaluing each other in efforts to decide whose version of feminism is the purest. Separatism will continue to be politically necessary for some women and for some of the time. Given that women are living in patriarchal societies, and that the choices open to them at present may be very limited, then living and working separately and taking political action separately from men may be the only way in which some women feel they can practise feminism. What is needed is a political connection between women who choose separation and women who make other choices. It is only in this way that effective political links can be established between radical and marxist feminists, and between reforming and revolutionary activists.

If women's lives cannot be liberated without simultaneous transformation of gendered production systems, then men cannot sensibly be left out of women's struggles. This does not mean that women who want to lead separate lives should have to work with men. The contradictions of feminist theory show quite clearly the need to struggle with men while simultaneously struggling against them. Men have to be engaged in struggle against patriarchy as well as against other forms of oppression. This means men becoming conscious of the parts they play, through their normal and legitimate behaviour, in oppressing women. Since men have a great deal of power to lose, they also need to be educated in what benefits they could gain from the liberation of women.

The difficulties of getting men to change and to engage in struggle make it imperative that women forge some basis of unity between each other which men can recognize. Otherwise men will continue to exploit the differences between women, and women's emotional involvement with men. Robin Morgan (1983: 303) has warned that women fear and mistrust each other, as a consequence of men's contempt for women. In societies which encourage misogyny, women can project their self-contempt on to other women. Feminists need to make women's fears explicit in order to dispel them.

If we look towards liberation in our various ways, we should all be addressing the need to change the way power is organized in production, reproduction, sexuality, and domestic and family life, and to connect these struggles. We cannot expect to overcome altogether the contradictions of feminism, but we need not be downhearted if we can accept them and, in particular, if we can accept the many situations in which women clearly share interests with men. Feminists should not be depressed because the concept of 'woman' has been shown to be fragmented. This theoretical development simply shows that feminist theory is catching up with the 'reality' of women's diverse and contradictory interests.

Western middle-class feminists can build bridges to working-class and impoverished western women who are engaged in their own struggles. Women can connect the struggles of different racial and ethnic groups, as well as making links between western and other women. We have to be careful not to develop a feminist politics that can appeal to middle-class women in Calcutta, but can offer nothing to women who are trying to raise their children on a strip of pavement. Feminist consciousness has also to come from the pavements. Third-world women have to consider how far their strategies for change should differ from those developed in the west, while taking the divisions of class, ethnicity, culture, and sexuality into account. It is quite possible to have an international movement which has a shared goal of liberation but which tackles the obstacles in different ways in different situations. Third-world women can make their varied needs known, and make alliances with other women. We have to find new ways of making connections which avoid the 'power relationship of the "helper/helped dyad" that has characterised white women's relations with black women' (Sykes 1984: 64). We have to find new ways of redistributing resources through changes in economic power relations. Liberal women can become aware of the political limitations of attempts to rectify inequalities which do nothing to change power relationships. Marxist feminists can become aware of the perils of party hierarchies and of factionalism. Western radical feminists can make connections with third-world women's economic needs. Every politically active group of women can seek understandings and alliances with others, rather than develop exclusionary practices.

Alliances need not be permanent or formally organized (Wood 1986: 198), but women can put their efforts into networking and connecting with each other as a way of counteracting the moral prescriptivism and fragmentation which currently endangers feminist politics. We have to listen ever more carefully to other women, and to broaden our awareness of other women's lives.

Philosophical discussions of human liberation have tended to pay too little attention to the problem of how the work of cleaning toilets, collecting food, preparing and clearing up after meals, sick nursing, laundry, and childcare can best be organized in transformed societies. When standards of living are low, the work of fetching water, collecting fuel, finding and preparing food, and controlling dirt and faeces can be arduous, time-consuming, and socially unvalued. Even where standards of living are high, and domestic labour is less demanding, these essential and time-consuming tasks will remain. As these are the most basic tasks of any society, women's liberation demands some critical attention to who shall perform them and why. Limited demands for men to share in domestic labour and parenting do nothing to connect domestic labour and childcare to changes in work outside the home, to racial difference, or to the emotional implications of change.

Struggles for liberation will continue to be painful. Miller (1976: 129) comments, 'it is clear that as women now seek real power, they face serious conflict.' Liberation entails transformation of women's most intimate experiences, of sexuality, motherhood, and family life. The prospect of such changes can make liberation seem fearful and dangerous. Feminism needs to be much more sensitive than socialism

191

to the emotional harm of change, to people's fears of loneliness (Rosenfelt and Stacey 1987), and to the enormous emotional difficulties of living in complex societies.

The prospects for women's liberation in the short term may be limited because of the scale of the changes that are required, but the short term may be all that we have left. We cannot afford to be utopian about the prospects for women's liberation when we live in a precarious world system dominated by private greed, competitive individualism, economic crises, sectional and international violence, the growing poverty and indebtedness of much of the third world, environmental disaster, and the prospect of nuclear pollution and war. But women's potential power to make changes, once a feminist consciousness has emerged, has no historical precedent.

Major changes which do something to resolve women's conflicting interests are probably least likely in the stable states of the west, where capitalism, individualism and male domination are entrenched, and the population is ageing. It is more likely that feminist politics can succeed in some of the more volatile parts of the third world, where war and economic deprivation have forged new values, and new forms of collective consciousness, in young populations. We should perhaps be looking for feminist successes in Eritrea and Nicaragua rather than in Europe or America. This is not to argue that feminist work should stop elsewhere, or that western feminists should instruct others on how to achieve what we have failed to achieve ourselves. Feminist resistance and struggle will continue wherever women develop feminist political consciousness. By looking towards liberation, by connecting struggles against oppression, by imagining a less oppressive future for all women, and by making connections between women, we can perhaps avoid getting bogged down in our differences and begin to deal more effectively with the problems of living together.

NOTES

1 FEMINISM AS CONTRADICTION

1 Engels (1970). There have been a number of critical appraisals of Engels's work (Sacks 1975; Sayers *et al.* 1987).

2 WHAT IS WRONG WITH FEMINISM?

1 Biological reductionism is the reduction of explanations of social behaviour to explanation in terms of underlying biological factors. Biological determinism is the argument that social behaviour is caused, or determined, by biological factors. Biological essentialism is, in this context, the argument that men and women have essential sexual natures rooted in their genes which help explain differences in male and female social behaviour. In practice there has been little difference in the outcomes of these arguments which lead to such conclusions as, for example, that women are by nature more caring, more nurturing, more creative, more co-operative, and less aggressive than men.

2 Reasonably sympathetic accounts of Firestone's intentions and achievements are given in Jaggar (1983), Eisenstein (1984) and Spender (1985).

3 While their examples are taken from English history, it is not clear how far the argument is intended to be a general one. It could be argued that English industrial history had a number of peculiarities which were not common to other capitalist societies.

4 Capitalism is widely discussed in feminist work, but is rarely defined. In using the term I have in mind the following definition. All societies which are recognized as capitalist must have these characteristics:

    1 private ownership of productive forces based on exploitation;

    2 general production of commodities for a market (things to be bought and sold);

    3 separation of people who produce things from the things that they produce, and from the means of producing them (in contrast to peasants with their own land, or craft workers);

    4 labour power as a commodity (that aspect of people's labour which is bought and sold for wages, as opposed to labour on

things which people produce and control themselves);
5 creation of surplus value. Surplus value is created when workers produce more value than they consume as wages, and this surplus is appropriated by a class of capitalists, as the basis of the accumulation of capital;
6 the expanded reproduction of capital. The continuation of the capitalist mode of production in any society depends on the continuous expansion of the processes of production and accumulation;
7 the operation of the economy and the political control of the economy are *apparently*, but not essentially, separated.

Any society which is dominated by the characteristics listed above will be a capitalist society. But each historical society will be a unique configuration of economic, political, and social factors. No two capitalist societies can, therefore, be exactly the same, and every capitalist society is in a process of change. The capitalist mode of production is an abstract notion and cannot be observed as such.

3 MAKING FEMINISM BELIEVABLE

1 Some of the ideas in this chapter appeared in an earlier version as Ramazanoglu (1987b).
2 See Kuhn (1970), Lakatos and Musgrave (1970), and Ravetz (1971) on the social character of science as produced by scientists in societies.
3 Social theorists are not agreed on how far social structures and relationships exist independently of people's understanding of them. Feminists by and large have taken a realist view. That is, they argue that the social, political, economic, emotional, and ideological mechanisms which maintain relationships of domination and subordination between men and women do 'really' exist, whether subordinated women know this or not. It is then the task of feminism to reveal these structures and processes beneath the appearance of the natural inferiority of women, and to change them (Cain 1986). This view of reality need not be simplistic. As Jane Flax has said (1987: 643), 'if we do our work well, "reality" will appear even more unstable, complex and disorderly than it does now.' This realist position has been criticized chiefly by those influenced by French post-structuralist philosophy. In the post-structuralist view, the reality of sexuality, production, or social relationships cannot be distinguished from the concepts with which people think about them. This view allows for multiple realities in social life, and so cannot give feminism any particular political direction.
4 Harding (1986) and other authors have used the term androcentrism as a way of characterizing knowledge which takes for granted that men are normally and naturally at the centre of the social world.
5 Social scientists, particularly sociologists and anthropologists, have developed methods of producing knowledge of society which do not

assume that the social scientist is objective. Nevertheless these methods still assume that the subjectivity of the social scientist can be controlled by reason. The control of passions is seen as intensely problematic, but still necessary.

4 WOMEN AGAINST MEN — FEMINIST KNOWLEDGE OF WOMEN'S OPPRESSION

1 One British example of such struggle is the independent political action taken by miners' wives during the coalminers' long strike in 1984–5 (Stead 1987).
2 These ideas were new in the context of new-wave feminism but the debates on reproduction and motherhood had existed previously, for example in the work of Simone de Beauvoir (1953).
3 Although much criticized as limited and ethnocentric, Betty Friedan's early study of dissatisfied middle-class American housewives exposed motherhood as less than fulfilling even for the affluent (Friedan 1965). Several novelists have done so with greater bitterness.
4 This explanation is teleological in that it explains the cause of housework by its effects; the benefits of housework for capitalism. The nature of housework is taken for granted rather than explained.
5 This contradiction is identified in contributions to the 'No nukes' section of Kanter et al. (1984).
6 A mass demonstration of women encircled the American air base at Greenham Common, in England, in 1982, before the establishment of American Cruise missiles at the base. There have been various mass demonstrations by women (some including men) since, but the Greenham Common protest is sustained by small camps of women protesters and their supporters who have survived outside the base ever since. These women have insisted on a women-only protest, and have survived physical assault, sexual and legal harassment, severe winters, and fluctuating support from the wider women's movement (Lowry 1983; Finch et al. 1986; Soper and Assiter 1983; Harford and Hopkins 1984).

5 WOMEN AGAINST WOMEN — CLASS, WORK, POWER

1 For a definition of capitalism see chapter 2, note 4.
2 The notion of intransitive is taken from Bhaskar (1979) to denote social objects, such as human relationships, which exist whether people are aware of them or not, as opposed to transitive objects which are constituted by people's knowledge of them.

6 WOMEN AGAINST WOMEN — NATIONALITY, ETHNICITY, RACE

1 The term black here should be qualified to include western women

who define themselves as black, but also those who define themselves
as women of colour, Asian, Latina, as members of ethnic minorities
in the west, or as women of the third world. Boundaries remain
unclear and, as Anthias and Yuval-Davis (1983) and contributors to
Phizacklea (1983) have pointed out, ethnic-minority women in the
west are oppressed in quite specific ways. Jewish and Irish women
also suffer from discrimination but not in the same way as black
women. The categories of inferior and superior are not static and are
continually contested.

7 WOMEN AGAINST WOMEN — CULTURE, IDEOLOGY, SEXUALITY

1 Rigoberta Menchu (1984) gives a moving account of how she had to
break out of the linguistic isolation resorted to by the Quiche Indians
in an effort to preserve their culture. She overcame her aversion to
learning Spanish (seen as the language of the enemy) and to revealing
the secrets of Quiche culture in order to seek support for the Quiche
cause from sympathizers outside Guatemala.
2 Clitoridectomy entails cutting off at least part of the clitoris, and may
include removing the whole organ and some surrounding tissue.
Infibulation goes further, as after removal the woman is sewn up,
leaving only a small hole for the passage of menstrual blood and
urine. She must be cut open to allow intercourse with her husband,
and for childbirth (Morgan 1984: 764–6; Thiam 1986).
3 Female circumcision predates Islam, and has also been practised by
non-Moslem peoples, but over the centuries it has become legitimated
by Islam as an Islamic practice which complicates women's struggles
against it.
4 Althusser (1971: 190) defined familial ideology as 'the ideology of
paternity-maternity-conjugality-infancy and their interactions'.
5 Toynbee's interview with Salihbegovic does not elucidate this position,
but ridicules it from the perspective of western culture.
6 The statement from which this quotation is taken was part of the
process of recognizing a split in the British National Abortion
Campaign. It was decided at the time that NAC should continue as a
single-issue movement for abortion rights, but that a separate
reproductive rights campaign should also be launched to address
broader issues (NAC 1984: 236).
7 Prior to modern methods of contraception, and still existing alongside
them, women have developed over the centuries various practical and
cultural means of limiting their fertility, but these tend to give women
less personal choice than modern methods of contraception.
8 For arguments in favour of sado-masochism see Califia (1981).
Comments on the debate are given in France (1984). The argument
that such practices are legitimated by consent is problematic. On these
grounds marriage could also be legitimated in its present forms, since
the majority of women marry willingly.

BIBLIOGRAPHY

Abbott, P. and Sapsford, R. (1987), *Women and Social Class*, London, Tavistock.

Abbott, S. and Love, B. (1972), 'Is women's liberation a lesbian plot?', in Gornick and Moran (1972).

Abel, E. and Abel, E.K. (1983), *Women, Gender and Scholarship: the SIGNS Reader*, Chicago, University of Chicago Press.

Acker, J., Barry, K., and Essevold, J. (1983), 'Objectivity and truth: problems in doing feminist research', *Women's Studies International Forum*, 6, 4: 423-35.

Adlam, D. (1979), 'The case against capitalist patriarchy', *M/F*, 3: 83-102.

Afkhami, M. (1984), 'Iran: a future in the past — the "prerevolutionary" women's movement', in Morgan (1984).

Afshar, H. (1984), 'Muslim women and the burden of ideology', *Women's Studies International Forum*, 7, 4: 247-50.

Afshar, H. (ed.) (1985), *Women, Work and Ideology in the Third World*, London, Tavistock.

Agosin, M. (1984), 'Chile: women of smoke', in Morgan (1984).

Alderson, P. (1988), 'Informed consent: problems of parental consent to paediatric cardiac surgery', unpublished PhD thesis, London, Goldsmiths' College.

Althusser, L. (1969), *For Marx*, London, Allen Lane.

Althusser, L. (1971), *Lenin and Philosophy and Other Essays*, New York, Monthly Review Press.

Amos, V. and Parmar, P. (1984), 'Challenging imperial feminism', *Feminist Review*, 17: 3-19.

Anthias, F. and Yuval-Davis, N. (1983), 'Contextualizing feminism — gender, ethnic and class divisions', *Feminist Review*, 15: 62-75.

Ardill, S. and O'Sullivan, S. (1986), 'Upsetting an applecart: difference, desire and lesbian sadomasochism', *Feminist Review*, 23: 31-57.

Arditti, R., Duelli Klein, R., and Minden, S. (eds) (1984) *Test-Tube Women: What Future for Motherhood?*, London, Pandora Press.

Assiter, A. (1983), 'Womenpower and nuclear politics', in Thompson (1983).

197

Badri, A.E. (1984), 'Sudan: women's studies — and a new village store', in Morgan (1984).

Balbo, L. (1987), 'Crazy quilts: rethinking the welfare state debate from a woman's point of view', in Sassoon (1987).

Barrett, M. (1980), *Women's Oppression Today*, London, Verso.

Barrett, M. (1984), 'Women's oppression: a reply', *New Left Review*, 146: 123–8.

Barrett, M. (1987), 'The concept of difference', *Feminist Review*, 26: 29–41.

Barrett, M. and McIntosh, M. (1979), 'Christine Delphy: towards a materialist feminism?', *Feminist Review*, 1: 95–106.

Barrett, M. and McIntosh, M. (1982), *The Anti-Social Family*, London, Verso.

Bassnett, S. (1986), *Feminist Experiences: The Women's Movement in Four Cultures*, London, Allen & Unwin.

de Beauvoir, S. (1953), *The Second Sex*, trans. H.M. Parshley, New York, Knopf.

Beechey, V. (1978), 'Women and production: a critical analysis of some sociological theories of women's work', in Kuhn and Wolpe (1978).

Beechey, V. (1983), 'What's so special about women's employment? A review of some recent studies of women's paid work', *Feminist Review*, 15: 23–45.

Beechey, V. (1985), 'Familial ideology', in V. Beechey and J. Donald (eds), *Subjectivity and Social Relations*, Milton Keynes, Open University Press.

Bellos, L. (1984), 'For lesbian sex, against sado-masochism', in Kanter *et al.* (1984).

Bengelsdorf, C. (1985), 'On the problem of studying women in Cuba', *Race and Class*, 27, 2: 35–50.

Benhabib, S. and Cornell, D. (eds) (1987), *Feminism as Critique*, Cambridge, Polity Press.

Benston, M. (1970), 'The political economy of women's liberation', in L.B. Tanner (ed.), *Voices from Women's Liberation*, New York, Signet.

Berer, M. (1986), 'Breeding conspiracies: FINNRAGE reviewed', *Trouble and Strife*, 9: 29–35.

Bhabha, J., Klug, F., and Shutter, S. (eds) (1985), *Worlds Apart: Women under Immigration and Nationality Law*, London, Pluto.

Bhaskar, R. (1978), *A Realist Theory of Science*, 2nd edn, Brighton, Harvester.

Bhaskar, R. (1979), *The Possibility of Naturalism*, Brighton, Harvester.

Bhavnani, K.-K. and Coulson, M. (1986), 'Transforming socialist-feminism: the challenge of racism', *Feminist Review*, 23: 81–92.

Birke, L. (1986), *Women, Feminism and Biology: The Feminist Challenge*, Brighton, Wheatsheaf.

Black Women for Wages for Housework (1988), 'Black women networking', *WEA Women's Studies Newsletter*, 8 (n.s.): 14–15.

Bleier, R. (1984), *Science and Gender: A Critique of Biology and its Theories on Women*, New York, Pergamon.

Bleier, R. (ed.) (1986), *Feminist Approaches to Science*, New York, Pergamon.

Bower, M. (1986), 'Daring to speak its name: the relationship of women to pornography', *Feminist Review* 24: 40–56.

Bowles, G. and Duelli Klein, R. (eds) (1983), *Theories of Women's Studies*, London, Routledge & Kegan Paul.

Brenner, J. and Ramas, M. (1984), 'Rethinking women's oppression', *New Left Review*, 144: 33–71.

Brittan, A. and Maynard, M. (1984), *Sexism, Racism and Oppression*, Oxford, Blackwell.

Brixton Black Women's Group (1984), 'Black feminism', in Kanter *et al.* (1984).

Brown, P. and Jordanovna, L. (1982), 'Oppressive dichotomies: the nature/culture debate', in E. Whitelegg (ed.), *The Changing Experience of Women*, Oxford, Martin Robertson in association with the Open University.

Brownmiller, S. (1975), *Against Our Will: Men, Women and Rape*, New York, Bantam Books.

Bruegel, I. (1979), 'Women as a reserve army of labour: a note on recent British experience', *Feminist Review*, 3: 12–23.

Bryan, B., Dadzie, S., and Scafe, S. (1985), *The Heart of the Race*, London, Virago.

Bujra, J. (1978), 'Female solidarity and the sexual division of labour', in P. Caplan and J. Bujra, *Women United, Women Divided*, London, Tavistock.

Bujra, J. (1986), 'Urging women to redouble their efforts', in C. Robertson and I. Berger, *Women and Class in Africa: Class, Gender and Capitalist Transformation in Africa*, New York, Africana Publishing House.

Bunch, C. (1981), 'Not for lesbians only', in The *Quest* Book Committee, *Building Feminist Theory: Essays from Quest*, New York, Longman.

Burman, S. (ed.) (1979), *Fit Work For Women*, London, Croom Helm.

Butler, J. (1987), 'Variations of sex and gender', in Benhabib and Cornell (1987).

Cain, M. (1986), 'Realism, feminism, methodology and law', *International Journal of the Sociology of Law*, 14: 255–67.

Califia, P. (1981), 'Feminism and sadomasochism', *Heresies*, 3, 4, issue 12.

Cameron, B. (1983), 'Gee, you don't seem like an Indian from the reservation', in Moraga and Anzaldua (1983).

Cameron, D. (1985), *Feminism and Linguistic Theory*, London, Macmillan.

Campbell, B. (1984), *Wigan Pier Revisited: Poverty and Politics in the 80s*, London, Virago.

Campbell, B. (1987), *The Iron Ladies: Why Do Women Vote Tory?*, London, Virago.

Caplan, P. (ed.) (1987), *The Cultural Construction of Sexuality*, London, Tavistock.

Carby, H. (1982), 'White woman listen: black feminism and the

199

boundaries of sisterhood', in Centre for Contemporary Cultural Studies, *The Empire Strikes Back*, London, Hutchinson.

Carmen, Gail, Shaila and Pratibha (1984), 'Becoming visible: black lesbian discussions', *Feminist Review*, 17: 53–72.

Carroll, B.A. (1976), *Liberating Women's History*, Urbana, University of Illinois Press.

Chapman, F.S. (1987), 'Executive guilt: who's taking care of the children?', *Fortune International*, 4: 18–25.

Chen, M. (1986), 'Poverty, gender and work in Bangladesh', *Economic and Political Weekly*, 21, 5: 217–22.

Chester, G. (1984), 'Why the Jewish question must be answered by feminists', in Kanter *et al.* (1984).

Chodorow, N. (1978), *The Reproduction of Mothering: Psychoanalysis and the Sociology of Gender*, Berkeley, University of California Press.

Clark, W. (1982), 'The dyke, the feminist and the devil', *Feminist Review*, 11: 30–9.

Clarke, C. (1983), 'Lesbianism: an act of resistance', in Moraga and Anzaldua (1983).

Cock, J. (1980), *Maids and Madams*, Johannesburg, Ravan Press.

Cockburn, C. (1983), *Brothers: Male Dominance and Technological Change*, London, Pluto.

Cockburn, C. (1985), *Machinery of Dominance: Women, Men and Technical Know-How*, London, Pluto.

Cockburn, C. (1986), 'The relations of technology', in Crompton and Mann (1986).

Cohn, C. (1987), 'Sex and death in the rational world of the defense intellectuals', *Signs*, 12, 4: 687–718.

Collette, C. (1987), 'Taking the lid off: socialist feminism in Oxfordshire', *Feminist Review*, 26: 74–81.

Collins, M. (1985), 'Silenced: black women as domestic workers', *Trouble and Strife*, 6: 15–16.

Combahee River Collective (1983), 'A black feminist statement', in Moraga and Anzaldua (1983).

Comer, L. (1974), *Wedlocked Women*, Leeds, Feminist Books.

Corea, G. (1985), *The Mother Machine*, New York, Harper & Row.

Coulson, M. (1980), 'The struggle for femininity', in Gay Left Collective (1980).

Coveney, L., Jackson, M., Jeffreys, S., Jaye, L., and Mahony, P. (1984), *The Sexuality Papers: Male Sexuality and the Social Control of Women*, London, Hutchinson.

Coward, R. (1983), *Patriarchal Precedents: Sexuality and Social Relations*, London, Routledge & Kegan Paul.

Coward, R. (1984), *Female Desire: Women's Sexuality Today*, London, Paladin.

Coward, R., Lipshitz, S., and Cowie, E. (1978), 'Psychoanalysis and patriarchal structures', in *Papers on Patriarchy*, Brighton, Women's Publishing Collective.

Croll, E. (1986), 'Domestic service in China', *Economic and Political Weekly*, 21, 6: 256–60.

Crompton, R. and Mann, M. (eds) (1986), *Gender and Stratification*, Cambridge, Polity Press.

Currie, D. (1986), 'Reproductive decision-making as reproductive strategies: a case study', paper given to the British Sociological Association sexual divisions study group.

Dahlerup, D. (ed.) (1986), *The New Women's Movement*, London, Sage.

Daniels, A.K. (1976), 'Feminist perspectives in sociological research', in Millman and Kanter (1976).

Daly, M. (1973), *Beyond God the Father: Toward a Philosophy of Women's Liberation*, Boston, Beacon Press.

Daly, M. (1978), *Gyn/Ecology: The Metaethics of Radical Feminism*, Boston, Beacon Press.

Davenport, D. (1983), 'The pathology of racism: a conversation with third world wimmin', in Moraga and Anzaldua (1983).

Davis, A. (1982), *Women, Race and Class*, London, Women's Press.

Delmar, R. (1986), 'What is feminism?', in Mitchell and Oakley (1986).

Delphy, C. (1974), 'The main enemy', in Delphy (1984).

Delphy, C. (1984), *Close To Home: A Materialist Analysis of Women's Oppression*, London, Hutchinson.

Delphy, C. and Leonard, D. (1986), 'Class analysis, gender analysis and the family', in Crompton and Mann (1986).

Dietrich, G. (1986), 'Women's movement and religion', *Economic and Political Weekly*, 21, 4: 157–60.

Dixon, M. (1983), *The Future of Women*, San Francisco, Synthesis.

Draper, H. and Lipow, A.G. (1976), 'Marxist women versus bourgeois feminism', in R. Miliband and J. Savile (eds), *Socialist Register 1976*, London, Merlin Press.

Duchen, C. (1986), *Feminism in France: From May '68 to Mitterrand*, London, Routledge & Kegan Paul.

Dworkin, A. (1981), *Pornography: Men Possessing Women*, London, Women's Press.

Dworkin, A. (1983), *Right Wing Women: The Politics of Domesticated Females*, London, Women's Press.

Edgerton, L. (1986), 'Public protest, domestic acquiescence: women in Northern Ireland', in Ridd and Callaway (1986).

Edholm, F., Harris, O., and Young, K. (1977), 'Conceptualising women', *Critique of Anthropology*, 9 and 10: 101–30.

Edmond, W. and Fleming, S. (1975) *All Work and No Pay: Women, Housework and the Wages Due*, Bristol, Falling Wall Press.

Edwards, A. (1987), 'Male violence in feminist theory: an analysis of the changing conceptions of sex/gender violence and male domination', in Hanmer and Maynard (1987).

Edwards, S.S.M. (1987), ' "Provoking her own demise": from common assault to homicide', in Hanmer and Maynard (1987).

Egerton, J. (1984), 'The goal of a feminist politics . . . the destruction of male supremacy or the pursuit of pleasure?, in Kanter *et al.* (1984).

Eisenstein, H. (1984), *Contemporary Feminist Thought*, London, Allen & Unwin.

Eisenstein, Z. (1979), *Capitalist Patriarchy and the Case for Socialist Feminism*, New York, Monthly Review Press.

Elson, D. and Pearson, R. (1981), 'Nimble fingers make cheap workers: an analysis of women's employment in third world export manufacturing', *Feminist Review*, 7: 87–107.

Engels, F. (1970), 'The origin of the family, private property and the state', in K. Marx and F. Engels, *Selected Works*, vol. 3, Moscow, Progress Publishers.

Ettorre, E.M. (1990), *Lesbians, Women and Society*, London, Routledge & Kegan Paul.

Fahmy-Eid, N. and Laurin-Frenette, N. (1986), 'Theories of the family and family/authority relationships in the educational sector in Quebec and France 1850–1960', in Hamilton and Barrett (1986).

Fairweather, E., McDonough, R., and McFadyean, M. (1984), *Only the Rivers Run Free — Northern Ireland: The Women's War*, London, Pluto Press.

Federici, S. (1975), *Wages Against Housework*, Bristol, Falling Wall Press.

Feminism and Nonviolence Study Group (1983), *Piecing It Together: Feminism and Nonviolence*, Buckleigh, Feminism and Nonviolence Study Group.

Feminist Anthology Collective (1981), *No Turning Back: Writings from the Women's Liberation Movement 1975–80*, London, Women's Press.

Ferguson, A. and Folbre, N. (1981), 'The unhappy marriage of patriarchy and capitalism', in Sargent (1981).

Fernea, E.W. (1985), *Women and the Family in the Middle East: New Voices of Change*, Austin, University of Texas Press.

Fesl, E. (1984), untitled article, in Rowland (1984).

Finch, S. and others from Hackney Greenham Groups (1986), 'Socialist-feminists and Greenham', *Feminist Review*, 23: 93–100.

Firestone, S. (1979), *The Dialectic of Sex*, London, Women's Press.

Flax, J. (1983), 'Why has the sex/gender system become visible only now?', in Harding and Hintikka (1983).

Flax, J. (1987), 'Postmodernism and gender relations in feminist theory', *Signs*, 12, 4: 621–43.

Foucault, M. (1979), *The History of Sexuality*, vol. 1, London, Allen Lane.

Fox-Genovese, E. (1982), 'Placing women's history in history', *New Left Review*, 133: 5–29.

France, M. (1984), 'Sadomasochism and feminism', *Feminist Review*, 16: 35–42.

Freedman, E.B. and Thorne, B. (1984), 'Introduction to the "feminist sexuality debates"', *Signs*, 10, 1: 102–5.

Friedan, B. (1965), *The Feminine Mystique*, Harmondsworth, Penguin.

Friedman, S. and Sarah, E. (1982), *On the Problem of Men*, London, Women's Press.

Gaitskell, D., Kimble, J., Maconachie, M., and Unterhalter, E. (1983), 'Class, race and gender: domestic workers in South Africa', *Review of African Political Economy*, 27/28: 86–108.

Gardiner, J. (1976), 'Political economy of domestic labour in capitalist society', in D. Barker and S. Allen (eds), *Dependence and Exploitation in Work and Marriage*, London, Longman.

Gay Left Collective (1980), *Homosexuality, Power and Politics*, London, Allison & Busby.

Ghandy, A. and Chaudhry, N. (1984), 'Towards a day when there will be no servants', in Kishwar and Vanita (1984).

Gilroy, P. (1987), *There Ain't No Black in the Union Jack*, London, Hutchinson.

Glendinning, C. and Millar, J. (1987), *Women and Poverty in Britain*, Brighton, Wheatsheaf.

Goodenough, G. and Dogsbody, E. (1984), 'On bringing up boys', in Kanter *et al.* (1984).

Gornick, V. and Moran, B.K. (1972), *Woman in Sexist Society: Studies in Power and Powerlessness*, New York, Mentor.

Gramsci, A. (1971), *Selections from the Prison Notebooks*, ed. Q. Hoare and G. Nowell Smith, London, Lawrence & Wishart.

Griffin, S. (1978), *Woman and Nature: The Roaring Inside Her*, New York, Harper & Row.

Griffin, S. (1982), *Made From This Earth: Selections From Her Writing*, London, Women's Press.

Grimshaw, J. (1986), *Feminist Philosophers*, Brighton, Wheatsheaf.

Hamblin, A. (1982), 'What can one do with a son? Feminist politics and male children', in S. Friedman and E. Sarah (1982).

Hamilton, R. (1978), *The Liberation of Women: A Study of Patriarchy and Capitalism*, London, Allen & Unwin.

Hamilton, R. and Barrett, M. (eds) (1986), *The Politics of Diversity: Feminism, Marxism and Nationalism*, London, Verso.

Hanmer, J. and Allen, P. (1980), 'Reproductive engineering; the final solution?', in Brighton Women and Science Group (1980), *Alice Through the Microscope: The Power of Science over Women's Lives*, London, Virago.

Hanmer, J. and Maynard, M. (1987), *Women, Violence and Social Control*, London, Macmillan.

Hanmer, J. and Saunders, S. (1984), *Well-Founded Fear: A Community Study of Violence to Women*, London, Hutchinson.

Harding, S. (1986), *The Science Question in Feminism*, Milton Keynes, Open University Press.

Harding, S. and Hintikka, M.B. (eds) (1983), *Discovering Reality: Feminist Perspectives on Epistemology, Metaphysics, Methodology, and Philosophy of Science*, Dordrecht, D. Reidel.

Harford, B. and Hopkins, S. (eds) (1984), *Greenham Common Women at the Wire*, London, Women's Press.

Hartmann, H. (1981), 'The unhappy marriage of Marxism and

feminism: towards a more progressive union', in Sargent (1981).

Hartsock, N.C.M. (1983a), *Money, Sex and Power: Toward a Feminist Historical Materialism*, London, Longman.

Hartsock, N.C.M. (1983b), 'The feminist standpoint: developing the ground for a specifically feminist historical materialism', in Harding and Hintikka (1983).

Hearn, J. (1987), *The Gender of Oppression: Men, Masculinity and the Critique of Marxism*, Brighton, Wheatsheaf.

Heilbrun, C.G. (1980), 'Androgyny and the psychology of sex differences', in H. Eisenstein and A. Jardine (eds), *The Future of Difference*, Boston, G.K. Hall.

Hellman, J.A. (1987), *Journeys Among Women: Feminism in Five Italian Cities*, Cambridge, Polity Press.

Herzog, M. (1980), *From Hand to Mouth: Women and Piecework*, Harmondsworth, Penguin.

Heyzer, N. (1986), *Working Women in South-East Asia: Development, Subordination and Emancipation*, Milton Keynes, Open University Press.

Hochschild, A.R. (1976), 'The sociology of feeling and emotion: selected possibilities', in Millman and Kanter (1976).

hooks, b. (1982), *Ain't I a Woman? Black Women and Feminism*, London, Pluto Press.

hooks, b. (1984), *Feminist Theory From Margin To Center*, Boston, South End Press.

Hull, G., Bell Scott, P., and Smith, B. (eds) (1982), *All the Women are White, All the Blacks are Men But Some of Us are Brave*, Old Westbury, New York, Feminist Press.

Hunt, P. (1980), *Gender and Class Consciousness*, London, Macmillan.

Hussein, F. (ed.) (1984), *Muslim Women*, London, Croom Helm.

Hussein, F. and Radwan, K. (1984), 'The Islamic revolution and women: quest for the Quranic model', in Hussein (1984).

Imray, L. and Middleton, A. (1983), 'Public and private: marking the boundaries', in E. Gamarnikow *et al.*, *The Public and The Private*, London, Heinemann.

Jackson, M. (1984), 'Sex research and the construction of sexuality: a tool of male supremacy', *Women's Studies International Forum*, 7, 1: 43–51.

Jaggar, A. (1983), *Feminist Politics and Human Nature*, Brighton, Harvester.

Janeway, E. (1977), *Man's World, Women's Place: A Study in Social Mythology*, Harmondsworth, Penguin.

Jaywardena, K. (1986), *Feminism and Nationalism in the Third World*, London, Zed Books.

Jennings, M. (1985), (talking to Ruth Wallsgrove) 'Between Marx, the border and the womb — Irish Women United', *Trouble and Strife*, 7: 47–52.

Kader, S.A. (1984), 'A survey of trends in social sciences research on women in the Arab region, 1960–1980', in UNESCO (1984).

Kaluzynska, E. (1980), 'Wiping the floor with theory — a survey of writings on housework', *Feminist Review*, 6: 27–54.

Kanter, H., Lefanu, S., Shah, S., and Spedding, C. (eds) (1984), *Sweeping Statements*, London, Women's Press.

Karpf, A. (1987), 'Recent feminist approaches to women and technology', in McNeil (1987).

Kazi, H. (1986), 'The beginning of a debate long due: some observations on ethnocentrism and socialist-feminist theory', *Feminist Review*, 22: 87–91.

Keller, E.F. (1983), 'Feminism and science', in Abel and Abel (1983).

Kelly, L. (1985), 'Feminists v. feminists — legislating against porn in the USA', *Trouble and Strife*, 7: 4–10.

Kishwar, M. and Vanita, R. (eds) (1984), *In Search of Answers: Indian Women's Voices from 'Manushi'*, London, Zed Press.

Kitzinger, C. (1987), *The Social Construction of Lesbianism*, London, Sage.

Koonz, C. (1987), *Mothers in the Fatherland: Women, the Family and Nazi Politics*, New York, St Martin's Press.

Kuhn, A. and Wolpe, A.-M. (1978), *Feminism and Materialism*, London, Routledge & Kegan Paul.

Kuhn, T. (1970), *The Structure of Scientific Revolutions*, 2nd edn, Chicago, University of Chicago Press.

Lacan, J. (1968), *The Language of the Self*, New York, Delta.

Ladner, J.A. (1976), 'Racism and tradition: black womanhood in historical perspective', in Carroll (1976).

Lakatos, I. and Musgrave, A. (1970), *Criticism and the Growth of Knowledge*, Cambridge, Cambridge University Press.

Landes, J. (1978), 'Teaching feminist politics', in T.M. Norton and B. Ollman (eds), *Studies in Socialist Pedagogy*, New York, Monthly Review Press.

Landes, J. (1980), 'Wages for housework — political and economic considerations', in Malos (1980).

Larrain, J. (1979), *The Concept of Ideology*, London, Hutchinson.

Latin American and Caribbean Women's Collective (1980), *Slaves of Slaves: The Challenge of Latin American Women*, London, Zed Press.

Leeds Revolutionary Feminists (1981), *Love Your Enemy: The Debate Between Heterosexual Feminism and Political Lesbians*, London, Onlywomen Press.

Lees, S. (1986), *Losing Out: Sexuality and Adolescent Girls*, London, Hutchinson.

Lerner, G. (ed.) (1973), *Black Women in White America: A Documentary History*, New York, Vintage Books.

Lerner, G. (1986), *The Creation of Patriarchy*, Oxford, Oxford University Press.

Lewenhak, S. (1980), *Women and Work*, London, Fontana.

Lewis, J. (1984), *Women in England 1870–1950*, Brighton, Wheatsheaf.

Lewis, J. (1985), 'The debate on sex and class', *New Left Review*, 149: 108–20.

Lewis, J. (1987), 'Abortion and the new conservatism', *New Left Review*, 162: 123–8.

Liddington, J. (1983), 'The women's peace crusade: the history of a forgotten campaign', in Thompson (1983).

Lieberman, L. (1970), 'The debate over race', in J.E. Curtis and J.W. Petras (eds), *The Sociology of Knowledge*, London, Duckworth.

LLOG (London Lesbian Offensive Group) (1984), 'Anti-lesbianism in the women's movement', in Kanter *et al.* (1984).

Loach, L. (1987), 'Can feminism survive a third term?', *Feminist Review*, 27: 23–35.

Lorde, A. (1983), 'Open letter to Mary Daly', in Moraga and Anzaldua (1983).

Loughran, C. (1986), 'Armagh and feminist strategy: campaigns among republican women prisoners in Armagh jail', *Feminist Review*, 23: 59–80.

Lown, J. (1983), 'Not so much a factory, more a form of patriarchy: gender and class during industrialisation', in E. Gamarnikow *et al.*, *Gender, Class and Work*, London, Heinemann.

Lowry, M. (1983), 'A voice from the peace camps: Greenham Common and Upper Heyford', in Thompson (1983).

McArthur, L. (1984), untitled article in Rowland (1984).

McDonough, R. and Harrison, R. (1978), 'Patriarchy and relations of production', in Kuhn and Wolpe (1987).

Macintyre, S. (1976), ' "Who wants babies?" The social construction of instinct', in D. Leonard and S. Allen (eds), *Sexual Divisions and Society*, London, Tavistock.

MacKinnon, C. and Hunter, N. (1985), 'Coming apart: feminists and the conflict over pornography', *Off Our Backs*, 15, 6: 6–8.

McMillan, C. (1982), *Women, Reason and Nature*, Oxford, Blackwell.

McNeil, M. (ed.) (1987), *Gender and Expertise*, London, Free Association Books.

McNeil, M. and Scott, S. (1986), 'Mothers to be or not to be: is there a question?', workshop given at the British Sociological Association annual conference.

Mainardi, P. (1980), 'The politics of housework', in Malos (1980).

Malos, E. (1980), *The Politics of Housework*, London, Allison & Busby.

Mama, A. (1984), 'Black women, the economic crisis and the state', *Feminist Review*, 17: 3–20.

Maroney, H.J. (1986), 'Embracing motherhood: new feminist theory', in Hamilton and Barrett (1986).

Marx, K. (1976), *Capital*, vol. I, Harmondsworth, Penguin.

Marx, K. and Engels, F. (1955), *Selected Correspondence*, Moscow, Progress Publishers.

Marx, K. and Engels, F. (1968), *The German Ideology*, London, Lawrence & Wishart.

Mattelart, M. (1980), 'Chile: the feminine version of the coup d'état', in J. Nash and H.I. Safa (eds), *Sex and Class in Latin America*, New York, J.F. Bergin.

Menchu, R. (1984), *I, Rigoberta Menchu: An Indian Woman in Guatemala*, ed. E. Burgos-Debray, London, Verso.

Merchant, C. (1982), *The Death of Nature: Women, Ecology and the Scientific Revolution*, London, Wildwood House.

Mernissi, F. (1985), *Beyond the Veil: Male-female Dynamics in Muslim Society*, London, Al Saqi books.

Midgley, M. and Hughes, J. (1983), *Women's Choices: Philosophical Problems Facing Feminism*, London, Weidenfeld & Nicolson.

Mies, M. (1986), *Patriarchy and Accumulation on a World Scale*, London, Zed Press.

Miller, J.B. (1976), *Towards a New Psychology of Women*, Harmondsworth, Penguin.

Millett, K. (1977), *Sexual Politics*, London, Virago.

Millman, R. and Kanter, R. (eds) (1976), *Another Voice: Feminist Perspectives on Social Life and Social Science*, New York, Octagon Books.

Mitchell, J. (1974), *Psychoanalysis and Feminism*, Harmondsworth, Penguin.

Mitchell, J. and Oakley, A. (1986), *What is Feminism?*, Oxford, Blackwell.

Moi, T. (1985), *Sexual/Textual Politics*, London, Methuen.

Molyneux, M. (1979), 'Beyond the domestic labour debate', *New Left Review*, 116: 3–27.

Molyneux, M. (1981), 'Women in socialist societies: problems of theory and practice', in K. Young *et al.*, *Of Marriage and the Market*, London, CSE Books.

Moraga, C. and Anzaldua, G. (eds) (1983), *This Bridge Called My Back: Writings by Radical Women of Color*, New York, Kitchen Table: Women of Color Press.

Morgan, R. (ed.) (1971), *Sisterhood is Powerful: An Anthology of Writing from the Women's Liberation Movement*, New York, Vintage.

Morgan, R. (1983), *The Anatomy of Freedom*, London, Martin Robertson.

Morgan, R. (ed.) (1984), *Sisterhood is Global: The International Women's Movement Anthology*, Harmondsworth, Penguin.

Moschkovich, J. (1983), '-But I know you, American woman', in Moraga and Anzaldua (1983).

NAC (National Abortion Campaign) (1984), 'The case for change: two views', in Kanter *et al.* (1984).

Nettl, P. (1969), *Rosa Luxemburg*, London, Oxford University Press.

New, C. and David, M. (1985), *For the Children's Sake*, Harmondsworth, Penguin.

Nicholson, L. (1987), 'Feminism and Marx: integrating kinship with the economic', in Benhabib and Cornell (1987).

Oakley, A. (1974), *The Sociology of Housework*, London, Martin Robertson.

O'Brien, M. (1981), *The Politics of Reproduction*, London, Routledge & Kegan Paul.

Okely, J. (1975), 'Gypsy women: models in conflict', in S. Ardener (ed.), *Perceiving Women*, London, J.M. Dent.

Omolade, B. (1980), 'Black women and feminism', in H. Eisenstein and A. Jardine (eds), *The Future of Difference*, Boston, G.K. Hall.

Omvedt, G. (1980), *We Will Smash This Prison: Indian Women in Struggle*, London, Zed Press.

Ortner, S. (1982), 'Is female to male as nature is to culture?', in M. Evans (ed.), *The Woman Question*, London, Fontana.

Ortiz, B.S. (1985), 'Changing consciousness of Central American women', *Economic and Political Weekly*, 20, 17: WS 2–8.

OWAAD (Organisation of Women of Asian and African Descent) (1981), 'Black women and health', in Feminist Anthology Collective (1981).

Pagels, E.H. (1983), 'What became of god the mother? Conflicting images of God in early Christianity', in Abel and Abel (1983).

Patriarchy Conference (1978), *Papers on Patriarchy*, Brighton, PDC and Women's Publishing Collective.

Pence, E. (1982), 'Racism — a white issue', in Hull *et al.* (1982).

Petchesky, R.P. (1986), *Abortion and Women's Choice: The State, Sexuality and Reproductive Freedom*, London, Verso.

Phillips, A. (1987), *Divided Loyalties: Dilemmas of Sex and Class*, London, Virago.

Phizacklea, A. (1983), *One Way Ticket*, London, Routledge & Kegan Paul.

Pinchbeck, I. (1981), *Women Workers and the Industrial Revolution 1750–1850*, London, Virago.

Pollert, A. (1981), *Girls, Wives, Factory Lives*, London, Macmillan.

Prescod-Roberts, M. and Steele, N. (1980), *Black Women: Bringing It All Back Home*, London, Falling Wall Press.

Ramazanoglu, C. (1985), 'Labour migration in the development of Turkish capitalism', in H. Ramazanoglu, *Turkey in the World Capitalist System*, Aldershot, Gower.

Ramazanoglu, C. (1987a), 'Sex and violence in academic life or you can keep a good woman down', in Hanmer and Maynard (eds) (1987).

Ramazanoglu, C. (1987b), 'Taking a feminist stance: some problems of the scientific character of social science', paper given at the British Sociological Association Annual Conference.

Ravetz, A. (1987), 'Housework and domestic technologies', in McNeil (1987).

Ravetz, J.R. (1971), *Scientific Knowledge and its Social Problems*, Harmondsworth, Penguin.

Raymond, J. (1987), 'Politics of passion: an interview', *Trouble and Strife*, 11: 38–42.

Redclift, N. (1985), 'The contested domain: gender, accumulation and the labour process', in N. Redclift and E. Mingione (eds), *Beyond Employment: Household, Gender and Subsistence*, Oxford, Blackwell.

rhodes, d. and McNeill, S. (1985), *Women Against Violence Against Women*, London, Onlywomen Press.

Rich, A. (1980), *Of Woman Born: Motherhood as Experience and Institution*, London, Virago.

Rich, A. (1983), 'Compulsory heterosexuality and lesbian existence', in Abel and Abel (1983).

Richards, J.R. (1982), *The Sceptical Feminist: A Philosophical Enquiry*, Harmondsworth, Penguin.

Ridd, R. and Callaway, H. (1986), *Caught up in Conflict: Women's Responses to Political Strife*, London, Macmillan.

Roberts, P. (1984), 'Feminism in Africa — feminism and Africa', *Review of African Political Economy*, 27/28: 175–84.

Rogers, B. (1980), *The Domestication of Women: Discrimination in Developing Societies*, London, Tavistock.

Rose, H. (1984), 'Hand, brain and heart: towards a feminist epistemology for the natural sciences', *Socialism in the World*, 8, 43: 70–90.

Rose, H. (1986), 'Beyond masculinist realities: a feminist epistemology for the sciences', in Bleier (1986).

Rose, H. and Hanmer, J. (1976), 'Women's liberation, reproduction and the technological fix', in D.L. Barker and S. Allen (eds), *Sexual Divisions and Society: Process and Change*, London, Tavistock.

Rose, J. (1983), 'Femininity and its discontents', *Feminist Review*, 14: 55–21.

Rose, S. with Rose, H. (1987), 'Biology and the new right', in S. Rose, *Molecules and Minds: Essays on Biology and the Social Order*, Milton Keynes, Open University Press.

Rosenfelt, D. and Stacey, J. (1987), 'Review essay: second thoughts on the second wave', *Feminist Review*, 27: 77–95.

Rowbotham, S. (1973), *Woman's Consciousness, Man's World*, Harmondsworth, Penguin.

Rowbotham, S. (1981), 'The trouble with "patriarchy" ', in R. Samuel (ed.), *People's History and Socialist Theory*, London, Routledge & Kegan Paul.

Rowbotham, S., Segal, L., and Wainwright, H. (1979), *Beyond the Fragments: Feminism and the Making of Socialism*, London, Merlin.

Rowland, R. (1984), *Women Who Do and Women Who Don't Join the Women's Movement*, London, Routledge & Kegan Paul.

Rowland, R. (1987), 'Technology and motherhood: reproductive choice reconsidered', *Signs*, 12, 3: 512–28.

Rubin, G. (1975), 'The traffic in women: notes on the "political economy" of sex', in R.R. Reiter (ed.), *Toward an Anthropology of Women*, New York, Monthly Review Press.

Rubin, G. (1984), 'Thinking sex: notes for a radical theory of the politics of sexuality', in Vance (1984).

el Saadawi, N. (1980), *The Hidden Face of Eve*, London, Zed Press.

Sacks, K. (1975), 'Engels revisited: women, the organisation of production, and private property', in R.R. Reiter (ed.), *Toward an Anthropology of Women*, New York, Monthly Review Press.

Sacks, K. (1979), *Sisters and Wives: The Past and Future of Sexual Equality*, Westport, Connecticut, Greenwood Press.

Saffioti, H. (1978), *Women in Class Society*, New York, Monthly Review Press.

Salman, M. (1978), 'Arab women', *Khamsin*, 6: 24–32.

Sargent, L. (ed.) (1981), *Women and Revolution: A Discussion of the Unhappy

Marriage of Marxism and Feminism, London, Pluto Press.

Sarsby, J. (1985), 'Sexual segregation in the pottery industry', *Feminist Review*, 21: 67–93.

Sassoon, A.S. (ed.) (1987), *Women and the State*, London, Hutchinson.

Sayers, J. (1982a), 'Psychoanalysis and personal politics: a response to Elizabeth Wilson', *Feminist Review*, 10: 91–5.

Sayers, J. (1982b), *Biological Politics: Feminist and Anti-Feminist Perspectives*, London, Tavistock.

Sayers, J. (1986), *Sexual Contradictions: Psychology, Psychoanalysis and Feminism*, London, Tavistock.

Sayers, J., Evans, M., and Redclift, N. (1987), *Engels Revisited: New Feminist Essays*, London, Tavistock.

Schor, N. (1987), 'Dreaming dissymmetry: Barthes, Foucault and sexual difference', in A. Jardine and P. Smith (eds), *Men in Feminism*, London, Methuen.

Scott, Sara (1987), 'Sex and danger: feminism and AIDS', *Trouble and Strife*, 11: 13–18.

Scott, Sue (1984), 'The personable and the powerful: gender and status in sociological research', in C. Bell and H. Roberts, *Social Researching: Politics, Problems, Practice*, London, Routledge & Kegan Paul.

Segal, L. (1987), *Is the Future Female? Troubled Thoughts on Contemporary Feminism*, London, Virago.

Seidler, V. (1986), *Kant, Respect and Injustice*, London, Routledge & Kegan Paul.

Sheffield Black Women's Group (1984), 'Black women — what kind of health care can we expect in racist Britain?', in Kanter *et al.* (1984).

Siltanen, J. and Stanworth, M. (eds) (1984), *Women and the Public Sphere*, London, Tavistock.

Slocum, S. (1975), 'Woman the gatherer: male bias in anthropology', in R.R. Reiter (ed.), *Toward an Anthropology of Women*, New York, Monthly Review Press.

Smith, B. (ed.) (1983), *Home Girls*, New York, Women of Color Press.

Smith, B. and Smith, B. (1983), 'Across the kitchen table: a sister-to-sister dialogue', in Moraga and Anzaldua (eds) (1983).

Smith, D. (1979), 'A sociology for women', in J.A. Sherman and E.T. Beck (eds), *The Prism of Sex*, Madison, University of Wisconsin Press.

Smith, D. (1983), 'Women, class and family', in R. Miliband and J. Savile (eds), *Socialist Register 1983*, London, Merlin Press.

Smith, D. (1986), 'Institutional ethnography: a feminist method', *Resources for Feminist Research*, 15, 1: 6–13.

Snitow, A., Stansell, C., and Thompson, S. (eds) (1984), *Desire: The Politics of Sexuality*, London, Virago.

Soper, K. (1979), 'Marxism, materialism and biology', in J. Mepham and D.-H. Ruben (eds), *Issues in Marxist Philosophy*, vol. II, Brighton, Harvester.

Soper, K. and Assiter, A. (1983), 'Greenham Common: an exchange', *Radical Philosophy*, 34: 21–4.

Spender, D. (1980), *Man-Made Language*, London, Routledge & Kegan Paul.

Spender, D. (1983), *Feminist Theorists*, London, Women's Press.

Spender, D. (1985), *For the Record*, London, Women's Press.

Spender, D. (1986), 'What is feminism? A personal answer', in Mitchell and Oakley (eds) (1986).

Stacey, M. and Price, D. (1981), *Women, Power and Politics*, London, Tavistock.

Stanko, E. (1985), *Intimate Intrusions: Women's Experiences of Male Violence*, London, Routledge & Kegan Paul.

Stanley, L. and Wise, S. (1983), *Breaking Out: Consciousness and Feminist Research*, London, Routledge & Kegan Paul.

Stanworth, M. (ed.) (1987), *Reproductive Technologies: Gender, Motherhood and Medicine*, Cambridge, Polity Press.

Stead, J. (1987), *Never the Same Again: Women and the Miners' Strike*, London, Women's Press.

Stimpson, C.R. and Person, E. (eds) (1980), *Women, Sex and Sexuality*, Chicago, University of Chicago Press.

Stowasser, B.F. (1984), 'The status of women in early Islam', in Hussein (1984).

Styrkarsdottir, A. (1986), 'From social movement to political party: the new women's movement in Iceland', in Dahlerup (1986).

Sydie, R.A. (1987), *Natural Woman, Cultured Man: A Feminist Perspective on Sociological Theory*, Milton Keynes, Open University Press.

Sykes, B. (1984), untitled article, in Rowland (1984).

Tabari, A. (1982), 'Islam and the struggle for the emancipation of Iranian women', in Tabari and Yeganeh (1982).

Tabari, A. and Yeganeh, N. (1982), *In the Shadow of Islam: The Woman's Movement in Iran*, London, Zed Press.

Te Awekotuku, N. (1984), untitled article, in Rowland (1984).

Te Awekotuku, N. and Waring, M. (1984), 'New Zealand: foreigners in our own land', in Morgan (1984).

Thiam, A. (1986), *Speak Out Black Sisters: Feminism and Oppression in Black Africa*, London, Pluto Press.

Thompson, D. (ed.) (1983), *Over Our Dead Bodies: Women Against the Bomb*, London, Virago.

Torkington, P. (1984), 'Black women and the NHS', in Kanter *et al.* (1984).

Toubia, N.F. (1985), 'The social and political implications of female circumcision', in Fernea (1985).

Toynbee, P. (1988), 'Behind the lines', *Guardian*, 4 February: 13.

Tsoulis, A. (1987), 'Heterosexuality — a feminist option?', *Spare Rib*, 179: 22–6.

UNESCO (1984), *Social Science Research and Women in the Arab World*, Paris, UNESCO and London, Frances Pinter.

Vance, C.S. (ed.) (1984), *Pleasure and Danger: Exploring Female Sexuality*, London, Routledge & Kegan Paul.

211

Valeska, L. (1981), 'The future of female separatism', in *Building Feminist Theory: Essays from Quest*, New York, Longman.

Walby, S. (1983), 'Women's unemployment, patriarchy and capitalism', *Socialist Economic Review 1983*, London, Merlin Press.

Walby, S. (1986), *Patriarchy at Work*, Cambridge, Polity Press.

Wallsgrove, R. (1983), 'Greenham Common — so why am I still ambivalent?', *Trouble and Strife*, 1: 4–6.

Ward, M. (1987), 'A difficult, dangerous honesty: Northern Irish feminism in the 1980s', *Trouble and Strife*, 12: 36–43.

Weeks, J. (1985), *Sexuality and its Discontents: Meanings, Myths and Modern Sexualities*, London, Routledge & Kegan Paul.

Weeks, J. (1986), *Sexuality*, London, Tavistock.

Welch, K. (1984), 'Racism in the feminist movement', in Kanter *et al.* (1984).

Westwood, S. (1984), *All Day Every Day: Factory and Family in the Making of Women's Lives*, London, Pluto Press.

Whitehead, A. (1984), 'Women's solidarity — and divisions among women', *IDS Bulletin*, 15, 1: 6–11.

Wilson, A. (1984), *Finding a Voice: Asian Women in Britain*, London, Virago.

Wilson, E. (1981), 'Psychoanalysis: psychic law and order?', *Feminist Review*, 8: 63–78.

Wilson, E. (1983), *What is to be Done About Violence Against Women?*, Harmondsworth, Penguin.

Wilson, E. (1986), *Hidden Agendas: Theory, Politics and Experience in the Women's Movement*, London, Tavistock.

Wolf, M. (1985), *Revolution Postponed: Women in Contemporary China*, London, Methuen.

Wood, E.M. (1986), *The Retreat from Class: A New 'True' Socialism*, London, Verso.

Zehra (1987), 'Different roots, different routes — ethnic minority lesbians', *Trouble and Strife*, 10: 11–15.

Zimmerman, B. (1984), 'The politics of transliteration: lesbian personal narratives', *Signs*, 9, 4: 663–82.

INDEX

abortion 157-61; control of 160; as
division 157, 160; general feminist
strategy 160-1; power relations of
157-8; racial attitudes to 131-2, 160;
related problems 158; third world
159-60
African women, and circumcision
143
AIDS, and feminism 165
alliances, forming 191
Althusser, L. 75, 82, 146
Alton, David 158
androgyny 184
appearance, classification by 123
Arab women, oppression 143, 145
Australia: sisterhood, divisions 126

Bangladesh, patriarchy in 113
Barrett, M. 28, 31, 32, 36, 62, 71, 77,
82, 83, 93-4, 130
biological determinism 29, 30, 35, 66,
164, 184-6
black women: and abortion 160;
criticism of white feminism
125-9, 137; invisibility 125;
kinship 131; specificity of
oppression 129
Black Women for Wages for
Housework 77
bourgeois women: lesbianism 161;
rights 99-100, 101
boycott, women's 175
Brazil, religious conflict 150
Brenner, J. 31-2
bridge building, women's 137, 190
Britain: feminism and sexuality 155;
racism and women 130-2

Brittan, A. 36, 135, 137

Cain, Maureen 53, 114, 135, 180
capitalism: and housework 77-8; and
patriarchy 31, 36-7, 39, 110;
women's work relationship 109,
110; work as service 104; as world
system 110-12
child abuse 68
child care 18, 70, 71-3; in rural society
73; by state 72-3
Chile, women's work relationships 113
China, domestic service in 109
Chodorow, Nancy 60, 80, 81
choice, women's 160-1, 183
Christianity, patriarchal 150, 151, 152
circumcision, female 143-6; and cross-
cultural generalization 145; as
subjugation 144
class: analysis, and women 96-8, 106,
113
division by 20, 95, 96, 113; and gender
98; marxist analysis 97, 99-101;
racism as 133-5; and work 103-6,
112-15
clitoridectomy 143, 144
colonial nations, feminism 126
colonialism: and immigrants 130;
kinship systems 131; knowledge of
130
Combahee River Collective 129, 161
contraception, racial attitudes to 131-2
contradictions: of class and work
112-15; of feminist theory 3-4, 9-10,
17, 58, 87-8, 117, 174; and
women's liberation 22-3; in women's
work 17-21, 87-8; *see also* divisions

INDEX

Hartsock, Nancy C.M. 87, 114, 168
heterosexuality: lesbian critique
165; patriarchal 162, 164; and
political lesbianism 162; and
subordination 85
hierarchy, in colonial societies 124
home, separation from workplace 71,
73, 99
housework 75, 107; and capitalism
77-8; as productive labour 78;
wages for 76-7; *see also* domestic
service

Iceland, feminism in 17-18
identity: cultural 152, 153; 'failure' 81;
feminine, contradictions of 83-4;
and motherhood 75; religion in 151,
152, 153; sexual 82, 83, 162, 163
ideology 146-8; as division 138; familial
148-9; historical variability 147;
marxist interpretations 146-7; sexual
82; *see also* patriarchal ideology
immigrants, as problem 130
imperial nations, feminism 126
India: divisions between women 17-18;
feminism in 17-18; religion and
feminism 152; struggles with and
against men 183; violence, male 17,
66
infertility 74-5
infibulation 143, 144
interests: common 30, 116-17, 177-8;
contradictory 177
internationalization of production
110-12
Islamic societies: circumcision, female
143, 144, 145; societies feminism
150, 152
Italy, radical feminism 10

Japan, working class 112
Jewish people 122; people religion and
feminism 150, 152-3

kinship 20, 40; and ideology 148; and
migration 130, 131; and religion
153; and power 182, 184
knowledge, feminist critique 62
knowledge, feminist: experience,
expressing 52-3; growth 57;
objectification of subjects 55; power
in 54; rules for production 51-5;
selection and interpretation 53-5;

subjective, validation 54-5;
validating 50-1; of women's
oppression 57-90, 95

labelling, racial 123
labour: domestic 77-8, 106-10; reserve
army 79; sexual division 76, 79,
110, 178
language, feminist critique 62
Latin America, liberation theology 153
Leeds Revolutionary Feminists 85
lesbianism: biological factors 162; and
heterosexuality 161-5; political 84-6,
162, 163-4; social construction 84;
as uniting factor 161
lesbians: ethnic minority 128-9; oppression 161, 165; sado-masochism
168-9, 188; separatism 162, 163-4
Lewis, J. 31, 32, 58, 160
liberal feminism 10-11, 16; and marxist
feminism 17; middle class appeal
16; political strategies 16; and
power 86-7; and radical feminism
17; and socialism 28
liberation, women's: achieving 188-92;
and contradiction 22-3; definition
21; goals, range of related 188;
means of achieving 175-6, 182,
187-8; and oppression 22-3; and
women's power 177-8; shared
conceptions of 176
liberty, personal and collective freedom
188
life: beginning of, definition 158; rights
to 157-8
lynching, as division 135

McIntosh, M. 36, 71, 130
Manushi journal 68
Marx, K. 26, 27, 40, 41, 77, 79, 105,
106, 116, 146, 187
marxism: and feminism, relationship
26-8, 41; and ideology 146-7
marxist feminism 10, 13-16, 26-8; and
biological reductionism 28, 31, 32;
class analysis 97, 99-101; class
oppression 115; and contradiction
105; and divisions between women
17, 20; and housework 75-6; and
liberal feminism 17; as 'marriage'
27; and patriarchy 34, 36, 38, 115;
political strategies 16; and power
87; and radical feminism 16, 17,

INDEX

ethnicity 122-3; and health services
131-2; institutionalization 131-2; as
personal responsibility 117;
reductionist argument 133, 137;
theoretical background 133, 135;
and violence 134-5

radical feminism 10, 11-13, 14, 16, 28;
biological reductionism 28, 29-30,
31-2; and capitalism 28;
contradictions 125; criticism of 28,
34; and divisions between women
17, 93; housework, paid 77;
lesbianism 84; and liberal feminism
17; and marxist feminism 16, 17,
28, 31, 42; and motherhood 30;
and new-wave feminism 26; and
oppression, diversity of 93; and
patriarchy 15, 16, 33-4, 36, 38, 86;
political strategies 16; and power
87; and sex-class 102; as social
theory 24

Ramas, M. 31-2
rape 66, 67, 68
reason: and emotion 48-9; as masculine
attribute 47; in science 46-7, 48-50
reductionism *see* biological reductionism
relativism, cultural 141-3, 144
religion 149-54; as division 149-50,
151; and feminism 153-4; as form
of false consciousness 152;
oppression within 154; patriarchal
150-1, 153; variations within 151
reproduction: in nature 74; and
production 75-6, 78-80; and sex
159; consciousness 71
reproductive technology 73-5; control of
74
revolutionary feminism 10, 11, 164
Rich, Adrienne 13, 30, 61, 67, 70-1,
84, 85, 158
Roman Catholic religion: and abortion
158; and the state 151
Rowbotham, S. 15, 37, 39, 58
Rubin, G. 82, 83, 167
rural societies, child care in 73

sado-masochism 167-9, 188
Scandinavia, radical feminism 10
science: feminist critique 48-50, 61, 62;
and reason 46-7
SCUM 102
selection and interpretation 53-4
separatism, lesbian 162, 163-4

service, women's work as 106-10
sex, and reproduction 159
sex-class, women as 101-3
sexes, relations between 11, 35; *see also*
power relations
sex/gender system 38, 59
sexual harassment 66, 68
sexual ideology 82
sexual pleasure 155
sexual politics 15, 35, 54-5, 155, 178
sexual power 155, 156; and abortion
158
sexuality: as division 138, 154, 155-6,
157, 165; and female violence
167-8; knowledge of 156; lesbian
86; and male violence 67, 68; men's
control of 143, 145; politics of 64-5;
social construction 64-5, 84, 163; as
unchanging biological essence 64,
65
sisterhood 3, 11, 20, 174; black
criticism of 125, 126; and class 112;
divisions in 126; foundations of
20-1; universal 127
Smith, Dorothy 38, 49, 52, 53, 96,
104, 152
social class *see* class
social democratic socialism 187
social security, dependence on 105-6
socialism, transformation 186-8
socialist feminism 15
Society for Cutting Up Men (SCUM)
102
sons, and separatism 163-4
South Africa, racism 134
Spender, D. 13, 24, 30, 35, 58, 62, 71,
85
spinning, as image 88-9
standpoints: class 114, 135; feminist
114, 136; incompatible 114; gender
114, 135, 136; race and ethnicity
135-6
strikes, women's 17
subjective knowledge, validating 54-5
subordination 22
Sudan, female circumcision 145

Thatcherism, and women's
maintenance 79
Third World: abortion in 159-60;
agriculture, transformation 111;
alliances with others 191; divisions
between women 126; domestic

service 108-9; feminism, future 192; individualism 145-6; production and reproduction 78, 79; relationship with Western women 110; resistance to feminism 181; rich and poor, gulf between 126
transformation of production 184, 186; socialist 186-8

Uganda, religious conflict 150
United States: feminism 10, 155-6; prescriptivism 156
universality, as problem 40-2

violence, in female sexuality 167, 168
violence, male 17, 51, 65-9; biological determinism 66, 69; causes 68; and peace 88; and physical superiority 69; politicization 67-8; and pornography 166; victim's responsibility for 67; women's role 68
violence, racist 134-5
visibility: minority 117; women's ethnicity 122

wages: for housework 76-7; levels for women 79, 80
West, the, and third world 110-11
Western thought, male bias 59-64
white women: oppression 125; racism, confronting 137
wives: battered, racism of 127; violence to 66

women: as biological category 33; as carers 77; choices 160-1, 183; and class analysis 96-8, 106; class, and work 103-6; common interests 30, 116-17, 177-8; divisions between 17-19, 20, 90, 93-4, 114, 117, 170; duties 158; as employers 104, 106-10; experience, expressing 52-3; and familial ideology 148-9; female nature 30; female oppression 4, 95, 117; and power 177-8; power relations 112, 115, 127; private domain 62-4; production and reproduction 75-6, 78-80; as reserve army of labour 79; as sex-class 101-3; sexuality 64-5; shared oppression 64-80; standpoints 114, 135, 136, 179-82; violence in 168; and violence, male 17, 51, 65-9; work, domestic 63-4, 75-80; work, paid 79-80; work relationship between 109, 110, 112-13, 114-15; working class 99, 100, 101, 161; working conditions 79; *see also* white women; wives
work: and class 103-6; domestic service 106-10; relationships, women's 109, 110, 112-13, 114-15; women's 78-80, 103, 104
working class: development, different 112, Japan 112; and lesbianism 161; nationalism 116